MEETING THE TRAIN

MEETING THE TRAIN
Hagerman, New Mexico and Its Pioneers

Facsimile of 1975 Edition

compiled by
The Hagerman Historical Society
with a new foreword by
Katherine Kitch Hagerman

SOUTHWEST HERITAGE SERIES

SANTA FE

New Material © 2007 by Sunstone Press. All Rights Reserved.

No part of this book may be reproduced in any form or by any electronic or mechanical means including information storage and retrieval systems without permission in writing from the publisher, except by a reviewer who may quote brief passages in a review.

Sunstone books may be purchased for educational, business, or sales promotional use. For information please write: Special Markets Department, Sunstone Press, P.O. Box 2321, Santa Fe, New Mexico 87504-2321.

Library of Congress Cataloging-in-Publication Data

Meeting the train : Hagerman, New Mexico and its pioneers : facsimile of original 1975 edition / compiled by the Hagernam Historical Society.
  p. cm.
  Originally published: Hagerman, N.M. : The Society, c1975.
  ISBN 978-0-86534-586-7 (softcover : alk. paper)
  1. Hagerman (N.M.)--History--Miscellanea. 2. Hagerman (N.M.)--Genealogy.
  3. Registers of births, etc.--New Mexico--Hagerman. 4. Hagerman (N.M.)--Biography.
  I. Hagerman Historical Society.

F804.H34M4 2007
978.9'43--dc22
                         2007016874

WWW.SUNSTONEPRESS.COM
SUNSTONE PRESS / POST OFFICE BOX 2321 / SANTA FE, NM 87504-2321 /USA
(505) 988-4418 / ORDERS ONLY (800) 243-5644 / FAX (505) 988-1025

The Southwest Heritage Series is dedicated to Jody Ellis and Marcia Muth Miller, the founders of Sunstone Press, whose original purpose and vision continues to inspire and motivate our publications.

CONTENTS

THE SOUTHWEST HERITAGE SERIES / I

FOREWORD TO THIS EDITION / II

FACSIMILE OF 1975 EDITION / III

I

THE SOUTHWEST HERITAGE SERIES

The history of the United States is written in hundreds of regional histories and literary works. Those letters, essays, memoirs, biographies and even collections of fiction are often first-hand accounts by people who wanted to memorialize an event, a person or simply record for posterity the concerns and issues of the times. Many of these accounts have been lost, destroyed or overlooked. Some are in private or public collections but deemed to be in too fragile condition to permit handling by contemporary readers and researchers.

However, now with the application of twenty-first century technology, nineteenth and twentieth century material can be reprinted and made accessible to the general public. These early writings are the DNA of our history and culture and are essential to understanding the present in terms of the past.

The Southwest Heritage Series is a form of literary preservation. Heritage by definition implies legacy and these early works are our legacy from those who have gone before us. To properly present and preserve that legacy, no changes in style or contents have been made. The material reprinted stands on its own as it first appeared. The point of view is that of the author and the era in which he or she lived. We would not expect photographs of people from the past to be re-imaged with modern clothes, hair styles and backgrounds. We should not, therefore, expect their ideas and personal philosophies to reflect our modern concepts.

Remember, reading their words and sharing their thoughts is a passport back into understanding how the past was shaped and how it influenced today's world.

Our hope is that new access to these older books will provide readers with a challenging and exciting experience.

II

FOREWORD TO THIS EDITION
by
Katherine Kitch Hagerman

Back when I was a child in the 1940s, my mother used to take me and my younger brother, Bill, from Dallas up to Denison, Texas where some older cousins of hers lived.

One of the ways the adults entertained the children on those visits was to take us down to the train station or depot in the evenings. If there was a train arriving or departing, we watched all the activity connected with that. When there were no arrivals or departures, we watched the switch engine moving cars around the train yard.

I remember that my brother was outfitted with a trainman's cap, a red bandana, and a toy lantern so that he could pretend that he was doing a brakeman's work. I got nothing because, of course, girls did not work with trains or wear trainmen's costumes. Still, I enjoyed the experience of watching the trains "up close."

At about the same time, back in Dallas, our father would from time to time take us out to Love Field to watch the airplanes arriving and departing. Even though we knew none of the travelers, the entertainment value of watching people coming from or going to distant places was considerable.

More than fifty years later, in 1999, my husband and I made a trip to Yucatan and Belize. On a Sunday afternoon, we prepared to fly home from Belize City. We were lined up with our fellow passengers, waiting to walk out across the runway to board the plane. I looked around at the crowd of people gathered on the terrace behind us, including many families with children, and realized that, while a few of those people may have been "seeing off" a particular traveler, the majority had come out to the airport simply to watch the planes and their passengers arriving and departing, a local form of free entertainment.

It would seem that, in any era or any place--whenever or wherever people and their children are/were not indoors glued to their electronic devices--watching the arrivals and departures of trains, airplanes, ships and boats, pack trains and caravans, and most recently rockets and spaceships has been and continues to be a focus of genuine interest and a source of pleasure. Small wonder that the Hagerman depot saw its share of this widespread and eternal human activity.

The southeast quadrant of New Mexico is bisected by the Pecos River which runs north to south, and the town of Hagerman lies in the Pecos River Valley. From 1869 to 1889 the entire quadrant was designated as Lincoln County, scene of the infamous Lincoln County War.

Due to the prevailing lawlessness and the fact that no railroads or major thoroughfares (except cattle trails) traversed it, the area remained remote and slow to develop until the late 1880s.

Pat Garrett, Charles Eddy, and a number of other residents of the Valley at that time had visions of developing irrigated farming and ranching--and, with it, a greater degree of "civilized living." (Of course, they also expected to make their fortunes from land and water sales.) Having begun, they soon realized that they were woefully underfunded.

They approached James John Hagerman of Colorado Springs, a wealthy mine owner and railroad builder who was experienced in organizing and financing large enterprises, and he was persuaded to share their vision.

In 1889, J.J. Hagerman took the reins of the original irrigation company and began building and expanding the dams and canals of the system. He also began building a railroad to link the Valley with the outside world without which, he knew, the Valley could never prosper.

It should be noted that 1889 was also the year that the Territorial Legislature created Chaves and Eddy Counties out of the enormous and unwieldy Lincoln County, thereby improving administrative and law-enforcement services and aiding development.

The Hagerman townsite was acquired by the Pecos Valley Town Company in 1893, and the town began developing as the railroad was completed through Hagerman up to Roswell, New Mexico in 1894.

Something should be said as well about the canal known today as the Hagerman Canal. When it was begun by Pat Garrett and others about 1887 or 1888, no one in the Pecos Valley had ever heard of J.J. Hagerman, and the town of Hagerman did not exist. After J.J. acquired the irrigation company, it was always known as the "Northern Canal." Finally, the canal (retained by J.J. in the irrigation bankruptcy settlement of 1898) was sold by him to the Hagerman Irrigation Company in 1907. And from this date it has been known as the Hagerman Canal.

◆ ◆ ◆

The question often arises: did J.J. Hagerman or any of his family ever live in the town of Hagerman? The answer is no.

During the entire decade (1889-1899) that J.J. Hagerman was involved in irrigation and railroad building in the Pecos Valley, his residence was in Colorado Springs.

He owned various farms and ranches in the Valley including the old John Chisum ranch at South Spring in Chaves County and Hagerman Heights east of Carlsbad in Eddy County. But these properties were occupied by resident managers and were operated as "demonstration showplaces" or simply as investments.

Following the bankruptcy of the Irrigation Company in 1898 and the completion of the last leg of the Pecos Valley Railroad up to Amarillo in 1899, J.J. Hagerman sold his Colorado Springs home and moved, with his wife, to South Spring where he proceeded to build a new home on the site of the old John Chisum headquarters.

Soon afterward, he sold the railroad to the Santa Fe and, within a year or so, bought a large ranch east of the Pecos River. During the last decade of his life (1899-1909), he lived the life of a "gentleman rancher."

Following J.J. Hagerman's death, his widow, Anna, lived on at South Spring. Their younger son, Herbert, lived with her and managed the properties until the early 1920s when his place was taken by grandson, Lowry Hagerman (Herbert's nephew). This arrangement lasted until Anna Hagerman's death in 1930 when all the Pecos Valley properties were sold and the last Hagermans moved away.

In 1992, the citizens of Hagerman were kind enough to include Lowry Hagerman's sons, Charles and H.L. "Bud" (my husband), as honored guests at their Old Timers' Day celebration.

It is always a pleasure to visit the town of Hagerman, to contemplate our shared history, and to enjoy the warmth, kindness, and genuine interest of the people who live there.

III

FACSIMILE OF 1975 EDITION

MEETING THE TRAIN
Hagerman, New Mexico and Its Pioneers

THE
HAGERMAN
HISTORICAL SOCIETY

The publication of this book has been
partially funded by the Bicentennial Commission.

Cover Painting by *Mickey Lavy*
From the Western Art Gallery Collection
Starline Corporation

Book Design by *Rachel Abrams*

Manufactured by
**SLEEPING FOX ENTERPRISES
P. O. BOX 2321
SANTA FE, NEW MEXICO 87501**

*Dedicated to the memory of
J. J. Hagerman
and the early pioneers who settled
the country.*

TABLE OF CONTENTS

Introduction	11
PART I - TOWN HISTORIES	**13**
The Beginning	15
The Railroad and the Hagerman Depot	24
A Short History of the Hagerman Schools	29
History of Hagerman High School Basketball	34
The Lighting System	37
Drug Stores	38
Newspapers of Hagerman	40
Hotel Hagerman	41
The Pecos Valley Alfalfa Mill	43
History of the Cotton Gins	45
Hagerman Garages	48
Earl Latimer - Hagerman Barber	50
Brief History of Hagerman Bank	52
The Volunteer Fire Department	54
Hagerman Water System	56
Gas Lines	57
The Telephone System	58
Hagerman Post Office	59
History of the Hagerman Canal	60
The Drainage System	65
River Fords and Bridges	67
Organization of the Presbyterian Church	70
Church of Christ	73
The Catholic Church	74
First Church of the Nazarene of Hagerman, New Mexico	76
History of the Seventh Day Adventist Church of Hagerman, New Mexico	77
First Baptist Church	80
Methodist Church	83
Order of Eastern Star Harmony Chapter No. 17	86
History of the Hagerman Masonic Lodge Felix Lodge No.29	88
Hagerman Thursday Club	91
Early History of the Hagerman Cemetery	92
The Felix Ranch	95

MAP OF HAGERMAN	98
PART II - FAMILY HISTORIES	**101**
W. J. Alter	103
Pioneers near Hagerman	104
Thomas Grant Andrews	108
Dub and Jane Andrus	110
The J. P. Andrus Family	112
The Marshall Bailey Family	114
My Memories of Hagerman - C. A. Baker	115
Felipé Banuello	119
The Levi Barnett's	120
George F. Baum	125
The J. Frank Bauslin Family	126
The Lewis Travis Bealer Family	127
E. L. Bitney Family	128
The Bledsoe Families	130
J. E. Blythe Family	132
Hal Bogle	133
My Memories of Hagerman - Elizabeth Bowen	135
The W. E. Bowen Family	137
The Buck Boyce Family	141
Harlan Boyce Reminisces	144
Mark Boyce	145
Rufus T. Boyce Family	147
The D. A. Bradley Family	149
The Bramblett Families	151
The Jim Bramblett's	153
The Brookshier Family	154
The Brown Families	157
Henry M. Brown, M. D.	159
The Burck Family	161
Uncle George Butler and the Pritchard Family	164
The John F. Campbell Family	168
Jack and J. P. (Pete) Casabonne	170
Clark-Atkinson Families	172
The John W. Coffee Family	175
History of the Charles Wallace Cole Family	177
Harry Cowan Family	182
The H. J. Cumpsten Family	184
The Charles W. Curry Family	190
The Davis Family	194
The Alpha Deason Family	195
The Tom Derrick Family	196
The Devenports	201
T.D. Devenport Family	203
The Fred H. Evans Family	205
The A. V. Evans Family	207
The L. E. Evans Family	208
The J. M. Fletcher Family	210
The O. J. Ford Family	212

The A. N. Franklin Family	214
Lawrence and Lela Garner	216
The B. F. Gehman Family	219
Demetro Gonzales Family	222
The W. R. Goodwin Family	224
The Calvin Graham's	226
W. E. Graham Family	227
The Greer Family	228
The Wiley Grizzle Family	229
The Zach Ham Family	232
Jim Hammons Family	233
The Richmond Hams Family	234
Carl R. Hanson	236
The M. E. Harshey Family	237
John I. Hinkle	240
The L. E. Hinrichsen Family	241
C. O. Holloway	244
The Charles G. How Family	245
The Ross and Josie Jacobs Family	246
Hugo Jacobson - Jim Michelet Families	248
The J. A. Jacobson Family	250
The William James Family Story	252
Will and Alla Jenkins	255
W. H. Keeth Family	256
The Key Klan in Hagerman	258
History of James H. King Family	263
James Luther King	266
The Kiper Family	268
The B. F. Knolls	270
The E. E. Lane Family	271
Leonard M. Lang Family	275
The Otto Lang Family	277
Ernest Langenegger	278
The John Langenegger Family	281
The Elton Lankford Family	285
The Frank Lattion Family	287
Harvey W. Little	292
The Loseys	294
The Lusk Family	296
The McCormick Families	297
The "Doc" McCormick Kids	304
About the McKinstrys	306
The Tom McKinstry Family	311
The Austin Swann Family and the Jim and Sam McKinstry Families	313
The John L. Mann Family	318
The Richard Mansfield Family	319
E. J. Mason Family	321
The Menefees	323
The E. D. Menoud Family	325
The A. N. Miller Family in Hagerman, New Mexico	329
Saga of Jacques L. Michelet	332
F. D. Mitchell Family	339
The Montaño Family and the Tony Trujillo Family	341

J. P. Morgan Family	343
The T. J. Nail Family	346
The George Berry Newsom Family	348
Remembrances of the Fred O'Dell Family	350
The Ned Aymer Palmer Family	355
The Frank Parks Family	356
A Sad Day for the Parks Family	358
J. W. Parks Family	360
The Warren N. Perry Family	361
William F. Phillips Family	363
The Pilley Families	364
E. M. Reed Family	366
The Rhodes Family	367
The W. E. Ridgley Family	369
Guy Robinson Family	370
The Arthur B. Russell Family	371
An Experience at Hagerman	375
Mr. and Mrs. James A. Sanders / Mr. and Mrs. J. Lester Ogle	378
Slayter - Dragoo Families	380
The Smith and Cox Families	382
The Stine Family	384
The Edward Van Sweatt Sr. Family	386
The Jack Sweatt Family	388
The Tanner Family	390
Miss Lucy Thomas	392
The R. N. Thomas Family	394
Truitt - Lemon Families	396
Henry Clay Lemon	398
Utterback Family History in New Mexico	399
The Utterbacks at Hagerman	401
The George Wade Family	403
The F. G. Walters Family	405
The Oscar Walters Family	406
The Walworths	408
The Ware Family	410
Rev. Angus E. Watford	414
The West Brothers	415
The Noah West Family	416
Ben Jack West	418
W. P. West Family	419
J. T. West Family	422
E. A. White, Superintendent of Hagerman Schools, 1920-1942	425
The Wiggins Story	429
The Jim Williamson Family	431
William Joseph Wilson Family	434
The J. E. Wimberlys	435
B. H. Wixom Family	438
W. P. Woodmas Family	439
The Wranoskys	441
The Adam Zimmerman Family	443
Post Script	445

INTRODUCTION

When W.E. Utterback began compiling the history of Hagerman, New Mexico, in 1968, he asked Mrs. B.W. Curry to help him. The two of them were doing fine until they discovered that Hagerman had more history than they had bargained for. It had become such a tremendous undertaking that others in the community offered to aid the struggling historians. From these volunteer sessions the Hagerman History Book Club was born, and from the efforts of the Club has come this book.

It is a unique achievement. No professional writers set about to search library stacks or interview "old timers." No professional writers, in fact, even saw the manuscript until it was finished. The "old timers," the Hagerman pioneers and their descendants, have written their own stories, weaving them into a colorful history. Each has become an author in his or her own way. There may be contradictions, perhaps some mistakes, but these are of little importance. This is the story of Hagerman as it was. It is history remembered and not necessarily history as it happened. Every effort has been made, of course, to verify names, dates and events, but should the reader find that his memory of a fifty-year old occurrence disagrees with the writer's — well, maybe you were standing on opposite sides of the street.

The original guidelines set up for the history have been followed as closely as possible. In order to be eligible for inclusion a family, business or public institution had to have been established in Hagerman before 1930. The first three generations of families represented are named and their histories given. The fourth generation is mentioned but not named. Editing has been kept to a minimum. The committee did, however, condense or delete some material, most of which did not pertain to Hagerman. Spelling and punctuation were checked and minor corrections made, but no major rewriting was done.

"Meeting the train" was a popular pastime in Hagerman "back then." Time and again people mention the evenings spent at the old depot — seeing who got off the train, who got on and who was there to watch. The passenger trains are gone now and the depot is just a memory. Many of the laughing young people who gathered there are gone, too. But, in the pages of this book, they live again, driving the buggies and the Model T's down to the depot "just to see what's goin' on."

William Farrington, Editor
October, 1975
Santa Fe, New Mexico

Part I
TOWN HISTORIES

THE BEGINNING
By Helen Curry

James John Hagerman was born on a farm near Port Hope, Ontario, Canada, on March 23, 1839, and died in Milan, Italy, on September 15, 1909. He was married to Anna Osborne in 1867 and they were the parents of two sons, Percy Hagerman, who was associated with his father in his enterprises, and Herbert J. Hagerman, also associated with his father until his appointment as governor of the Territory of New Mexico in 1906-07. He later served in important capacities for the Navajo Indians as a representative of the federal government.

The town of Hagerman which was named for J.J. Hagerman, is located in historic southeastern New Mexico, on the main line of the Santa Fe Railroad and State Road 2, formerly U.S. Highway 285. It is located near the junction of the Felix and Pecos Rivers, about halfway between Roswell and Artesia.

Mr. Hagerman had made his fortune from iron ore in Michigan and gold mines in Colorado. No other man gave more in time and money for the development of the Pecos Valley than he did.

On September 9, 1892, at the land office in Roswell, George F. Pennebaker made the final payment for all of Section 10, in Township 14, south of Range 26 east of New Mexico Principal Meridian, containing 640 acres. This was a desert land grant from the U.S. government and was sold for $1.25 per acre.

Water rights for this land were purchased from the Pecos Valley Irrigation and Improvement Co. on November 16, 1891.

Pennebaker then sold the southeast quarter of Section 10 to W.H. Austin of El Paso, Texas, on January 5, 1893. Austin sold the land to the Pecos Valley Town Co., on

March 9, 1893.

This company had been formed in April 1889 and the names of the incorporators were: Joseph C. Lea, Charles B. Eddy, Arthur A. Mermod, Patrick F. Garrett and Edgar B. Bronson.

In 1894, J.J. Hagerman was building the railroad from Eddy (Carlsbad) to Roswell. By this time he had become president of the Pecos Valley Town Co. and had decided on the location of the town which was to be known as Hagerman.

The town site is situated in the southeast quarter of Section 10 described above. Mr. Hagerman had the land surveyed and platted. It contained 67.02 acres. One of the men who worked for Mr. Hagerman at that time was William J. Wilson, who married Jessie (Birdie) Cowan. Their daughter, Mrs. Florence Wilson Loudon, who resides in Ruidoso, remembers her father telling about helping survey and planting the cottonwood trees that lined the streets. He told her that the townsite had to be fenced in order to keep the antelope from eating the trees.

Aberdeen Street was to be the north boundary and Oxford Street was the west boundary of original Hagerman. York and Aberdeen Streets were wider than some of the other streets. Alleys varied in width as did business lots. Residence lots were to be 50 by 150 feet. After the town was incorporated in 1905 several additions were made to the original plat.

Mr. Hagerman had artesian wells dug on the lots across from the depot and ditches made to water the trees. Some people used the water for drinking but for most it contained too much sulphur.

Excursion trains brought people from the Midwest, east and north. Promotional advertising in newspapers in other parts of the country interested many adventurous persons. Many came, some stayed a short while, others remained several years and some hardy souls remained for the rest of their lives.

Mrs. Harry Cowan who came to Hagerman in 1895 made the following statement: "After spending seven years of drouth in Kansas, the valley around Hagerman looked

Mr. J.J. Hagerman.

like a haven of rest to the people who were brought here on an immigrant train. The beautiful trees and grass were an invitation to get off the train and settle here."

Mr. J.T. West had this to say: "I came with an immigrant group which brought household goods, dogs and mules. The country between Amarillo and Roswell discouraged me to the point that I decided that I would only be in Hagerman for one week. After leaving Roswell the scenery began to get better and I was completely overcome by the difference in the countryside south of Roswell and north of Roswell. The closer I got to Hagerman, the better I liked the country. I have never been sorry that I decided to make my home in Hagerman."

The following news item, in part, appeared in *The Hagerman Irrigator* on August 3, 1895:

THE CITY OF HAGERMAN

Favorably located near the center of the finest and most fertile valley in the arid region is the beautiful city of Hagerman, which though less than a year old promises to be the most prominent town in the entire Pecos Valley.

Several substantial buildings have already been erected and the town at present has two general stores, post office, blacksmith shop, lumber yard, drug store, depot and section house, two real estate offices, several dwellings and one of the nicest brick school houses in Chaves County.

The educational facilities of the town are as good as the Valley affords. Another pleasing and beneficial feature is the character of the society which is perfect and pure. The people are refined pleasant people.

In 1905, there were enough people to petition the County Commissioners for the incorporation of Hagerman. On the 5th day of July, 1905, Hagerman was declared an incorporated town.

An election was held and the following trustees were elected: N.J. Fritz, Edward C. Miller, M.C. Moore, J.W. Langford and O.R. Tanner. Mr. Fritz was elected Mayor by his fellow trustees and O.R. Tanner was named Clerk. It has been said that Mr. Tanner was an excellent clerk and held the position for a number of years.

Summaries from the ordinances passed by this first town board in 1905:

Misdemeanors and Offenses:

Section 11. Against keeping or maintaining any public dance house, or hall or free and easy house for the mingling of the sexes.

Section 9. Any person who shall race horses at a speed to exceed eight miles per hour.

Section 12. Any saloon, gambling hall or retail liquor store must be screened or curtained from public view.

Section 13. No music in any saloon or in any billiard hall, restaurant or upon the sidewalk in front of such place.

Section 14. Unlawful for any woman to enter any saloon.

Section 21. Unlawful to spit on sidewalks or floors.

Section 26. Any person who shall walk, ride or drive on any public street with any lewd woman.

Another decision in the early years was to build sidewalks and street crossings. In 1906 the trustees agreed to pay Mr. Hagerman $900.00 a year for the use of his wells providing he would keep the wells in repair. At the end of ten years the wells would belong to the town.

In 1909 the school population had grown and five teachers were employed. It was determined that a new school house was needed. A school bond issue met with success.

About this time the water wells began to cave in and the mayor, N.S. West, O.R. Tanner, clerk, and the trustees, W.E. Bowen, H.C. Barron and J.C. Wranosky were forced to look in a different direction for a water supply. A special bond issue election was held for $4,300 for a water system. The election carried but then it was discovered that the town lacked enough residents. A town needed a thousand people before voting such a bond issue.

1910 saw the town experiencing a period of growth. The alfalfa mill had been constructed, the new school house was built, an undertaking establishment was opened by H.H. Henninger and Company, John Hogan opened a shoe repair shop; all of this in addition to the already established businesses.

Another question now faced the town officials. The citizens had voted the town "dry" in 1908, but some of the enterprising merchants of Dexter were making deliveries of beer into Hagerman twice daily.

The New Mexico Wool and Hide Company made application for a franchise to sell beer in Hagerman. The franchise was granted by the trustees, but if it had been left up to the people it probably would have been defeated. This was the nearest thing to a scandal that the people of Hagerman had ever witnessed in their government.

The town officials of 1910 negotiated a contract for the first electric lighting system for the town.

In the spring of 1911 there was a highly contested election of officials. C.W. Major was elected mayor over E.L. Jones by a bare majority of one.

In 1911 the first volunteer fire department was organized.

In 1912 the new depot for the town was completed. The town was jubilant and declared a day of celebration. (See story else where in book.)

Hagerman had its greatest fire loss in property in 1915 when the Hagerman Hotel, the Joyce-Pruit Company and the Hagerman Drug store burned to the ground.

The men are working on one of the first artesian wells drilled in the valley, near Hagerman. (Used by permission of Mrs. A.O. Miller.)

Artesian Well J.J. Hagerman had drilled in town across from depot.

One of the first immigrant trains to Hagerman.

Main Street, 1906

When Hagerman was still fenced to keep antelopes from eating trees.

Also in 1915 the town was hit by a diphtheria epidemic and the health officer, Dr. Brown, set up strict quarantine. Conditions were soon better and people could go back to the local movie which was operated only on Saturday nights.

When the United States entered World War I, Hagerman sent their boys off to war with the sound of band music and various homemade refreshments. The whole town turned its effort in a patriotic direction. The Rev. H.J. Cumpsten appeared before the town council with a suggestion that the town lower the water rates so every one could raise a garden. It was done for the months of June, July and August. W.A. Losey suggested that every man over the age of 18 be gainfully employed. The council approved that also.

An influenza epidemic hit the small town of Hagerman in 1918. All public gatherings were discontinued and schools and churches were closed for a time.

These interesting items of Hagerman's early history were taken in part from G.Y. Fails *Study of the Development of Town Government of Hagerman* and used with his permission.

As has been noted above, many of the early residents were intelligent and well educated, talented people. During the early years local talent put on many entertainments. When some organization needed funds they would have an evening of music and readings or an ice cream social. The town nearly always had a band that would give concerts on Saturday nights.

In later years Chautauqua and Lyceum provided entertainment. Then there were horse races and rodeo events. Baseball was very popular in bygone days.

The population reached its peak in the 1960's. But in the 70's there began a slow decline. However, there is reason for optimism and hope.

Farming and cattle raising is the source of most of the income. Crops are being tried now that have never been tried here before and if they are successful perhaps cotton will not be the main crop. At present alfalfa is still the most important crop. Summer wheat was planted and sunflowers and safflowers are being raised for their seed from which oil is made.

Now, too, many cars of cubed hay and pellets are being shipped from here to other markets.

MAYORS OF THE TOWN OF HAGERMAN

1905	N.J. Fritz
1906	J.W. Langford
1907-08	James McConnel
1909-10, 1944	N.S. West
1911	C.W. Major
1912-14	E.W. Powell
1915-18	R.I. Lochhead
1919-26	H.M. Brown
1927-28	H.R. Miller
1929-36, 1946-52	J.T. West
1937-42	C.G. Mason
1952-53	R.L. Higgins
1953-56	Wayne Graham
1956-60	D.T. West
1960-62	John Garner
1962-	Leonard George

CLERKS OF THE TOWN OF HAGERMAN

1905-14, 1918-34	O.R. Tanner
1914-18	James Cowan
1934	R.W. Connor
1935-36	J.T. Sweatt
1936-38	C.G. Mason

TOWN MARSHALS AND DEPUTY TOWN MARSHALS

D.L. Lang	1905
W.E. King	1905
L.R. Burck	1906
John Bryan	1907
J.M. Pulliam	1907
C.W. Autrey	1908
L.M. Lang	1909
James Cowan	1910, 1914
Joe West	1911
T.S. Seegraves	1912
J.B. McCormick	1918-1920, 1923
J.M. Brown	1921
L.B. Heick	1925-1928
Jim Williamson	1928-1938

THE RAILROAD AND THE HAGERMAN DEPOT
By Helen Curry

J.J. Hagerman was a man who saw great possibilities for irrigated farms in the Pecos Valley, and it was he who brought the railroad to the valley. Construction began in 1890 at Pecos, Texas, and continued northward to the state line. After completing the railroad between the state line and Carlsbad (Eddy), the road was officially opened in 1891.

By October 6, 1894, construction had inched on to Roswell. By March, 1898, the road was completed through Portales to Cameo, and when a 13.2 mile stretch from Cameo to Texico was completed, rail service over the whole line was opened March 1, 1900. Passenger service was first offered from Amarillo to Pecos on February 10, 1899. Not until 1908 was a line built from Cameo to Texico through Clovis and then the original line from Cameo to Texico was abandoned.

In 1901 control of the Pecos Valley and Northeastern Railway (Hagerman's line) passed to the Santa Fe when it bought the securities from Hagerman, including more than two thirds of the bonds and ninety-six percent of the stock for a little more than two and a half million dollars. Complete ownership was acquired later.

In 1906 the Pecos Valley lines were integrated into the Santa Fe's system operation and after 1907 a Santa Fe subsidiary, the Eastern Railway of New Mexico, held title to the property. The present Santa Fe system acquired title in 1912.

Traffic on the Pecos Valley line for many years was basically agricultural products, livestock and later petroleum products, until discovery and opening of the potash mines near Carlsbad.

Building Felix Railroad Bridge.

Hagerman Depot.

The Town of Hagerman was listed as a non-agency station in the Santa Fe's official records prior to 1901.

The first depot was a wooden structure built on a level with the loading platform. The first agent was M.H. Jones. A few years later D.W. Crozier became agent and served in that capacity for a number of years. His son Arthur was telegraph operator.

Around 1910 Hagerman experienced a boom. *The Hagerman Messenger*, the town's first newspaper, which began publication in 1904, carried a headline in the September 30, 1910 edition, "A Reality — A New Hagerman." At the time the Alfalfa Growers Association was operating successfully, the town had a good hotel, a new alfalfa meal mill, a broom factory operated by Albert Bledsoe, a brush factory, a boot and shoe factory, a new dam in the Felix River, new Wool and Hide building, First National Bank, new school house and the printing office. New sidewalks were under construction, also.

During that year, 1910, a new depot was assured for Hagerman. An article in the *Messenger* of February 11, 1910, states that G.C. Starkweather, superintendent of Eastern Railway, and J. Brinker, freight and passenger agent, were in Hagerman and gave out the good news that they had scheduled a new depot for Hagerman, New Mexico, this year.

The September 30 issue of the paper stated that work would begin as soon as the workmen could get to it. No further mention is made concerning the depot in any other issues of the paper for that year, and no 1911 papers are available.

Evidently the depot was built during 1911. It was built of brick — three bricks wide — on a concrete base and floor. The roof was of tile and the outside was stuccoed with wood trim painted green. Several years ago it was painted yellow with red trim.

The building was supposed to have cost $12,000 but there is a story that the man in charge of the building exceeded that amount and lost his job because of it. However, the Hagerman depot was the best and prettiest depot on the line. In the days before cars were so numerous and television was unheard of, the depot was a gathering place for people to watch the train come in. There was always somebody there when the passenger trains arrived, to see who came in or left. On occasion there were large crowds, as when the boys were leaving to go to war or coming home after being discharged. Young people, especially in the evening, would go to the depot to see the trains, as they did in small towns all over the country.

The Washington Spur was built about two miles south of town on the curve at the Washington Ranch about 1890. When the lease was up on the land occupied by the Washington Spur it was abandoned and it was then that the Mossman Spur was built. The Mossman Spur was about five miles south of town and the stock holding corrals were east of the railroad track. In the early days this spur was a popular place for thousands of head of livestock to be shipped to market. Some of the early days shippers were Dee Jones Ranch, Four Lakes Ranch owned by J.P. White Sr., Joe Lane Ranch, Carl Sams, Adam Zimmerman, Stephens and Cap Mossman. Mossman's shipments were by the train load as he was the manager of the large Turkey Track Ranch east of the Pecos River as well as the manager of the Diamond A Ranch west of Hagerman. The corrals have all been torn down with just a windmill left of the site, as hauling of cattle by trucks has replaced the trains.

Mossman Spur was named for Captain Burton C. Mossman. The story is told that after loading cattle all day long for shipment, Cap Mossman and Earnest Bowen had returned to the depot to do the paper work on the shipment with the help of Hamp Cosper. Hamp was the Western Union boy for Earnest and always pushed the mail cart. As the paper work progressed that night Hamp kept watching Cap spit his tobacco stream on the floor and, knowing that he was the one who would have to clean the floor, he became extremely upset. Hamp got up and walked over to Cap, tapped him on the shoulder and asked Cap to stop spitting on the floor or else. Cap, being a much larger man that Hamp's 100 pounds, looked up at Hamp and said "Or else what will you do?" Cosper then said "I guess I will just have to take it away from you." For many years after that incident Cap Mossman would mention the big little man who was going to take his chewing tobacco away from him.

New Mexico Place Names has this to say about Russell Spur: "A Spur on the AT&SF Railroad two miles northwest of Hagerman, built about 1912. Named for Howard Russell, who along with his neighbors used it for hay hauling."

A large barn was built under the direction of C.W. Curry for the storage of hay awaiting shipment. There were stalls for each person storing hay in the barn. The barn no longer stands but the hitching post still shows at Cassabonne Curve (Russell Spur).

The U.S. Mail was taken from trains #25 and #26 in 1955. The company streamlined their trains hoping to stimulate passenger traffic, however, these expectations were not realized. Passenger trains were discontinued with August 29, 1967 being the final day for passenger service between Clovis and Carlsbad.

After D.W. Crozier left the agent was H.A. Dicken, followed by C.F. Hurley. Following Hurley was E.S. Bowen who held the position from 1921 until he retired in 1966. Altogether, he worked for the Santa Fe for fifty years. H.E. Boydston was the next agent, then for a short time a man named Haddox was the agent. Following him came Jim Alsup, who served until May 14, 1971, when the depot was closed. Now the building has been torn down and the site will be cleared, much to the sorrow of Hagerman residents.

An old program booklet, belonging to E.S. Bowen, tells of a festive occasion that occured on March 19, 1912, when the Hagerman Chamber of Commerce sponsored a big banquet for the officials of the A.T.&S.F. Railroad. This banquet was in honor of the completion of the new depot and was given at the Hagerman hotel. The committee of arrangement consisted of; John I. Hinkle, O.R. Tanner, Frank Anderson, Robert N. Miller and W.E. Bowen. The committee of finance were Howard Russell, D.E. Bryant and T.B. Platt. The committee of reception were D.W. Crozier, E.E. Hoagland, and H.F. Johnson. The Imperial Orchestra from Roswell played during the banquet hour. The menu was very impressive with turkey and all the trimmings. Some of the speakers on the programme were; Ex-Governor Hagerman, John I. Hinkle, G.C. Starkweather, Dr. Frank Talmadge and Col. I.H. Elliott.

A SHORT HISTORY OF THE HAGERMAN SCHOOLS
By R.A. Welborne

The first organized school in the town of Hagerman began September 23, 1895. Miss Hannah Blackstone was the teacher. School year ended May 15, 1896. The school building was located at the corner of Inverness and Winchester Streets. The register shows that there were eighty-five children who attended, ranging in age from five to nineteen. The youngest was Ralph Smalley, age five, and Seraphine Lattion, age nineteen, was the oldest. Louie Burck was also a student, age fourteen, and he lived the remainder of his life here.

Also listed in the register of 1895 were the names of: Winnie Cowan; Hattie and Clara Spencer; Bessie Mae and Mabel Bailey; Roxie, Ethel and Maude Russell; Maude and Mabel Stratton; Mary and Walter Gill; Loyd and Scott Thompson; Susie and Jimmie Cowan; Charlie and Ethel Tanner; Bert Bailey; Henry and Ella Mills; Rachel, Nellie and Mabel Amis and Eunice Bowen.

The records are rather incomplete; in fact, there are no records until about 1910, at which time a new building was erected. The "Burro," a school publication, published in 1906 and 1907, lists Professor W.F. Osborne as Superintendent of the high school that year. Board members were: W.E. Bowen, President; Dr. J.A. Farnsworth, Vice President; and G.C. Stanford, Secretary.

The "Burro" also shows that Blanche Osborne and Frank Wimberly were in a play. They were children about 8 or 10 years old at the time.

About 1910 a two-story building was erected. C.S. Waggoner of Roswell was the contractor. The building was wooden frame with red brick facing and measured sixty by sixty feet. The first floor had four 23'x30' classrooms; the second floor had one 60'x60' room with a stage on the east end and across the south were two classrooms, a stairwell, and a small office in the center at the top of the stairwell. A colored postal card picture of this building, in the display case in the present high school lobby, shows that the roof was four-sloped with a belfry and dormer windows. Later, an addition to this building was made, the outside was stuccoed and the roof was changed to a low-pitch fire wall type. This portion served as an elementary grade school for many years. It was razed in December, 1968, during the school holidays.

In 1920, at a cost of about $20,000, a new auditorium with eight classrooms and a basement was joined on the north of this original building. An architect by the name of Carr designed this building. The walls were poured concrete with wooden floors and mostly wooden trusses for the ceiling. During 1970 the old auditorium was remodeled into a modern, 500 seat auditorium.

About 1925, following a state basketball championship season, a gymnasium was built. This building had poured concrete walls, two classrooms on the south and a shop building on the north. The total cost of the erection was about $13,500. This building was torn down in 1953 to make room for the present high school building.

Appearing as board members for these early years were: N.S. West, Harry Cowan and W.E. Bowen. Of course these records are not complete.

In 1936 the Home Economics Cottage was constructed with W.P.A. labor. At the same time the school — in conjunction with the town of Hagerman — erected a rock stadium on city property. This was to have been a joint W.P.A. project with the city and school. The city ran out of money, and the school finished the project. The stadium was dedicated about 1936 with a speech by the governor, John Miles. C.G. Mason was Mayor of Hagerman and E.A. White was Superintendent of the Schools. Board members at

First school house. Back part built in 1895.

Second school building, 1910.

the time were: H.A. Kiper, N.S. West, Charlie Michelet and Levi Barnett.

E.A. White became superintendent in 1920 and remained in this position until 1942. Other names that appear on the record that indicate they may have been superintendents are: (1) D.A. Paddock, (2) R.C. Bonney and F.A. Adair, (3) McClung-Lugibihl, (4) W.N. Kelsey, (5) O.R. Gable and (6) Parkhurst. Also Ruth Pettigrew was principal. D.A. Paddock's daughter, Grace Paddock, who is now Mrs. Kern Jacobs of Roswell, was a teacher in the Hagerman school during the 1930's.

In 1948 a new and larger gymnasium, including 3 classrooms, was erected. The architect on this job was Max Plato, the contractor was Rhyan Brothers and it cost about $103,000. The building was built with a $75,000 bond issue plus money from the operational fund.

In 1953 the old gymnasium was torn down and a new administrative unit and library, a laboratory and a number of classrooms were erected on the site of the old building. This building was joined to the gymnasium.

The cafeteria and classrooms were added in 1957. This contract amounted to $130,000. The contractor was from Carlsbad and Vorhees and Frank Standhart were the architects. They were also the architects on the administrative building which joined to the gym.

In 1964 a band room was added to the north side of the gymnasium. This projected the band room into St. Charles Street, and the city gave the school the south half of the street.

A year later an agricultural shop was added to the north side of the school, adjacent to the band room. The following year, the two lots of the Newsom property were purchased to square out the school grounds. Those are the two lots on which the Distributive Education Building and a small green house are located.

About 1947 a metal building was purchased from an oil company in Roswell at a cost of $3,600. This building was made into an agricultural shop and was used as such for several years. It was later joined to the gymnasium to make additional shower rooms.

R.A. Welborne became Superintendent in 1942 and continued in this position until 1970. Board members during this time were: H.A. Kiper, Robert Conner, Sam McKinstry, Charles Michelet, Bernice Barnett, O.J. Ford, T.A. Bledsoe, Stanley Utterback, Richard Lang, Tony Trujillo, Jim Langenegger and Willard Watson. In 1969 Lindell Andrews and Frank Rhodes were elected. Other board members during the building years, who took an active part, were Vencil R. Barnett and H.R. Menefee.

Hagerman High School must have been started about 1906. It was probably a two- or three-year high school until 1914, at which time it became a four-year high school. I believe the records show that Bayard Curry graduated twice — once from a three-year high school and then the next year from a four-year high school.

The high school became, and continues to be, a member of the North Central Association in 1923. The curriculum for these many years has been a complete one for a small high school.

Many of the past years we have boasted a sixty-piece band and a winning basketball team. We were state champions in basketball in 1923 and 1924, went to the state tournament twice during the 1930's and twice during the late 1950's and early 1960's.

At present Gordon L. King is Superintendent and W.E. Knoy is Principal.

HISTORY OF HAGERMAN HIGH SCHOOL BASKETBALL

Basketball in the early days was different in many respects from the basketball which is played today. It was largely the center of all athletic activity. The high school enrollment in the old days never exceeded more then seventy-five or eighty and it was difficult to find enough men to develop a team. All games were played on outdoor courts and often on gravel courts. There was no protection for the players, other than heavy knee pads, against the scuffles and falls which usually developed because of almost vicious competition.

The outdoor game assisted the Hagerman team in becoming state champions during the years 1923 and 1924 to the extent that the Hagerman boys developed unusual wind and could outplay most any indoor team. The team was accustomed to playing in strong winds and shooting at basketball goals and backstops which were always moving back and forth.

The early basketball games were somewhat slower and much rougher than present day basketball. There were fewer rules and regulations and the players were considerably older. No one bothered about the team's respective ages and sometimes they averaged between twenty-two and twenty-four years. There were no rules about bringing in out-of-state players and providing them with compensatory jobs. All high schools were in one category regardless of size and when Hagerman became state champs, they had out-played and out-scored every team in the state from the smallest to the largest high school.

Hagerman High School State Basketball Champions - 1923. Back row: Boucher Brookshier, Horton White, Ross White, Curtis Baker. Front row: Elton Thompson, Wilbur Lyles, Dwight Robinson, Johnny Bowen.

Hagerman High School State Basketball Champions - 1924. Back row: Elton Thompson, Johnnie Bowen, Coach R.N. Thomas, Albert McKandles, Wayne Adams. Front row: Bill Lyles, Dwight Robinson, Ross White, Curtis Baker.

When Hagerman won the state basketball tournament in 1923 they had no official coach. The townspeople were so elated that they raised $1800.00 to send their team to Chicago for the National Basketball Tournament. New green and white uniforms were bought and the town proudly sent them off in style. The 1923 team consisted of Horton White, Ross White, Boucher Brookshire, Dwight Robinson, John Bowen, Elton Thompson, Wilmer Lyles and Curtis Baker. (Mr. Baker was unable to go to Chicago with the team.) They lost their first game at Chicago but the famous team brought respect and admiration to the citizens of Hagerman.

In 1924 Mr. R.N. Thomas came to Hagerman to teach and coach. Again Hagerman won the State Tournament. The members of this team were Ross White, Albert McKandles, John Bowen, Wayne Adams, Elton Thomas, Wilmer Lyles, Dwight Robinson and Curtis Baker.

During the 1930's Hagerman returned to the state tournament twice. All schools in New Mexico were still in the same class, as far as athletics were concerned.

By 1963 basketball had a new look and rules and regulations changed. Small and large schools were classed by their enrollment. Hagerman sent to the state tournament a team made up of the following boys: Jake Trujillo, John Sparks, Bobby Chaves, Ishmael Dela Rosa, J.D. English, Joe Gomez, Bobby Harrison, Teddy King, Frances Romero, Larry Turpen and Valois Torres. This team placed third in the state and was coached by Bill Turner.

The 1964 team also returned to state competition with great determination, placing second. They were Jack Langenegger, Freddie Gibson, Jackson Wiggins, Charles Foster, Billy Gomez, Lee Ledbetter, Paul West, Buddy Adair, Ervin Huddleston and Ray Barela.

Sportsmanship throughout the winning years of basketball for Hagerman has always been on a respectful level and teams and townsmen have maintained an enviable record of good will, companionship and wonderful cooperation.

— Information for this story was furnished by Curtis Baker, Wayne Adams and records of the Hagerman School.

THE LIGHTING SYSTEM

The first settlers in Hagerman probably used candles, coal oil lanterns and lamps for lighting their tents or homes. After the discovery that a circular wick as opposed to the flat wick gave more light the Rayo lamp became very popular.

Then came the Coleman gasoline lanterns and lamps. These burned gasoline which was under pressure. A little pump came with the lamp and each had to be pumped up with air in order to burn.

Shortly after Mr. O.R. Tanner and his son Charlie built and opened a garage in 1914, a horizontal Primm engine was installed to furnish electricity to homes and businesses. Poles were erected and wires strung to light the business houses and most of the homes, churches and other meeting places. The electricity was turned on at dark and off at 10 p.m. Some times the engine would stop but soon Charlie would have it going again and those at the movie would patiently wait to see "who got the girl."

In 1925 the Southwestern Public Service Company came to the valley and furnished electricity twenty-four hours a day. Then the residents could buy electric refrigerators, irons, washers and other appliances that operated with electricity.

Street lights were installed and later improved until now we have a well lighted town and enjoy many conveniences that the pioneers never dreamed of.

DRUGSTORES

According to Jim Cowan, a real old-timer, the first drugstore in Hagerman was in the house now owned by Jim Bowman at 300 West Argyle. A man named Tomlinson operated it and presumably lived there.

In 1903 Mr. R.S. Cravens opened the Hagerman Drug Store in the building where the L&K Cafe is presently located. Cravens was assisted by N.J. Fritz.

The ownership changed hands frequently as did the location. The name of Branstetter was the next on the list of druggists, then in 1910 The Messenger carried an advertisement of the Pecos Valley Drug Co., and George L. Baber was the pharmacist. At one time there was a drugstore on the east side of the Joyce-Pruitt Mercantile Co., which also housed the hotel. At another time there was a drugstore in the lobby of the hotel. There may have been two drugstores in the town at times.

The next druggist or owner was a man named Dohoney. He was followed by T.E. Hall.

Mr. George Sasser bought the drugstore in 1915. His store was located in the building now used as Latimer's barber shop. Mr. Sasser sold out in 1921 to Richmond Hams. Mr. Hams operated the store until 1927 when he sold to Mr. W.W. McAdoo of Carlsbad. McAdoo moved the drugstore across the street to the building now used by Valley Grocery. A Mr. McCall became a partner of Mr. McAdoo and the store was known as the McAdoo-McCall Drug Store.

They in turn sold to a Mr. Brown of Artesia and in 1930 Mr. Frank McCarthy bought the store and moved back across the street. Early in the 1940s, Mr. Hams again acquired the store and later sold to E.C. Smith (better known as Smitty), and he operated under the name of Smitty's Rexall Drug.

Sam Osborn was the next buyer when he took over in 1950. He employed Tucker Collins as pharmacist. In 1952 Cathey-Jacobs of Roswell bought the store and employed various pharmacists to take care of the business. In 1953 they moved the prescription merchandise to Roswell and sold the sundry items to Drike Bealer.

In 1953 Dillard Irby of Artesia opened the Irby Drug Store in a new building which Steve Mason had built next to the movie theater. After seven years Mr. Irby sold out to J.C. Wallace of Hobbs, who moved his Exchange Drug to Hagerman and consolidated the two stores under the name of Wallace Drug. Mr. Wallace continued in business several years, even after there was no doctor in town. When the last doctor left it was not long until he, too, decided to look for greener pastures. He closed out the store in 1969, much to the regret of all Hagerman citizens.

NEWSPAPERS OF HAGERMAN

Hagerman's first newspaper was called *The Irrigator*. William N. Mullane was the editor. The earliest copy found at the Chaves County courthouse was August 21, 1895. It contained mostly news from the large cities of the world, Paris, New York, Chicago, etc., large advertisements of land for sale in the Pecos Valley, surveyors and notary public ads, train schedules, and a very small column of local news.

J.E. Wimberly from Hale Center, Texas, came to Hagerman in 1904 to publish *The Messenger*. It is not known when he published the first paper, though probably in 1904 or 1905. At the time the type had to be set by hand, one letter at a time. Mr. Wimberly was interested in all the news from world wide to the local entertainment. He had strong opinions on most every subject and many articles in this book have been based on his printing. Under Mr. Wimberly's guidance other people, including his two sons, worked in the editing and publishing of *The Messenger*. In 1928 his sister-in-law, Mrs. Ethel Mae McKinstry, was employed by the newspaper company. She continued to work there for a few years after Mr. Wimberly retired in 1939.

Hagerman was without a newspaper for awhile until Mr. and Mrs. Earl Stratton came in 1957. The Strattons began publishing the *Hagerman Star* in July of that year.

HOTEL HAGERMAN

Hotel Hagerman opened its doors to the public in October, 1906. The beautiful brick building was one of the grandest hotels in the Pecos Valley. Located in the downtown area on the corner of Argyle and Cambridge, it cost $19,000.00 to build. A news item from a 1915 *Messenger* states that it was built by local parties. The furniture was birdseye maple, oak and mahogany of a very good grade. All of the furnishings were in harmony with the building.

The upper story was used as a hotel. On the first floor there was lobby and dining room. The Joyce-Pruitt general store and the Hagerman Drug Store occupied other rooms in the downstairs area. Mrs. Ella Davidson was the first person in charge of the hotel although over the years of its service many different people were managers and in charge of the dining room. A Mr. and Mrs. Allison were managers in 1907 and *The Messenger* says that Mr. Allison was an experienced cook. In 1910 H.E. West was manager and Mrs. Kate Waterman and Edna Blocker were directors of the dining room.

On February 4, 1915, the hotel burned to the ground. The fire was discovered about 1:30 a.m. by a Mr. Hall, who was manager of the Hagerman Drug Co. He lived in a room of the hotel. An alarm was given but the fire had gained such headway that an attempt to save the building was a hopeless task. The cause of the fire was unknown. It seemed to have started in the wing of the Joyce-Pruitt store where the hardware stock was kept. The company sustained a total loss, but the drug company saved a considerable amount of their goods. At that time the upper story was under the management of Mason and Devenport, who owned the furnishings of the hotel. The building was then owned by A.D. Garrett of Roswell, New Mexico. Mr. E.E. Hoagland was the manager.

Members of the St. Peter's Catholic Church in Roswell bought the brick that remained from the fire to build their church.

— Information for this article was found in a 1906, 1907 and a 1915 *Messenger*.

Hotel Hagerman and Joyce—Pruitt Store in 1912.

Hotel Hagerman burning in 1915.

THE PECOS VALLEY ALFALFA MILL

An important business development to help start and keep the growth of Hagerman was the Pecos Valley Alfalfa Mill. Although there are no records of whether the mill was started in 1910 or 1911, Mr. Roy Lochhead was the first manager and later bought the mill.

It was operated by a 100 horsepower Corliss engine and later equipped with electric lights which almost doubled its capacity.

In September, 1911, the plant employed about twelve men and turned out thirty-five tons of meal daily. There were two large warehouses — one for hay storage and one for meal which was sometimes held until the market was right. The price in September, 1911, was $16.00 per ton.

By 1915 the owner, Mr. Lochhead, had customers in the northeastern part of the United States, Cuba, Norway and many other countries. The standing of the business was such that when a car of alfalfa meal was loaded, the bill of lading was taken to the bank, a draft drawn and the deposit was credited as a cash item.

Ground alfalfa became more and more favorable as a feed, especially as a mixed feed element. The food value of the Pecos Valley alfalfa product, recognized the world over, was much higher than that produced in any other section of the country. Customers learned that the uniform rules of grading were the same as those used for flour and other mill products.

There were few other successful alfalfa mills in the country. The many failures in the industry were not due to a lack of capital or bad business management but the inferiority of the raw product. The Pecos Valley still grows the best alfalfa in the country.

Alfalfa Feed Mill, 1912.

Mr. Hal Bogle eventually bought the mill from Mr. and Mrs. Roy Lochhead.

Roy I. Lochhead was a well-known resident of the Pecos Valley. He arrived in Hagerman in 1907 and established the Pecos Valley Alfalfa Milling Company with Ray Levers as a partner. Mr. Lochhead was active in a number of business enterprises in the area.

Mr. Lochhead married the former Odessa White who had been a teacher in the rural schools of the county. They had one son, Jim, and Mr. Lochhead had another son, Roy Jr., by a former marriage. In 1941 Mr. Lochhead died at the age of fifty-four and Mrs. Lochhead died two years later as a result of a car accident.

— Information for this article was taken from a 1915 *Messenger* and *The National Land and Irrigation Journal* of 1911.

HISTORY OF THE COTTON GINS
By O.J. Ford

The first cotton was grown in the Hagerman area around 1918. At that time the nearest gin was at Carlsbad where the cotton was taken by wagon and team. This was quite a chore as most wagons would only hold one bale. However, cotton growing at that time was an experiment and only a very few bales were harvested. In the early twenties a number of farmers indicated that they were going to plant several acres and persuaded the banker and a few other prominent citizens to build a gin. This plant was built at York and Perth Streets (where the south gin now stands). The group responsible for the building of this gin was: W.A. Losey, Noah West, Jack Sweatt, Van Sweatt, Sr., Ben Jack West, J.T. West, Tom McKinstry, Jim McKinstry, Sam McKinstry and J.W. Pardee. The manager was John Campbell.

This gin was a two-story plant with Continental machinery, 4-70 Pratt stands and feeders with one overhead cleaner and a "contraption" known only as a mockingbird, which choked down about three times on each bale. This, together with the usual suction, separator, lint flue, condensor and press was about the extent of the machinery used. The power plant for the first year's operation was a steam powered Hart-Parr tractor which was purchased from Mark Boyce who used it in operating his thrashing machine. This tractor was stationed behind the gin building and pulled the machinery by means of a long belt. This was not the best arrangement in the world but as there was not too much cotton ginned that first year, they managed to get by very well.

The second year a 100 HP Twin Cylinder Fairbanks-Morse diesel engine was purchased and installed in the new engine room which was of adobe construction with walls eighteen inches thick. This addition was the gin plant, modern in every respect.

By 1925 considerable cotton was being grown in the valley and several gins had been built. There had been quite a bit of concern about an infestation of pink bollworms which had reportedly been brought in or blown in from Old Mexico. The U.S. Department of Agriculture made rules and regulations to the effect that all gins would have to sterilize the cotton seed at the time of ginning. This sterilizer was made of sixty feet of twelve inch well casing with sixy feet of ten inch casing on the inside. This was welded together at the ends in order to hold steam. There was a nine inch conveyor installed inside the ten inch pipe. Steam pipes were connected to the boiler and as the seed was conveyed through the pipes it was heated to a minimum of 160 degrees. Near the discharge end of the pipe a thermometer was inserted into the sterilizer where it would come in contact with the seed and then record the temperature on a chart in the clock which was on the wall. This clock was locked and the Government inspector held the key. The chart was changed every twenty-four hours. After this installation the ginner was "hotter" than the cotton seed, the Government was mad because the ginner didn't get the seed hot enough and the farmer was mad because he got 'em too hot. Whether this regulation was of any benefit or not we will never know, but the ginner knows one thing: there were always more inspectors seen around the gin than there were pink bollworms.

In 1925 a Company was organized and built a second gin in Hagerman. It was known as Farmers Gin Company. Harry Cowan was president and C.W. Curry was secretary-treasurer and manager. Lester Hinrichsen was bookkeeper for several years. Other officers and directors' names were not obtainable. A new modern plant was erected with the latest machinery installed. It was a Continental 5-80 outfit complete with electrical power. It was also equipped with a fourteen foot Hardwicke-Etter Burr Machine, which, in my opinion, was the best on the market

Hagerman's first Gin.

at that time. This was probably the most up-to-date plant in the valley. They had a fine business and did a good job of ginning. This gin was operated by the original company until about 1941 when it was sold to Hal Bogle.

The Hagerman Gin Company sold it's property to W.W. Akin in 1928. O.J. Ford was employed as manager. The plant was operated four years with the original machinery, then was re-designed. The building was enlarged, the old machinery taken out and replaced with Lummus equipment which was installed on a ground floor. This plant was operated as W.W. Akin Gin from 1928 to 1944 when it was sold to the newly formed Farmers Cooperative Association. This Association was chartered in March, 1944. The first Board of Directors was composed of Jim Michelet, A.W. (Bill) Langenegger, W.E. Utterback, Roscoe Fletcher and Sanford Knoll. Original membership consisted of sixty farmers who pledged $100.00 each to get the Association started. After purchasing the Akin Gin, the Association bought the Bogle Gin in Hagerman (formerly Farmers Gin Co.) and three gins from Greenfield Gin Co. One was located in Greenfield and two in Dexter. O.J. Ford was the first manager of the Farmers Co-op Association, a position he held for 21 years. He retired in 1965. J.H. Baxter has been manager since 1965.

HAGERMAN GARAGES
By B.W. and Helen Curry

The first garage in Hagerman, so far as we are able to determine, was owned and operated by A.J. Hicks. In March, 1912, Mr. Hicks opened a garage in a building which had been used by a lumber company and was located on the property where the Nazarene Church now stands.

In 1914 Mr. O.R. Tanner and his son, Charlie, built a building on a lot west of the railroad track on Argyle. The foundation and floor of concrete were put in by L.R. Burck. The building was 26 feet by 60 feet.

This was the Tanner garage where Charlie did electrical and mechanical work and later installed a light plant which furnished the first electric lights for the town of Hagerman. He obtained a Ford dealership and sold many cars in the area. He sold Ford parts and accessories and made repairs.

Around 1917-18, T.D. Devenport and Clay Lemon opened a garage on the south side of Argyle in the business district. A couple of years later they sold it to Jess Turner who in turn sold out to Earl Camp and Bayard Curry in 1921. This was the start of the C and C Garage.

In the spring of 1926 they moved the business across the street to the building now occupied by Gibson's barber shop. In 1927 they rented the Tanner building and Mr. Tanner put an addition on the east side of the building. In 1930 Earl Camp sold his interest in the garage to Curry and moved to Carlsbad.

Curry bought the Tanner building in 1934 and in 1946 built an addition to the west side of the building. During the 1930's Curry obtained a franchise to sell Chevrolets. Several carloads of new cars were sold. H.C. Babb was the salesman.

Between 1915 and 1920, Ben Lampton opened a garage in a building located where the Conoco Station now stands.

Several garages opened and closed over the years. Bert Dority had a garage in the building at Argyle and Cambridge, now occupied by the HELP Center. Later, he sold out to Basil Barnett, who operated the business until 1968 when he sold to his brother, V.R. Barnett.

That same year V.R. Barnett also bought the C & C Garage, remodeled and built on to the building and operated it for a few years. At the present time the garage is closed and there is no garage in Hagerman.

Others who had garages at various times were Dugan Taylor, Delbert Dennis, Dudley Stephon and Jerry Young.

Some of the men who worked for the C & C Garage during the forty-seven years of its existence were: Earl Bratcher; Howard Brown; Clyde Gant and his brother-in-law, "Pee Wee" Hartley; Earl Berryman; Charlie Troublefield; Delbert Dennis; Shorty Dennison; Henry Basden; Pat Wylie; Fernando Ramirez; Bill Dearholt; Raynal Cumpsten and Walter Elliott. There were others too numerous to mention who worked for shorter periods.

EARL LATIMER — HAGERMAN BARBER

*By Audre Latimer King
and Dianne Latimer Andress*

Our father, Earl Latimer, came to Hagerman in 1908 and did farm work. He tells of jogging five miles into town to play pool at night after working in the fields all day. He became acquainted with Al Jones, who owned the barber shop and pool hall, located where the Valley Grocery is now, on the south side of downtown Argyle Street. Because he had always been interested in cutting hair he kept on asking Al Jones where he could learn to barber. After sometime Al decided he was serious and taught him the trade.

Earl started his career as a barber in the Al Jones' shop in 1912. After he had mastered the trade he taught his brother Everett to barber. The two had been close all of their lives and continued this closeness in their business careers.

Shortly after Everett's return from World War I, in 1920, the two brothers bought the shop in Hagerman. Everett married Vesta Whitman, barbered and lived in Hagerman. Later the brothers bought the Old Mission Barber Shop in Roswell.

In the present Hagerman shop, located on the north side of downtown Argyle Street, the back bar and lavatory are the same fixtures that were in the original shop. Another permanent fixture of the shop is the large painting, "Custers Last Stand," which was given to the Hagerman shop by the makers of Budweiser Beer — long before the days of national prohibition.

Our father has always been interested in sports and he played on the Hagerman baseball team when he was a young man. Many people can attest that he has never hesitated to fight for what he strongly feels is right. Also, in his younger years, he never missed a dance if he could manage in any way to get there. He tells us about renting horses and a buggy to take his date to one of those famous dances at the Felix Ranch.

In 1915 Earl and Johnie Parks were married and they established their home in Dexter.

Now after 63 years he is still barbering and operating his own shop in Hagerman, and who could possibly know the number of people that he has "clipped."

Glenn Latimer, Earl and Johnie's son, is serving the people as a barber just as his father has.

BRIEF HISTORY OF HAGERMAN BANK
By Mabel Nail

The Hagerman Bank, a corporation, was incorporated the ninth day of November, 1904, in the County of Chaves and Territory of New Mexico. The Board of Directors were: E.D. Balcom, E.A. Cahoon, H.J. Hagerman, George M. Slaughter, A.R. Teeple, John W. Warren, W.M. Waskom. John W. Warren was elected president of the corporation; H.J. Hagerman, vice-president; W.M. Waskom, cashier.

Cashiers' salary was set at $1,200.00 per year, with clerks' salary of $40.00 per month. Currency would be issued in denominations of $10s and $20s.

Bids for the construction of a brick building in the town of Hagerman were opened on December 16, 1905, and a contract was awarded to G.N. Amis with a bid of $7,126.00, with instructions to veneer the front of the building with press brick. The bank building was accepted as finished by the contractor on May 4, 1906.

A statement of condition dated June 30, 1907, shows the total assets of the bank to be $5,971.89.

E.A. Cahoon was president of the bank in 1910. John I. Hinkle was cashier from 1906 to 1912. George W. Losey was elected cashier in December, 1912. W.A. Losey was appointed cashier on September 4, 1914. George W. Losey was elected president of the bank in January, 1915.

At a meeting of the Board on April 15, 1907, the stockholders of the Hagerman National Bank, a corporation, voted to amend the section of the article giving the name of the bank, "The First National Bank of Hagerman."

In 1918 the Board was unable to have its regular meetings for three months of October, November and

December due to the prevalence of influenza and general quarantine.

Failure of banks in Artesia and Lake Arthur, and the effect it would have on the bank at Hagerman, was the main topic of discussion at the February, 1919, Board meeting.

The bank continued to show steady growth over the years. In 1946 Mr. Clifford Helms was appointed Vice-President.

A new bank building was built on the corner of Argyle and Oxford Streets and completed in August, 1961. On July 17, 1964, The First National Bank of Hagerman was sold by its stockholders to the First National Bank of Roswell, its official name now being Hagerman Branch, First National Bank of Roswell.

Mr. Helms passed away in February, 1969, and was succeeded by Max Malone of Olton, Texas. Mr. Malone left the bank December 1, 1971, and was replaced by Bill Strickland from the Roswell bank. At the present time Billy J. Petree is Vice-President and Branch Manager.

First National Bank, built in 1906.

THE VOLUNTEER FIRE DEPARTMENT

By Joe Mann

From Minutes of Town Board Meetings.

At a meeting on October 11, 1911, the Town Board decided to purchase a thirty-six inch fire bell weighing 580 pounds. The first fire engine was a hand drawn cart with two thirty-five gallon chemical tanks on it. On April 8, 1912, the board decided that the volunteer firemen should be exempt from street tax. Mayor Powell appointed Mr. Ehret and Mr. Jones as a Fire Protection Committee at the May 13, 1912, meeting.

Mayor Powell called a special session on November 24, 1913, for the purpose of talking over the completion of the fire house. Mr. Walton made a report that it would take $439.00 to complete. A motion was made by Mr. Walton, seconded by Mr. Wranosky, to finish the fire house.

On December 11, 1922, a Ford fire truck was purchased from the Roswell Auto Company for $474.00. In August, 1944, while Wayne Graham was fire chief, a new department was established and a new truck costing $3,419.00 was bought.

Ordinance No. 79, passed March 21, 1950, holds that the fire chiefs be appointed by the mayor with the approval of the town trustees. H.E. Porter was appointed fire chief April 10, 1950. Amos Hampton followed him in 1955. Wayne Graham became chief again in 1956 when Amos Hampton resigned to move. S.A. "Corky" Andrus served from about 1960 until 1963. C.D. "Dee" Eastham was next and when he resigned the mayor and trustees appointed Joe Mann. He served until his retirement in 1974. Gary Boyce was the next fire chief and at the present time Cassie Mason heads the department.

The fire bell was replaced by a siren but the old bell is still in place. About the only time it is rung now is on Halloween. But those who remember its loud ring will never forget it.

The town now has a modern well equipped building, two tanker trucks with from twelve to fifteen volunteer firemen.

Hagerman's first Fire Department.

HAGERMAN WATER SYSTEM

By Joe Mann

In the early days of Hagerman water was brought up from Carlsbad in a tank car for use by the residents. In the late 1890's artesian wells were being dug to supply water. The artesian wells that Mr. Hagerman had dug across from the depot contained too much sulphur for most people, but others thought the water was very healthful.

As farms developed nearly everyone had a surface well for domestic use, and often townspeople would haul water from one of the surrounding farms.

In October of 1914 the town board decided to offer Mr. L.E. Evans $750.00 for two eight inch wells and one-half acre of land west of town. Mr. Evans accepted the offer.

In November the board agreed to have a storage reservoir constructed. The tank was to be of cement, ten feet high and thirty feet wide. The contract for construction went to L.W. McBride.

Water lines were laid into the town and in the early part of 1915 water meters were installed. James Cowan was appointed the first water superintendent.

In 1934 a $35,000.00 bond issue was approved by the voters to extend the water lines. D.P. Chappell was hired as superintendent. Soon after this the town installed a sewer system.

Several others served as water superintendent and in 1948 Joe Mann became town manager. He continued in this position until he retired in 1974. Roger Salas now holds the position.

GAS LINES

The town records do not show when the Gas Company laid the pipelines in Hagerman. The following accounts appeared in The Messenger, the local newspaper. The June 11, 1929, issue carried the proposed gas franchise by the Pecos Valley Gas Co., also a proclamation by Mayor J.T. West asking all who were interested in obtaining gas for the town of Hagerman to register their vote at the town hall and to make a ten dollar deposit. The vote was almost unanimous in favor of the gas lines. In November of 1929 an ad appeared from Pecos Valley Gas Company asking customers to have their appliances checked by their serviceman to make sure that they were properly adjusted.

The Southern Union Gas Company bought the Pecos Valley Gas Company and had an office in Artesia. In 1952 Southern Union opened an office in Hagerman on South Cambridge Street. In 1968 a new office building was erected in the same location. In December of 1972 the Hagerman office was closed and all work now is done in the Roswell office.

THE TELEPHONE SYSTEM
By Helen Curry

The first mention of a telephone system for Hagerman was found in the minutes of a town board meeting on October 9, 1905, when Mr. E.D. Balcom asked for a franchise. On November 13 of that year Ordinance No. 7 was read and passed, granting a franchise for a period of twenty-five years to Mr. Balcom or his successors and assigns. There was an amendment to section 1 as follows: provided that no wires shall be strung on poles less than eighteen feet from the ground.

Evidently this was for the lines in town as old-timers tell us that some of the wires were strung on fences in the early days.

We do not know how long Mr. Balcom operated the telephone system, but in 1911 Mountain States Telephone and Telegraph Company entered New Mexico by taking over the Colorado Telephone Company with exchanges in fourteen New Mexico towns including Hagerman.

Mountain States acquired, along with the Roswell exchange, a long distance line from Roswell to Clovis and from Roswell to Artesia. Roswell had been connected with Albuquerque in 1910. Roswell was made headquarters of the Mountain States District office.

Hagerman had dial phones installed in 1939 with equipment still housed in the upper floor of the bank building. That, of course, eliminated the need for an operator.

In 1958 a new equipment building was built on Argyle Street, just east of the town hall. In December of 1973 we got direct dialing. We now have 609 telephones in operation in Hagerman.

Mr. Tom Campbell is the telephone repairman and has lived in Hagerman for eight years.

— Thanks to Mr. Bill O'Dowd of the telephone business office in Roswell for some of this information.

HAGERMAN POST OFFICE
By F.K. Boyce

The Post Office was established in 1894 as Felix, New Mexico, with A.B. Phillips as its first postmaster. On February 27, 1895, the name was changed to Hagerman with John H. Langford as postmaster. Other postmasters were Alfred N. Miller, April 4, 1899; Thomas B. Platt, January 29, 1908; Charles M. Sanford, October 1, 1914; Maggie E. Wimberly, December 17, 1919; Helen McBride Wimberly, September 30, 1921; Cassius G. Mason, April 17, 1922; Robert Cumpsten, March 1, 1935 until April 24, 1965 when he retired. Francis K. Boyce was appointed acting postmaster April 24, 1965, and was commissioned July 27, 1966.

Some of the buildings in which the post office was housed included the A.N. Miller store, the north end of the old bank building and the Lang building on Argyle.

Now a new modern building on the south side of Argyle houses the post office. The dedication of the new building took place on October 9, 1964, at 3 p.m. John Garner was master of ceremonies and the address was given by the honorable Joseph M. Montoya, United States Congressman. Congressman Montoya presented a flag that had flown over the Capitol in Washington, D.C. The Boy Scout Troop #20 conducted the flag raising ceremony. The high school band provided the music. A tour of the building was conducted by the postal clerks and refreshments were served by ladies of the community.

Some of the clerks who have worked in the post office through the years are Mary Mason, O.J. Atwood, Mrs. Mary Brannon, Polly Cumpsten, Slick Boyce, Bob Hart, Zan King, Ruby Arnold, Leona Mayberry, Jean George, Mary Smith, Mae White, Katie Langston, Ruth Brown, Eulalia Campbell, Lila Heitman and Billie Eastham.

Rural carriers included Mr. Black, E.O. Reed, J.E. Wimberly, J.C. Wyman and Jean George.

HISTORY OF THE HAGERMAN CANAL

The Hagerman Canal was constructed in about 1888 to transport surface water and spring flow of the Rio Hondo and its tributaries and South Spring River in the Roswell area to lands in the vicinity of Hagerman. At the time of the canal's construction there was no irrigation from wells and the Carlsbad Irrigation project or the Pecos River compact had not been considered.

Pat Garrett, C.D. Bonney and others formed a company and capital was secured from Chicago. Two large machines were purchased to dig the canal. The machines plowed a furrow and carried dirt on an endless belt. Fourteen horses and mules and three men were needed to operate the machines.

The canal was originally designed to be thirty feet deep and handle 100 second feet of water. It was never deeper than ten feet. It took several years to build and was not a success at first. It has been said that it took two months for the water to get to the end of the canal because Hondo flood water had not yet coated the bottom with mud.

Charles B. Eddy started the Carlsbad Irrigation project, and he and Mr. Garrett decided to become partners. In looking for financial aid they contacted Mr. J.J. Hagerman from Colorado. Mr. Hagerman came to the Pecos Valley and decided to invest in the enterprise.

A company called the Pecos Irrigation and Improvement Company was formed. The Northern Canal was finished in 1891, and the McMillan dam on the Carlsbad project was finished in 1893.

No real development was made under the canal until the spring of 1893, when several hundred acres were planted to alfalfa and various other crops. Water rights for land could be purchased at $7.00 to $10.00 per acre. The holders of the water rights received, during the irrigating season, thirty acre inches of water or so much as they required, at $1.25 per acre per year. However, if they wanted a greater amount of water it was obtained as excess water on the basis of 3630 cubic feet or one acre inch at five cents — sixty cents per foot.

All did not go well with Eddy and Hagerman and in 1895 they dissolved partnership, Eddy taking the Carlsbad Irrigation project and Mr. Hagerman the Northern Canal.

In 1907 Mr. Hagerman offered to sell the canal to the water rights owners for $50,000.00. It required but two weeks to enter into arrangements for taking over the property and the Hagerman Irrigation Company was formed.

At first, two ditch riders were employed. The south side of the Felix ranch was the dividing line. A two wheeled cart pulled by one horse was used. The cart carried a shovel, pitch fork, grabbing hook, saw, hammer and nails. All weirs and headgates were wooden. Delivery ditches were dirt and had to be cleaned out by hoe hands.

Cleaning the Canal with teams and scrapers in the early days.

A dam-flood.

The Northern Canal in 1909.

In the winter the entire canal was cleaned out with teams and scrapers. From fifteen to twenty-five teams were hired. Camps were set up with sleeping tents, a cook tent, and one for horse feed and odds and ends. Men worked as long as there was daylight and were paid $3.25 per day and board. Horses and mules were sometimes down on their backs in ditches or nearly lost in mud and water.

Most of the land in the early days was rough and it took a determined man to irrigate his plowed land. When the canal had plenty of water, a user could order a head of water and keep it until he finished. Now the water is on rotation and one hour per acre is the general rule.

After landowners began to drill wells, the water table began to drop and the springs nearly stopped flowing. The canal company was forced to drill artesian and shallow wells and purchase drainage lines.

It was first planned to irrigate 15,000 acres from the canal. Now there are 9,026 acres of land watered by the canal and 106 water rights. The main canal is thirty-two miles long and there are thirty-six miles of delivery ditches. Thirty miles of these ditches are cemented.

W.E. Bowen was the first Superintendent of the Hagerman Irrigation Company. He also used his surveying ability to plot ditches and farms in the area. He had been connected with the canal since 1894.

Clay Lemon was a long time manager of the canal company. Bert Bailey worked for many years for the company. His job was keeping ditches clean and repairing and building forms for head gates and weirs. Many will remember Buck Boyce who worked by the day with a team and as a cook.

The following are men who have served as members of the Board of Directors of the Hagerman Canal. The last four are serving in that capacity at this time.

H.C. Barron
J.B. McConnell
Harry Cowan
A.E. Macy
O.D. Whitney
J.E. Fife
Howard Russell

B.H. Wixom
M.M. Brayshaw
W.F. Greenwood
N.S. West
E.H. Jones
A.G. Mills
Sam McKinstry
G.L. Truitt
George Losey
J.W. Davidson
W.E. Bowen
Levi Barnett
T.B. Platt
J.E. Blythe
Fred Mielenz
R.C. Reid
M.Y. Monical
Hal Bogle
F.L. Mehlhop
Jim Michelet
Harold Hanson
J.D. Mitchell
Stanley Utterback
Max Wiggins
Bob McNeil
Bobby Michelet
P.R. Monical
John H. Reid
Bill Bogle
Lawrence Lathrop
V.R. Barnett
John Garner

— News items from a 1907 *Messenger* were used to write the history of the canal. Ernest Bowen, W.E. Utterback and Bill Bogle furnished information.

THE DRAINAGE SYSTEM

A petition was filed in the District Court on February 8, 1913, petitioning for the establishment of a drainage district. The general description of the proposed work was that ditches would be constructed to drain the lands from seepage water and carry away the alkali.

This needed improvement meant much to the future of the Pecos Valley. The system was to reclaim thousands of acres of waterlogged land and guarantee the future against deterioration from the effects of alkali. It insured the permanency and stability of farm values.

Under the drainage law, the arrangements for repayment of bonds were to be liberal. The first five years there was to be no assessment except interest which was six percent. After the sixth year the principal was payable in fifteen annual payments.

Including the main drains and the laterals, the system had about sixty-five miles of tiling from six to twenty-one inches in size. One-hundred-seventy-five train car loads of tiling and other materials were used in the construction.

Ditching machines were brought in after attempting to dig by hand to the eleven foot depth. Mr. Bill Hart ran the digging machine. There was much trouble with sand filling the lines and later open ditches had to be made on some of the lines.

Walter S. Dickey contracted to construct the work in June, 1915. The preliminary survey work was started October 13, 1913. There were many engineers who worked on the system which was not completed until 1917.

— The 1913 *Messengers* published articles about the drainage system and most of the information for this story was found in the old newspapers.

Digging system, between 1914 and 1917.

RIVER FORDS AND BRIDGES

Before there were bridges on the Pecos River fords were used to cross. Because of high banks on one side or the other and because of quick sand, a place to ford the river had to be carefully chosen. Sometimes when the rivers were up, men and teams were carried several hundred yards below the crossings.

One crossing east and south of Hagerman was called the Hagerman ford. This crossing was used by ranchers and freighters. There was a crossing farther south called Bonine, later called the Bruce ford. The next ford south was called the Haynes or Jim Miller crossing.

Through the efforts of some of the citizens of Hagerman, enough funds were raised in 1907 to build a ferry. This was a great convenience to the people living east of the river. The ferry was built as an experiment and it accidently sank. A new ferry was launched on May 31, 1907. The name of the new boat was "It," and the people were looking forward to a bridge being constructed.

The first Pecos River bridge near Hagerman was a cable bridge, built about 1908, at a cost of $10,380.00. It was located just south of where the Felix River empties into the Pecos River. This bridge fell when a herd of cattle belonging to the Turkey Track ranch was crossing. The weight of the cattle was more than the bridge could hold.

The next Pecos bridge was finished in 1924 and was located east of Hagerman. This was a wood piling bridge. Flood water damaged it beyond repair in 1954. The present bridge, built in 1955, is located east of the 1924 bridge on Highway 31.

Felix River Bridge, under construction, 1916.

A picture of the first Felix bridge appeared in a 1907 *Messenger* with this description: "A suspension steel bridge over the pure cool water of the Felix River. The stream is 200 feet wide and has a depth of two to twenty feet. It never goes dry being supplied by underground springs." No one knows for sure when this bridge was constructed. In April, 1915, flood water washed the bridge away. The Harshey and Heitman crossings were used until a new bridge was completed in 1915 or 1916. Mrs. Alta Gehman Evans recalls a cement ditch near the bridge on the north side of the Felix. She knew it as the "Little Dam" and used to go there to pick watercress. This bridge lasted until the late 1940's when a camper under the bridge left his campfire and the wooden part of the bridge floor burned.

When Highway 285 from Roswell was paved, a new Felix River bridge east of the old one was erected. This was in 1926.

— Information furnished from 1907, 1908 and 1915 *Messengers* and W.E. Utterback, Alta Evans and Ernest Langenegger.

Pecos River Bridge, 1907.

ORGANIZATION OF THE PRESBYTERIAN CHURCH

The record of the First Presbyterian Church begins as follows: January 25, 1905, First Presbyterian Church of Hagerman organized. By request of a number of Christian people of Hagerman, New Mexico, and after several years of services furnished by Dr. C.E. Lukens, pastor of the First Presbyterian Church of Roswell, New Mexico, a meeting was called January 25, 1905, for the purpose of organizing a Presbyterian Church.

The record goes on to say that there had been a special revival meeting for the past five days during which Dr. Lukens preached and the Rev. John Meeker of Portales led the singing.

Dr. Lukens presided over the organizational meeting and the Rev. Meeker was appointed secretary.

The following persons presented themselves for charter membership, coming from other churches: Mrs. A.A. Cooper, Mrs. H.C. Carter, Mrs. Arrita Woodman, Mrs. L.W. Mitchell, Miss Helen Mitchell, Robert Gardiner, Margaret Gardiner, Eva Gardiner, Mrs. James T. Gardiner, Mr. and Mrs. R.L. Clark and Mr. and Mrs. J.E. Wimberly. Those persons who presented themselves for baptism were: Winnie Mason, Mellie Mason, Lillie Tucker, Mrs. Fannie Tucker, Arthur Cooper, Ellen Cooper, Horace Cooper, and Mrs. W.E. Washington. These were all charter members, but a footnote states that the Gardiner family left Hagerman shortly after the church was organized and were never fully identified with this body. The organization of the church was authorized by the Rio Grande Presbytery at a meeting held in Santa Fe in October of 1903, at a meeting of the Synod.

Presbyterian Church, 1906.

The original building, which was built in 1906, is still being used. The building was struck twice by lightning and once the ceiling around the stove pipe caught fire, but, in all cases, quick action held the damage to a minimum. In 1934 a basement was put under the building, containing a fellowship hall, a kitchen, four classrooms and a restroom. When the restroom was in the basement, the basement was flooded several times causing extensive damage to furniture and books. Later the restrooms were added to the back of the church at ground level.

At the time the basement was put in, the upper part of the building was remodeled with two rooms added on each side of the pulpit. The Lake Arthur church building was bought from Presbytery, and that lumber was used in the remodeling and in the basement. The pews from that church were painted and are now in use. Mr. Harry Steinberger assisted by L.E. Hinrichsen built and installed the pulpit furniture and communion table as a gift to the church.

Many of the early members were here only a short time, others stayed for longer periods of time. But one man whose service to the church from its beginning until about 1942, who served as Sunday School superintendent, elder, and in other capacities, must be mentioned. J.E. Wimberly, who gave so much to keep the church going, in good times and bad, remained faithful until his health failed and he moved to Roswell, where he passed away in 1943.

The church was at first a National Mission church, financial aid being received from that board. Later the church became self-supporting. But due to the decrease in membership and the rising cost of operating a church, the Hagerman and Dexter Presbyterian churches formed a yoked parish with one minister. It has worked very well for both churches.

Pastors who served the church in order of service were: W.M. Carle, B.C. Meeker, J.H. Doran, J.C. Turner, D.B. Simpson, H.J. Cumpsten, E.E. Mathis, C.T. Walker, Samuel Mayne, William Eadie, J.C. Hughes, J.A. Hedges, Emory Fritz, a Mr. McCrory, Harry Cox, C.E. Powell, Mebane Ramsay, R.B. Sherman, and Howard Holland. The present pastor is Charles Fullinwider.

CHURCH OF CHRIST

The first Church of Christ to be organized in Hagerman was due to the efforts of O.C. Lusk and Oscar Walters and families. Others who were members when the church was organized were Mr. and Mrs Elvin Lusk, Mrs. Devenport, affectionately known as Grandmother Devenport, and her daughter, Mrs. Iola Lemon.

Organization took place in 1923 after a meeting held by Brother Thomas F. Thomasson, who served as first preacher. Services were held first in the Adventist Church, later in a movie house and then in a room over the bank.

In 1928 a building was purchased from the Kemp Lumber Company and moved to the corner of Argyle and Winchester Streets. The building is still being used today.

Through the years the membership grew and at one time the congregation was quite large. In the 1950's another church was organized which took some of the members from the first one.

A number of members moved away, other passed away and now the membership is small. However, those who remain are faithful and services are held each week. Kenneth Ward is now the leader for the church.

THE CATHOLIC CHURCH

The first Catholic Church in Hagerman was built mainly through the efforts of the Wranosky family. Mr. and Mrs. John Wranosky and his brother Frank brought their families to this town in the spring of 1905.

John Wranosky bought up most of the lots in the southwest part of town which was known as the Wranosky Addition. He gave lots on which to build a Catholic Church and it was situated on the site of the present St. Catherine's Church. He then contacted other Catholic families in the area, two of which were the Frank Walters and Krukenmier families. He also solicited aid from the Catholic officials in Roswell. With assistance from them the church was built. It was called St. Mary's Church.

When the church was completed, Mr. Wranosky told his daughters that if they would give their organ to the church, he would get a piano for them. They agreed and it was done. Since the church was not being used at the time of their departure from this area in 1920, they took the organ with them. It is still being used in the home of Winnie Wranosky Kebble's daughter-in-law in Texas.

Quoting from a letter from Mabel Wranosky Reed, concerning the first service in the little church; "A Sister came down from Roswell and taught me to play the introductory hymns, also a couple of the more important hymns. I'll never forget that service—The kindness and understanding of the priest and sisters!"

During the early years several Franciscan priests, including, Fr. Sixtus Kepp, Fr. Bernard Espelage, the future bishop of Gallup, New Mexico, Fr. Theodosius Meyer and others served the church at Hagerman as part of a string of missions that included Clovis, Portales and Elida. The priest lived at St. Peter's in Roswell. He would board the train to

Hagerman on Saturdays, stay over night, offer Mass on Sunday and return to Roswell by train.

For some reason services had to be discontinued, and in 1923 the original church building was sold to Mr. Alf Deason for two hundred and fifty dollars. Mr. Deason removed the building from the property and for many years it was used as a barn.

In 1958 a barracks was acquired by the Catholic community and services and instructions were held in it until the present building was ready for use.

Construction on the present structure was begun in 1961, under the direction of Bruce Bailey, local carpenter, and the present pastor, Fr. Joyce Finnigan. Generous donations from the Catholic Extension Society, the Franciscan Fathers of Cincinati and the Clement Hendricks family of Flying H Ranch were added to steady donations of parishioners to finance the project. An interest-free loan of six thousand dollars was obtained from the Franciscan Missionary Union.

The building was begun in September 1961. By Christmas Fr. Julian Reusseau was able to give the first mission or revival in it.

St. Catherine's Church was formally dedicated by Archbishop Byrne of Santa Fe on September 16, 1962.

Originally the church was planned to accommodate approximately eighty families in and around Hagerman and to seat 250 people. It was more than adequate for the congregation. Beginning in 1966, Catholic boys from Villa Solana school, who previously had attended Mass in Dexter, began attending services in Hagerman and the added seating was put to good use.

At present a small dedicated group of men are forging ahead with a series of improvements on the church. Carpeting has been added to the middle aisle, the sanctuary remodeled, and grass has replaced gravel in the churchyard. The church is served by a Franciscan priest, Fr. Joyce Finnigan, who lives in the church building in Dexter. Mass is offered each Sunday at 9:15 a.m. and usually on Thursday evenings.

— Information supplied by Tony Trujillo and Mabel Wranosky Reed.

FIRST CHURCH OF THE NAZARENE HAGERMAN, NEW MEXICO

The Rev. T.V. Cox came from Artesia to Hagerman as a missionary and started the work of the Church of the Nazarene.

On January 17, 1923, the Rev. C.W. and Florence Davis, district superintendent, began a revival that lasted through February 3. On that date the Hagerman church was organized with twenty-eight members. The Rev. David Mickey was called as the first pastor. Services were held in the Christian Church, which was not being used at the time, until the construction of the present church building was completed in the spring of 1925.

Charter members were: Mrs. Irene Bailey, J.W. Baugh, Mrs. Zora Baugh, Francis Beeman, Mrs. Ruth Beeman, Lucille Beeman, Beauford Green, Mrs. Acey Green, C.G. Howe, Mrs. Nellie Howe, Glendon Howe, Mrs. Bessie Hoyt, Helen Hoyt, H.A. Olive, Mrs. Rosa Olive, Mrs. Sally Pilley, Gladys Pilley, Fred Pilley, Dick Pritchard, George Weaver, Mrs. Hannah Weaver, Alda Weaver, Ethel Weaver, Frank Reinecke, Mrs. Opal Reinecke, C.J. Wild and Mrs. Margaret Wild. Living charter members in the vicinity are Fred Pilley, Mrs. George Lewis (Opal Reinecke), and Lucille Beeman (Mrs. Willie Pilley).

Ministers who have served the church are: T.V. Cox, David D. Mickey, John F. Robersts (later District Superintendent), Mary E. Hartline, W.A. Huffman, W.J. Bell, E.E. and Ora J. Turner, Warn A. Henry, Walter Orr, C.W. Gardner, E.L. Askins, P.B. Wallace, Harold W. Morris (later District Superintendent), J.S. Collins, V.S. Wheeler, C.E. Hagemeier, H.E. Russell, E.M. Culberson, J.A. Deville, C.H. Lucas, Marvin L. Ford, Larry J. Webb (now missionary in Barbados Islands), Alvin Keswater, Wiley Whitt, Lucille Stockton, James Pettigrew, and Ray Morrison.

— Information received from Mrs. Fred Pilley.

HISTORY OF THE SEVENTH DAY ADVENTIST CHURCH OF HAGERMAN, NEW MEXICO

By Grace Cole Greer

The Hagerman Church is the oldest organized Seventh Day Adventist church in the state of New Mexico — and perhaps in the Texico Conference, which includes a portion of West Texas and the state of New Mexico. Among the oldest families who were members of the church were the Arvid Johnson family, H.C. Barron family, the Frank Green Family, J.M. Cowles, Mrs. L.J. Black and family — Mr. Black later joined the church, Mrs. J.E. Jacobson and family, John Anderson and family, Dr. Brayshaw and family, the C.W. Cole family and perhaps others. It was an organized group of about four or five of these families on May 16, 1896. Their first meeting place was the old brick public grade school building, the remains of which are now a residence in the northeast part of Hagerman. Elder Milo D. Warfle held the first S.D.A. series of meetings in Hagerman in this old public school building.

However, it was a few years before they were able to build a church of their own. It was erected mainly through the means and labor of the church members and that which was generously donated by citizens of the town of Hagerman. The church building at that time consisted of one main room, without the division that is now in the rear of the room. The heating system was a coal stove which sat in the middle of the aisle. The lighting was produced by coal oil lamps with reflectors attached to the windows on each side of the church. There is no record in the local files or in the conference files as to the actual date of dedication of the building, but, as near as can be determined, it must have been in the latter part of 1907.

The first one teacher church school was organized in 1909 in the original church room with a brown chintz curtain drawn across the front of the rostrum. The teacher's desk was a handmade table which is still in use at the church. Two of the present chairs are part of the original furniture. They served as the teacher's chair and were used by the elders and visiting ministers on the platform. The student desks were folding desks attached to the back of handmade benches, which are still used in the church. There was room for two students at a desk if needed. I always considered myself a charter member of the Hagerman church school, for I started in the first grade the first year the school opened. Miss Ida Brown was the first teacher.

Since the heating system was the coal stove in the middle of the aisle, it was quite often the habit of the teacher and students to gather around it closely during recess and noon periods in order to get warm. One day after the teacher had given a talk on how a person should think three times before saying anything, the class was standing around the stove, the teacher with her back to it. Ernest Truitt made the remark to her, "I think, I think, I think, your dress is burning."

The following year it was necessary to have two teachers, therefore, the south room was added during the summer. A sliding door about eighteen feet wide was placed between the two rooms. The door could be raised to accommodate large meetings. During the 1920's the school again had only one teacher, but the room was too small to accommodate the number of students. An enlargement was added to the west side of the schoolroom. In the 1930's it was again necessary to have a two-teacher school, and, since the desks had been removed from the church benches, the west room was then added for the other school room.

Church school was held continuously with one or two teachers from the time it was organized in 1909 until

1941-42. We again had church school during the term of 1954-55 with only one local member to start us off, but other students were registered from Roswell and other nearby towns. The school term in the early years always ended with a school picnic which was usually held on my father's farm. This was an event to which we all looked forward.

Elder V.B. Watts and Elder R.B. Coberly who were New Mexico Conference presidents just after the state had been considered a mission field to the Colorado Conference, chose Hagerman for their residence because it was the only church in the field that had a church school. During their stay a number of workers' meetings were held in Hagerman and many ministers and workers in the field attended. Elder H.M.J. Richards, father of H.M.S. Richards of the radio Voice of Prophecy program, was among the early conference presidents and he visited several times.

After the Texico Conference was organized, and the office moved to Clovis (later to Amarillo), there was very little help for the conference ministers. There were no district pastors; so often it would be months between visits from any ministers. In 1943 the district pastors were organized and Elder J.L. Ditberner was the first district pastor.

A number of people have gone from the little church and church school to enter into some phase of denominational or medical work. Missionaries from this church have served in Central America, Korea, South Africa, China, Puerto Rico, Cuba, India and Pakistan. Many others have spent their lives serving as ministers, teachers, administrators, doctors or nurses, often in church-related institutions.

We hope the influence of the little Hagerman, New Mexico, church will continue in the future as it has in the past.

FIRST BAPTIST CHURCH

The First Baptist Church of Hagerman was organized on September 15, 1895, although it was not incorporated until June 24, 1904. The R.N. and A.N. Millers were instrumental in the founding of the church. The American Baptist Convention with whom the church was affiliated gave a loan to erect the first building which was located one block east of the present location. The American Baptist Convention also paid half of the pastor's salary. The first pastor is believed to have been Rev. J.B. Atkinson. First trustees of the church were: A.N. Miller, C.F. White, and R.W. Terril.

Some early members included: Millers, Browns, Pulliam, Dodd, Moors, Reeves, Carter, Bush, Lang, Malone, Donner, Roberts, Walworth, Newsom, Davidson, West, Thomas, Greens, Buenning, Furr, Jack Bagley, Atkinson, Bankston, Austin Swanns, Ehret, Harvey Little, Earl Camp, Ollen Walters, John Campbell, Nellie & Francis Hines, Roland, Sanders, and Ogle families.

The auditorium of the early church had a capacity of one hundred people and there were facilities in the back rooms which served as living quarters for the pastor. These rooms were also used for Sunday School classes.

Settling of the Territory came, bringing more Baptist families who helped in the progress of the church. After the Territory became a state in 1912, the church withdrew its affiliation from the American Baptist Convention and became a part of the Southern Baptist Convention.

Some of the early records of the church were accidently destroyed, therefore, much of this report has been received from old-timers and *The History of New Mexico Baptists*.

People kept coming west and the membership grew. The church became self-supporting in the early 1930's. Harold Dye was the pastor in the late 20's and early 30's.

First Baptist Church, 1908.

In 1943, Mrs. Floto's home on Indiana Street was purchased for the parsonage. By 1947 the church building was too small and more classrooms were needed for Sunday School. The building was sold to Jim Michelet and he moved it to be used as the Hagerman Legion Hall.

The church bought two lots at 211 North Cambridge and started the new building in the spring of 1947. The congregation met at the schoolhouse during the construction. Services were held in the new building in the fall of 1947, even though it was not actually completed until the early part of 1948. The pastor at this time was Rev. L.C. Tucker.

The membership grew most rapidly from 1948 to 1952 and again the membership outgrew the educational facilities. A new educational unit was completed in March 1954. The new new building consisted of Nursery, Beginner, Primary Departments downstairs with Intermediate Department and Pastor's study upstairs. This is the south wing of the present building and cost about $17,000. Rev. Scott New was the pastor at this time.

In 1955 during the pastorate of R.A. Long, the church sponsored a Spanish Mission. The building for the Mission was donated by V.R. Barnett. With the help of the members there were Sunday morning services and Sunday School every Sunday. The mission is not in use at this time.

Because of population shifts, church membership goes up and down. The church has Sunday School, Training Union, Prayer Meeting, W.M.U., R.A.'s, and G.A.'s.

Some of the pastors include:

1900	H.C. King
1906	William J. Gordon
1911	E.S. Atwood
1912	D.C. Barb
1917-18	D.B. Jackson
1919	Rev. Bowls
1929	Harold Dye
1934	W.C. Garrett
1936	G.E. Toby
1941	Earl Landtroop
1943-44	C.M. Brister
1945-46	W.E. Wyatt
1946-47	L.C. Tucker
1947-48	John Stout
1949-52	D.A. Benson
1952-54	Scott New
1954-55	Bruce Giles
1955-57	R.A. Long
1957-62	C.O. Haile
1962-64	J.H. Brister
1964-65	Jerry Isaacs
1965-70	Jack Albright
1970-72	Virgil Drewery
1972-74	Tracey Patterson
1974-	Walt Isaacs

— Information from Mrs. Maxine Dennis

METHODIST CHURCH

The first religious services, held in the freight room of the railroad depot, brought preachers of many faiths to conduct them. Nail kegs and twelve inch boards were used for pews. It is not remembered who preached the first sermon here. Some revivals were held in the old Wool and Hide Building on West Argyle, which no longer stands. C.C. Edington, Presiding Elder of the Pecos Valley District, from Carlsbad, N.M., was the first to hold Methodist services on occasions when he visited the Hagerman community. O.R. Tanner was the first Superintendent of the Sunday School.

The records show that September 13, 1896, marked the organization of Hagerman Methodism. Ira S. Patterson was pastor. Following is a list of the Charter Members showing date of reception and manner: September 13, 1896, by vows: Hannah Blackstone, Susie Cowan, Winnie Cowan, Mary S. Cowan, Harry Cowan, Thomas A. Godwin, Martha Godwin, Eva Hitchcock, George M. Reams, Burt Robinson and Hattie Spencer; by certificate: Mrs. Abbie Harshey; September 18, by vows: Ora Amos, John W. Brookshire, Louie R. Burck, Bertie J. Cowan, Grace E. Cowan, Walter B. Coryell, Rosa Coryell, Virgie Laughinghouse, Anna M. Spencer, B.W. Stockwell; by baptism: Ancil M. Clogston, Sylvia Godwin, Howard Laughinghouse, Edith McGuinn, John Nesbit, Edith Russell, Fred Spencer, Clara Spencer, and William J. Wilson.

Reverend Patterson had served only a few weeks when he was succeeded by C.J. Oxley, who served both Roswell and Hagerman. Services were held in the schoolhouse for several years, until in 1905, during the pastorate of Charles L. Brooks, the church building was erected on East Argyle at a cost of $1,112.45. A two-room parsonage was erected. Later several rooms were added and other improvements made. Harry Cowan served as the first superintendent of the

Sunday School for nineteen years. It was during the pastorate of W.W. Turner that the annex to the church was built for Sunday School rooms. This was some time between the years of 1913 and 1916. Rev. M.F. Bell was pastor when the Education Building was erected in 1927-1928.

In 1945 local workers, led by the late Rev. J.W. Riley, pastor, constructed a sanctuary on the east of the building. The kitchen and classrooms had been built prior to this time. The first service was held in the new church on Mothers Day, in 1945, with Bishop W. Angie Smith officiating, assisted by the pastor, Rev. A.A. McCleskey, E.A. Paddock, chairman of the official board, Rev. A.C. Douglas, District Superintendent, members of the congregation and Mrs. L.E. Hinrichsen, organist.

This church was destroyed by fire on Friday, November 16, 1962. Members of the Church unanimously agreed to change the location of their church home to the corner of Morgan and South Cambridge Street. Plans for the new building were turned over to C.O. Holloway, Jr., contractor of Roswell, New Mexico, who had the low bid of $40,890.00. A modern and beautiful church with the latest furnishings and equipment was constructed. Services were held in the Seventh Day Adventist Church until the new church was completed.

Ground-breaking ceremonies were held at 12:00 noon on May 6, 1962, with the Rev. Miller H. Stroup, Pastor, directing the ceremonies. Participating were A.D. Menoud, lay leader; R.A. Welborne, chairman Official Board; Mrs. A.D. Menoud, president WSCS; Dacus Parker, chairman Board of Trustees; H.R. Menefee, chairman Building Committee; Earl Bass, Church School Superintendent and Mrs. A.A. Bailey, who has been a member of the local church longer than any other member.

The official opening and consecration of the new church was observed on Sunday, December 9, 1962, with Dr. M. Buren Stewart, District Superintendent of the Carlsbad District, the Reverend Miller H. Stroup, Pastor, and the congregation participating in the service.

The record shows the following pastors have been appointed to the Hagerman Church: Ira S. Patterson, C.J. Oxley, G.G. Hamilton, W.F. Burck, J.C. Gage, George R. Ray,

Charles L. Brooks, W.B. Evans, J.T. O'Bryant, G.H. McAnally, A.C. Bell, W.W. Turner, John Hendrix, H.W. Carter, John S. Rice, I.D.S. Lee, M.F. Bell, A.E. Watford, Bryan Hall, J.W. Slade, J.H. Walker, Rollo M. Davidson, Arthur Shaw, A.A. McCleskey, John W. Riley, Sam Freeman, Hardin Atkins III, G.H. Wolf, James G. Wayne, Miller H. Stroup, Frank E. Curry, Robert Whitis, Mark Dorff, R.A. English, Bill Stamper and Floyd Richardson.

First Methodist Church, 1905.

ORDER OF EASTERN STAR
HARMONY CHAPTER #17

Harmony Chapter #17 was instituted August 11, 1908, and chartered October 19, 1908, with twenty-one members.

From the first minutes book we learn that at the first anniversary meeting of the chapter there were visitors from Artesia, New Mexico and the following bills were presented:

$1.00 to the Hagerman Hotel for four meals for Artesia visitors.

$2.00 for a rig for the use of Artesia visitors.

In 1910 the meeting night was changed from the first Saturday to the first Wednesday night following the first full moon of the month.

From 1906 to 1919 meetings were held above the bank building. In 1919 the chapter moved to the Odd Fellows Hall, which stood on the present location of the Masonic Hall. This building was a tall, narrow, two-story wooden building with steps to the second floor on the outside of the building.

In the early days oyster stew suppers were served, following joint installations, all prepared on a two-burner kerosene stove.

In 1923 a very special program was held following the meeting with Lake Arthur, New Mexico chapter as guests. Cecil Barnett entertained with his radio. This was the first time most of the members had heard a radio.

Early day Past Matrons and Past Patrons were as follows:

1906 and 1907 .....Alice Mason ....Herman J. Thode
1908 and 1909 .....Margaret Thode ....Howard Russell

Year	Name	Name
1910 and 1911	Maude Anderson	E.E. Hoagland
1912	Annie Hoagland	Henry Johnson
1913	Eva West	W.S. McClung
1914	Eva West	George Ream
1915	Edith West	C.G. Mason
1916 and 1917	Mary Mason	C.G. Mason
1918 and 1919	Mayre Losey	J.T. West
1920	Pearl Miles	Ed Lane
1921	Pearl Miles	W.H. Miles
1922	Ethel Van Arsdol	Harold Miller
1923	Celia Hanna	Harold Miller
1924	Alberta Lane	Harold Miller
1925	Olive Holloway	Jack Sweatt
1926	Ann Wortman	J.C. Hughes
1927	Alice Mason	Robert Miller
1928	Maggie Wimberly	Robert Miller
1929	Lucy Russell	W.P. Woodmas
1930	Anna K. Miller	C.O. Holloway Sr.

HISTORY OF THE HAGERMAN MASONIC LODGE FELIX LODGE #29
By Ernest Bowen

Felix Lodge #29 was chartered in October, 1905. The members who signed the charter were: Frank Anderson, M.C. Moore and Charles Barnett. The first Master of the Lodge was Myron C. Moore. He served from 1905 through 1906. Mr. Moore was a blacksmith in Hagerman at that time, which was an important occupation in those days.

The second Master of the Lodge was L.L. Holt. He served in the year 1907. He was a farmer and had a good orchard.

The next Master was Henry C. Barron and he served in 1908. Mr. Barron lived west of town on a small farm and his principal occupation was honey beekeeping.

Howard Russell followed Mr. Barron, serving in 1909 and 1910. He had a small farm and bought and shipped alfalfa hay. He was a very enthusiastic Mason and ready to serve his Lodge in any capacity.

In 1911 Emory E. Hoagland was the Master. He was manager of Joyce-Pruitt Store.

The next Master was George Ream who served in 1912. Mr. Ream was a bachelor and a tailor. He was one of the most proficient men in those days and he gave almost all the proficiencies in his tailor shop while he was doing his cleaning and pressing.

George Shepard served in 1913. He was the bookkeeper for Joyce-Pruit Company and a very fine man.

Noah S. West served in 1914 and in 1918, 1921 and again in 1936. He was a farmer but also sold real estate.

In 1915 Cassius G. Mason was Master. He also served more years than anyone else. He held the office in 1920, 1939 and 1940. He was always the backbone of the Lodge as long as he lived.

Elza Powell served in 1916. He was a farmer and served as clerk at the Santa Fe Depot for many years.

In 1917 Earl Love became Master and he also served in 1919 and 1927. He was in the lumber business in Dexter.

During 1942 the lodge became more active and the present Lodge Hall was built. Pete Losey, Tollie West and Ernest Bowen spent two afternoons canvassing all the members of the Lodge and raised enough money to build and pay for the new building.

I would like to mention one of our secretaries, Ramon Welborne. He has been a very efficient Secretary of the Lodge for about thirty years. He has been present at almost every meeting.

The following men also served as Masters:

Frank Wortman 1922
Mr. Miles 1923
Harold Miller . . 1924 & 1925
Henry Hanna 1926
Ed Howell 1928
E.S. Bowen . . . . 1929 & 1938
Ed Lane . . . . 1930 & 1931
Isaac Wortman 1932 & 1933
C.O. Holloway 1934
W.A. Losey 1935
R.W. Connor 1937
W.F. Kerr 1942
Mr. Parker . . . . 1943 & 1944
Paul Whitman 1946
Rufus King 1947
Kern Jacobs 1948
Leonard George 1949
Bill Cook 1950
Raynal Cumpsten 1951
Royce Lankford 1952
John Garner 1953

Richard Lang ..1954 & 1955
Robert Cumpsten 1956
Howard Menefee 1957
Jack Menoud 1958
Bill Jack Graham 1959
Clifford Helms 1960
Jack Langenegger 1961
Bob Utterback 1962
Mr. Ackerman 1963
Warner Thomas 1964
Ben Kerr 1965
John F. Wortman 1966
Dee Eastman 1967
Fletcher Campbell 1968
George Losey 1969
John Rhodes 1970
T.A. Bledsoe Jr. 1971
W.H. Ledbetter 1972
W.W. Thomas 1973
W.H. Graham 1974
Jack Langenegger 1975

HAGERMAN THURSDAY CLUB
Commemorated Sixty Years Of Organization in 1968
By Alta G. Evans

Turn the pages of New Mexico history to the year 1908—those were Territorial Days. Hagerman was a new town. Many of those who came with their families and ambitions to this new settlement had already been successful in their former homes. Among them were the schoolteachers, the missionary pastors, the doctors, the merchants and the farmer and fruit grower.

That year, 1908, a group of ladies of this community organized the Hagerman Thursday Club. They drew up a constitution and by-laws to guide the new club. Their stated purpose was "to continue intellectual improvement and for social communication."

In the fourth year of organization we find that the Thursday Club gave a musical benefit for the local school. Through the years the members have continued to support worthwhile projects and have elected to study a variety of subjects.

Foreign countries have been a popular choice for lessons. Because of the changes made by two World Wars, some countries have been reviewed several times. Since the creation of the United Nations the club has studied a number of the newly formed nations.

A few of the other subjects for lessons have been: Operas, The Art of Conversation, American Writers, Contemporary Writers, Presidents of the United States, Types of Architecture, Rivers and Islands. The state of New Mexico is a popular subject.

The club's motto, "Still I am learning," taken from the writings of Angelo, which was selected by the charter members, applies as well now as when chosen sixty years ago.

EARLY HISTORY OF THE HAGERMAN CEMETERY
By Dorthea Cowan Johnson

The first public cemetery in the Hagerman area was located east of the school buildings on the farm owned by John W. Langenegger. It was later changed to the present location west of Hagerman and some the graves were moved.

On November 2, 1907, Hagerman citizens met in mass at the Methodist Church for the purpose of organizing a cemetery association. Mrs. George C. Stanford was elected temporary president and Mrs. M.E. Harshey temporary secretary. The first business was the election of permanent officers which were as follows: President, Mrs. C.W. Davisson; Vice-President, Mrs. M.E. Harshey; Secretary, G.C. Stanford and Treasurer, Mrs. Harry Cowan. A committee of three was appointed to formulate by-laws and to work up an interest in the association. They were: Mrs. A.R. Teeple, Mrs. W.T. Holloway and Mrs. Harry Cowan. This committee was also empowered to arrange entertainments for the purpose of raising funds.

At a meeting November 14, 1907, by-laws were adopted and a committee was appointed by the chairman to survey and plot the cemetery grounds. Harry Cowan and W.T. Holloway, with C.R. Tanner selected to assist, comprised that committee.

In 1909 officers were again elected as follows: President, Mrs. A.R. Teeple; Vice-President, Mrs. D.W. Crozier; Secretary, Mrs. G.C. Stanford and Treasurer, Mr. W.T. Holloway.

The first lots were sold for $20 per lot, $12.50 per half lot, and $7.50 for a quarter lot. The dues and donations were set at $1.00 per year.

On February 6, 1919, the old association was reorganized and new officers were elected as follows: President, Mrs. Harry Cowan; Vice-President, Mrs. Jim Williamson; Secretary and Treasurer, Mrs. C.W. Curry. Committees were appointed as follows: Membership, Mrs. Tom McKinstry, Mrs. Henderson, and Mrs. Tom Platt; Grounds, Jim Williamson, R.N. Miller, and C.W. Curry; Finance, Mrs. Oscar Walters, Mrs. Jim Williamson, Mrs. Sam McKinstry and Mrs. Ollie Durand. Those present at this organizational meeting were: Mr. and Mrs. Jim Williamson, Miss Roberta Williamson, C.G. Mason, R.N. Miller, H.W. Little, Mrs. Henderson, Mrs. C.W. Curry and Mr. and Mrs. Harry Cowan.

It was in this year that the ground was surveyed and it was found that the part of the cemetery then in use could be irrigated by the gravity system from the canal. A plant was installed a short time later in the same year for $233.40, and a cement block house was built to protect it in 1921.

The cemetery was enclosed with fence in the early days. In 1929 it was voted by the Association to take down the iron fence. However, a fence across the front remained until 1950.

Meetings were held frequently at the homes of various members when needed. Some of the homes used for meetings in the early years were: A.F. Clark, Jim Williamson, Thos. McKinstry, Charles Michelet, Harvey Little, A.A. Bailey, Harry Cowan, C.W. Curry, Perry Crisler, Lang, Nail, L.E. Harshey, J.P. Morgan, C.G. Mason, E.A. Paddock, G.C. Stanford, and W.E. Utterback. C.G. Mason worked closely with the Association during the many years that he was the local undertaker.

There were many ways that the Association earned money during those first years when the trees were bought and set out as the cemetery expanded. Ice-cream socials, box suppers, dinners served to organizations such as the Hagerman Alfalfa Growers Association, and the Business Men's Club and lunches at farm sales were a few of the ways. Clean-up days were frequently held when the public was asked to assist in the work of keeping the cemetery free of weeds.

Some early sextons were: Harvey Little, J.M. Frier, N.C. Smith, J.P. Morgan, H.W. Hayes, J.F. Campbell, Ed Pilley and A.A. Bailey. More recently Jess Huff and Elvin Lusk have served in this capacity. The first rate of pay was 25¢ per hour.

In March, 1945, it was voted to donate four lots to the American Legion Auxiliary for the purpose of erecting a monument to the memory of the soldiers of all wars.

The cemetery continues to be cared for through the loyal support of the many people in the Pecos Valley who have family and friends interred there, and also by those who have moved away but keep in touch. Work days are still held at which time many participate.

THE FELIX RANCH

The Felix Ranch - Sec. 32, TWP. 13S, Rge. 26 E. Original patent from U.S. to Minnie H. Gibson, December 1, 1891. Miss Gibson was a secretary to the Pecos Land and Improvement Co. This corporation was controlled by James J. Hagerman. Hagerman formed a corporation called the Felix Land and Cattle Co. which held the property until November 17, 1903. At this time the farm was sold to Cartwright and Warren. James Williamson purchased ten percent interest in the property in 1904. He kept this interest until 1923. Cartwright and Warren lived in Terrell, Texas. Jim Williamson managed the farm for them for many years. E. Van Sweatt later managed this property until it was purchased by Hal Bogle in 1931.

The following information was supplied by Mrs. A.A. Bailey, nee Alline Williamson, who remembers vividly arriving in a snow storm at Greenfield on Jan. 27, 1904. The family moved into the four room house at the ranch that had recently been vacated by Mr. and Mrs. Gil Amis.

During the early years of residence Mr. Williamson added four large rooms, 16 x 16, and a bathroom to the house.

An artesian well was drilled and orchards were planted. There was a bunk house for the hired men and another building containing a kitchen and dining room with living quarters above for the cook. A milk house was also built. The bunk house is the only one of the original buildings left. The original house burned and was replaced with a lovely new house by Mr. Bogle.

The ranch was a busy place and many workers were needed to bale the hay, pick and box the apples for shipping. All the farm work was done with horses and mules. There are several "straw bosses" that are well remembered including T.D. Devenport, Lee Fortenberry, Jim Pridemore and Charlie Studyvan. The cooks were an important factor in the life at the ranch and Mrs. Bailey remembers especially Pop Scoggins for his sour dough biscuits. Mrs. Pridemore was cook while her husband was foreman.

Mrs. Bailey met her future husband, A.A. "Bert" Bailey, while he was in charge of the irrigation of the farm.

The first haybalers required horses or mules to operate. One team remembered by one old timer was a couple of horses, one white and one dappled grey, known as Dutch and Eagle and a fine mule team, Pete and Bird.

The Williamson children attended school in Hagerman, Mrs. Bailey being one of a class of four to graduate from the tenth grade in 1908.

— Contributed by Bill Bogle and Mrs. A.A. Bailey.

Felix Ranch House. Jim Williamson on the horse.

MAP OF
HAGERMAN, NEW MEXICO

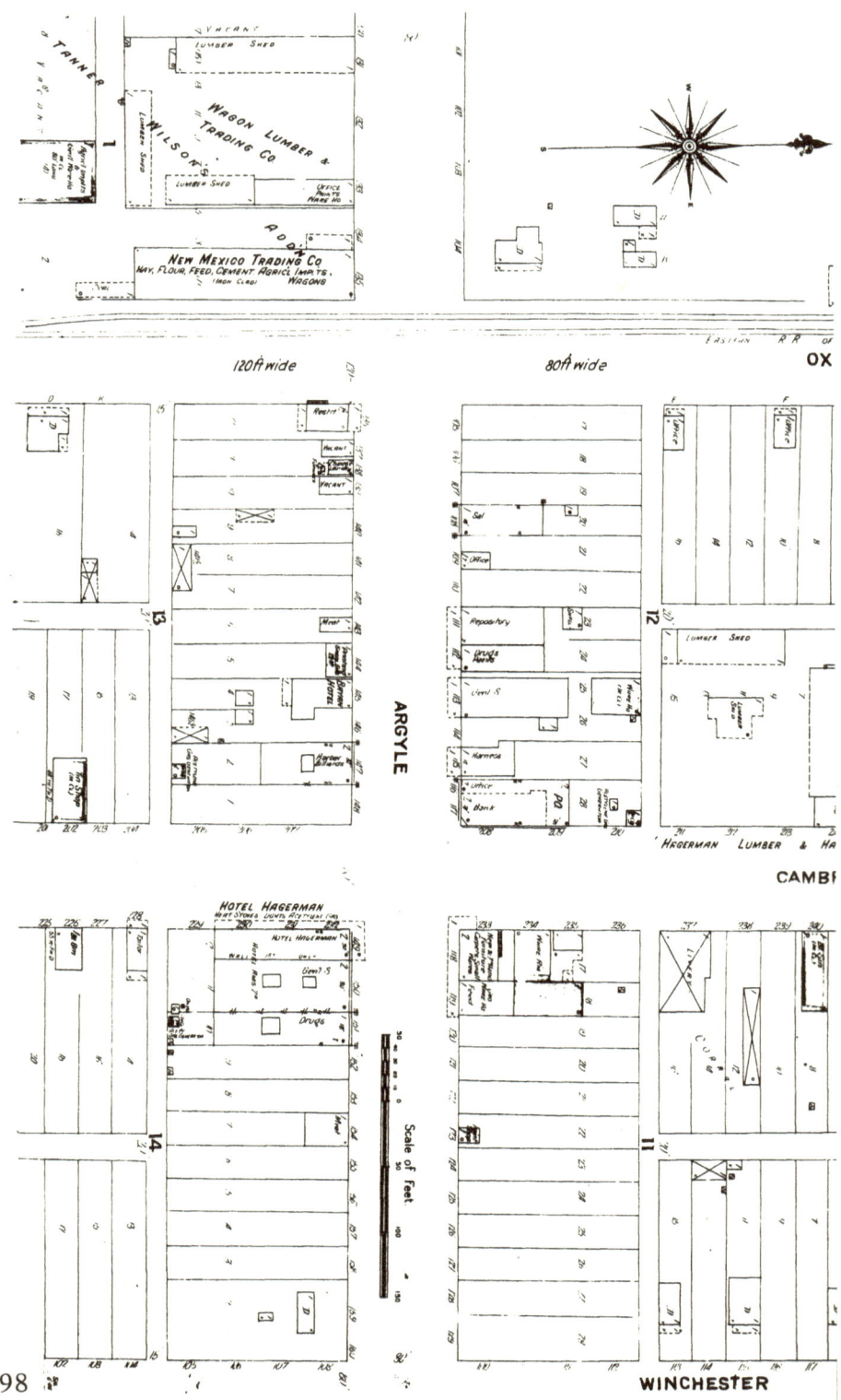

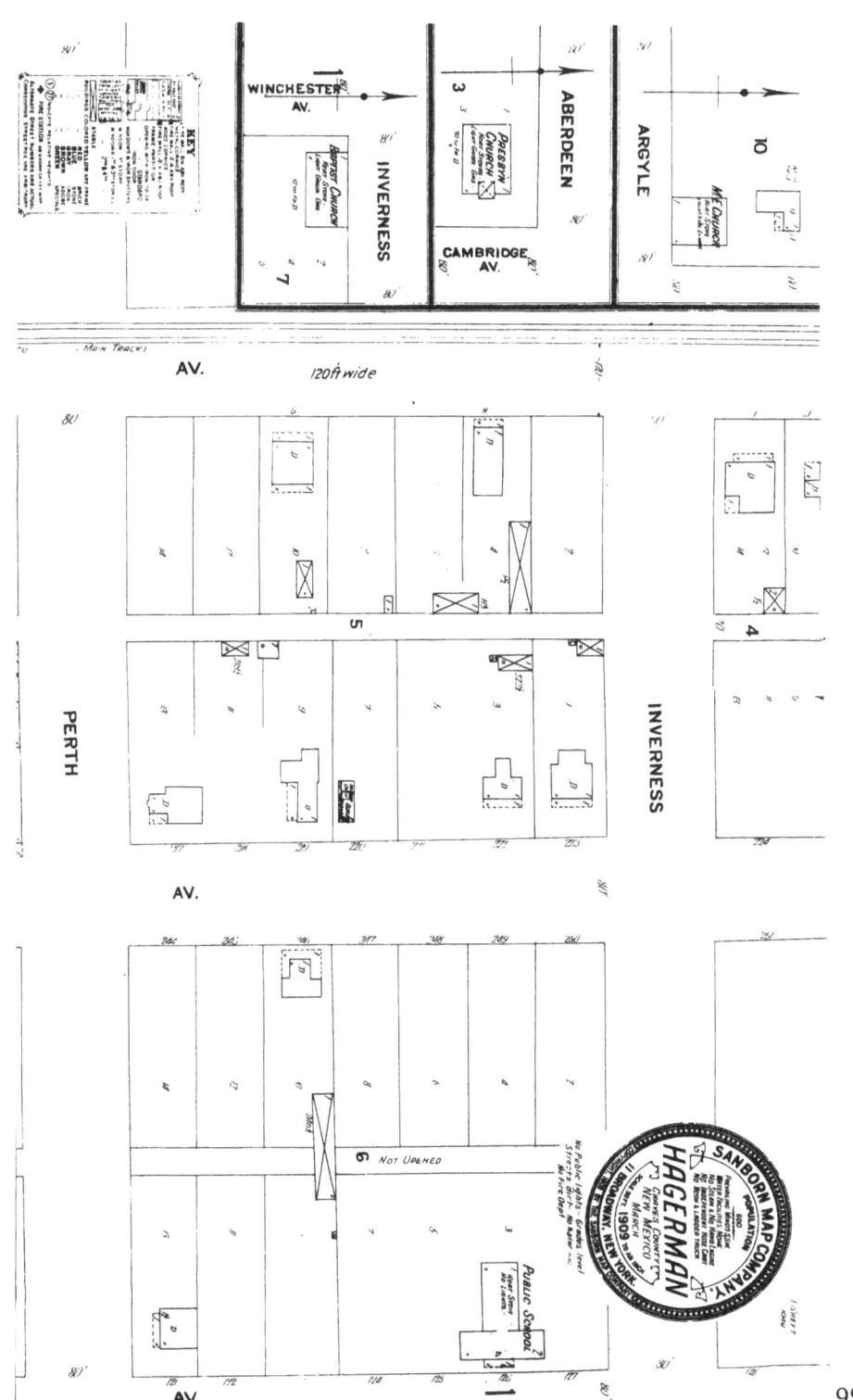

Part II
FAMILY HISTORIES

W.J. ALTER
By Katherine Farkus Gerhard

Wilton Justus Alger and wife, Katherine "Kate" Alice, came to Hagerman from Rubio, Iowa, because of Kate's poor health. A son, Cecil, was raised in Hagerman and graduated from the high school. He died during World War I in the flu epidemic.

Wilton was an ordained Congregational minister and a cheese maker. He started a cheese factory on a twenty acre farm west of town. Due to the lack of water the cheese business failed.

He then raised turkeys for several years. He would bring the turkeys into town where they were dry-picked (sometimes employing as many as fifty people) and then shipped out by box car. A bad freeze wiped out the turkey business.

A farm partnership with Jim Michelet was his most successful New Mexico business venture though he sold his share to Jim in later years when he moved to Roswell.

Kate died in 1934 and was buried in Rubio, Iowa. Later Wilton married Oma B. St. John from Roswell, New Mexico. He died in 1952 and is buried in Roswell, New Mexico.

Ethel Irene Haralson was engaged to Cecil Alter when he died. She was loved as a daughter by Wilton and Kate and lived with them for two years before she married Joseph A. Farkus from Birmingham, Alabama.

Joseph Farkus started a carbon paper and typewriter ribbon business in a small adobe building he had built across the street and east of the railroad depot in Hagerman.

Ethel died in Hot Springs, New Mexico, leaving two daughters, Katherine and Patsy. The Alters took these two young girls and raised them as their own grandchildren.

Katherine Farkus married Chester Gerhard of Cherokee, Kansas. He is now retired from the Air Force and they are living on a farm in Ozark, Missouri. She is a neo-nate intensive care nurse at L.E. Cox Medical Center, Springfield, Missouri. They have a son and a daughter.

Patsy married Alton Henry Tew. They live in Beaumont, Texas where he is a surgeon and she is active in nursing. They have four sons and two daughters.

PIONEERS NEAR HAGERMAN
By Carrie J.A. Robbins, M.D.

Christina Frederickson, who had migrated from Denmark with her parents in 1874 and later took the nurses course in Battle Creek, Michigan, was living in Iowa. She was kept very busy nursing friends and neighbors who were sick or in other ways needed help.

After several years with long hours of work and frequent exposure to inclement weather and disease, she broke down in health and was advised by a doctor to go to New Mexico. She arrived in Hagerman about the turn of the century and soon made friends with the Jacobson family and others in the community. About six months of rest and the New Mexico sunshine had the desired effect and her health returned. She was afraid to go back to Iowa, so took up a quarter section homestead three and one-half miles west of Hagerman. Claude Barron built a one room claim shanty for her to live in. This was on the present Bill Jack Graham place.

Soon after getting settled, Christina decided to visit her family in Iowa. At her father's farm there was a young man from Sweden by the name of John Anderson, who was helping with the work. He was very shy and she didn't pay much attention to him.

One day when she went to the well to get some water for the house, John was there watering the horses. He spoke to her in his quiet way. She answered, "Good Morning," but by this time her pail was full of water, so she hurried back to the house without a backward glance and probably thought nothing of the incident.

Not so with John. He had seen the desire of his heart. While driving his team home that night he dreamed of a happy home with Christina as its queen, but how to get her attention was his problem. The more he thought about it the more he was determined that the next time he saw her he would have a longer conversation and get better acquainted.

However, this was not to be. The next thing he knew she had returned to New Mexico. This was discouraging, but he had a vision and decided not to give up so easily. After thinking and praying about the problem for some time, a carefully worded letter found its way to Hagerman.

Christina was surprised and thrilled to receive it. She knew John and considered him a wonderful Christian man but had never dreamed that he was interested in her. She was too practical a person to spend much time day-dreaming, so back went an encouraging letter to Iowa.

In the next few months many letters were exchanged and plans were made. In 1903 Christina Frederickson and John Anderson exchanged marriage vows in the home of Mrs. Selma Jacobson.

Among the things that John had brought with him from Iowa was Christina's pump organ which her father had given her several years earlier. It crowded the little one room shanty.

One day when Christina returned from a trip to town, she found John in the back yard digging a hole. She wondered what he was up to, and he patiently explained that they needed a well. So far, they had hauled water from a nearby river—the Old Felix. When the hole got too deep for him to throw the dirt out anymore, John rigged up a bucket on a pulley, and hitched one of his horses to it. Christina would lead the horse out to bring the bucket up then empty it and send it back down into the well. In this way they worked together day after day until at forty-five feet John struck a good vein of water and had to hurry out of the well as it rather quickly filled up to about fifteen feet from the surface. This open well was a bit dangerous, so a few months later John put down a pipe and pump and set up a windmill on top and then filled the sides with rocks and dirt. Later, a large cement reservoir was built which was always full. Here was plenty of water for the stock and a one acre garden, besides a wonderful back yard swimming pool for the children for years to come.

Now the house was too small, so one day John started making adobe bricks and dried them in the sun. After he had enough to make a 16 x 16 foot room, he put this up as a living room with the old shanty as the kitchen. The new room was plastered on the outside to protect the mud bricks, and inside Christina covered the walls with cheese cloth and then papered them. When it was furnished, they had a very comfortable little house and room for the organ. Here they lived happily for many years.

One day in 1906 a letter arrived at the Frederickson home in Iowa from John Anderson. They knew John well, and when he stated that a little girl had come to live with them, and that she seemed to like it quite well and would probably stay, they figured John and Christina had decided to adopt a child, since they had been married for three years and neither was very young. Finally at the end of the letter when John made it clear that the baby was really their own, it was a happy surprise to Grandma and Grandpa.

Six more years rolled by. Carrie, as the baby had been named, was growing up, a happy but lonely child. Now they did seriously consider adoption, and sure enough, a three year old boy by the name of Lewis, whose mother had died, came into their lives. When they went to the train to meet him, Carrie was so thrilled to have a brother she could hardly contain herself. Lewis fitted into the family right from the start. And what fun they had out on the farm with Moss, the half Shetland pony, the calves, chickens and kittens. Also they had the reservoir to swim in, and the garden to work in.

More years flew by; 1920 was a sad year for the family. Christina was called away to Iowa because her mother was very ill. In her absence John began to have symptoms of rheumatic fever. He would not let Carrie write to mother about his illness until they had word that Grandma was better. By this time he was so ill that neighbors, especially George L. Truitt, would come and sit up with him at night. They wired Christina to come home which she did as soon as possible, but John kept getting worse and about ten days later went to his rest, leaving a lonely, heartbroken little family.

Christina started nursing again occasionally, and the children would care for the stock and chickens. One time when they were about twelve and fifteen years of age they even put up a crop of alfalfa in Mother's absence. They were real proud of themselves over this, and mother was proud of them too.

Finally it came time to go away from home to school. Carrie went to Keene, Texas, for two years. Then both of them went to Minnesota to live with Uncle James and go to school. Mother went back to Iowa to care for Grandma in her last years, so the Hagerman home was broken up, but there is still a warm spot in their hearts for all the old Hagerman friends when they meet them anywhere in the world. Carrie has met them in California, Oregon, Nebraska, Washington D.C., Texas and India. Lewis has met them in Minnesota, Washington state, Texas and Arizona.

Lewis married a Minnesota girl, settled on a farm there and raised seven beautiful children, among them a nurse, a farmer, a mechanic, two secretaries, a business man and a minister who is now a missionary in Korea.

Carrie took the medical course and practiced for several years in Colorado and Nebraska. She married later in life and went with her husband, Charles Robbins, as a missionary to India, where she has spent around twenty-two years in Medical Missionary work. There a little girl, Marian, was born who is now a minister's wife in North Dakota. She also adopted a little Pakistani girl by the name of Valynda, who is still living with her in Texas and going to school.

THOMAS GRANT ANDREWS
By Lindell Andrews

T.G. Andrews was an active farmer in the Pecos Valley for over forty years and is believed to have drilled the first shallow well for irrigation purposes east of the canal in the Hagerman area.

Thomas Grant Andrews was born in Wiseman, Arkansas, in 1895, to David and Rebecca (Bell) Andrews, one of five children. Tom received his formal education in the Wiseman Public Schools. In 1916, he was married to Maude Montgomery, and the couple established their home near Morriston, Arkansas, where in 1918 their first child, Phyllis Veta, was born.

In 1920 the T.G. Andrews family moved to Chaves County, New Mexico, locating about seven miles northwest of Dexter, farming on a sharecropper basis. During this two year period in 1921, his son, Lowell David, was born. In 1922 the family, now consisting of four, returned to Arkansas to a point near Morriston where Tom continued to farm. In 1923 another daughter, Mary Willine, was added. In 1925 thirst for Pecos Valley water drew the family back to Chaves County, New Mexico, this time locating east of the Pecos River on the Elliott farm near the headquarters of the Calumet Ranch. In 1927 another son, William Archie, was born. The eldest child began formal schooling in the little rock schoolhouse nearby, a portion of which still stands.

In 1929 the Andrews family moved to a new location about three miles west of Hagerman where Mr. Andrews had purchased a 140-acre plot from a Mr. Clayton Stewart. Here on the Rio Felix was 80 acres of canal-right land and 60 acres of undeveloped land thriving with a goodly growth of mesquite.

Plenty of hard work went into the carving out of a productive farm at the new location. They strove to establish a farming unit that would provide a livelihood and make the annual payment on the land. Very soon came the depression of the 1930's. Now the task became more formidable, but the family became a cohesive unit and met the problems in stride. The family now consisted of the parents and five children; Tommy Lindell, a son, having been born in 1933. Even with the hardships, by careful planning and hard work, the homestead was cleared of all debts and encumbrances and became recognized as one of the leading small farms of the area.

Mr. and Mrs. T.G. Andrews, in their quiet and unassuming way, were active, extremely interested and participated in the community life of the Hagerman area. They continually sought to maintain safeguards within a society of the nation that would preserve the American heritage for their children's children and those of their neighbors.

In the 1930's he became interested in strenghtening his church, the Church of Christ. He and his family worked diligently for years with the local congregation, and in the 1950's he and his wife, Maude, became instrumental in the construction of new church facilities which are presently known as the Oxford Street Church of Christ in Hagerman.

Mrs. Maude Andrews died in 1957 following a highway accident. Mr. Andrews died of natural causes in 1961. Both were interred in the Hagerman Cemetery.

Two members of the T.G. Andrews family, Archie and Lindell, remain in the Hagerman community. Lindell has served as a member of the Hagerman Board of Education.

DUB AND JANE ANDRUS

A.C. (Dub) Andrus came to Hagerman in May of 1926 from Seagraves, Texas. He came to manage People's Mercantile store for A.J. Crawford of Carlsbad. With him came his mother, Mrs. Ophelia Andrus, and two sisters, Mrs. Lizzie Rice and Mrs. Tinnie Chestnut.

On June 23, 1926, Dub and Jane Weir were married in Seminole, Texas. Jane was a member of a pioneer family and had lived most of her life on a ranch near Monument, New Mexico. She came to live with Dub and his family in the house on the corner of Argyle and Indiana Streets. In a short while the house was put on the market for about a thousand dollars and Jane wanted to buy it. Dub wouldn't consider it at all as he said he wasn't about to live in Hagerman the rest of his life. But he did. Jane helped in the store and in 1931 they bought the business and ran it for eighteen years. Later they bought a farm from M.D. Menoud, Sr., and, also, the home and acreage of Ben Jack West where Jane still resides.

Both Dub and Jane were active in community affairs. Dub taught Red Cross Life Saving classes for eleven years. He felt well repaid for this volunteer work when one of his pupils from Lake Arthur saved a friend from being electrocuted by giving artificial respiration. There were many amusing incidents in the classes. One story Dub liked to tell was about a test he gave in which the students were asked to trace the blood. One answer was, "the blood goes up one leg and down the other."

Dub also served on the Town Council for several years. Every time he wanted to quit, Jane would tell him he couldn't because she liked the delicious fruit cakes they got for Christmas. She says she can taste them still.

Both Dub and Jane were active members in the Order of the Eastern Star. Dub was Worthy Patron for eight years and

Jane was Worthy Matron for several years. Dub was also a member of the Masonic Lodge. Dub was of the Baptist faith and Jane was a member of the Christian Science Church for many years, later becoming a member of the Presbyterian Church in Hagerman.

Jane recalls her first impression of Hagerman as being favorable. She liked the town and the people. Her first social affair came about a week after she arrived in town. She was invited to a bridge party at Loveta West's home. She doesn't remember who made the highest score but does recall the fact that she wasn't introduced to a single person present. She also remembers the main recreation in those days was playing basketball and softball against the high school girls. These games were played after work and on weekends and furnished amusement for the townspeople.

Dub and Jane had no children of their own but when Dub's nephew, Frank Dub Hardin, was seven years old he came to live with them and go to school.

Dub passed away February 11, 1961, and is buried in the Lovington Cemetery.

THE J.P. ANDRUS FAMILY
By Cork Andrus and Lillis Mae Conley

In their model T Ford came Perry, Eula (Jack) and their 3 children, Jess, Lillis Mae and S.A. (Corky) to the Pecos Valley in 1927. They first settled in Dexter for six months after leaving their home in New Home, Texas. The valley was not new to mother, Eula Holden Andrus, as she had worked in the Greenfield post office in 1914. Like many other families they were seeking a more prosperous life and Hagerman was attractive to them because Grandmother Andrus, Uncle Dub and Aunt Lizzie were living at Hagerman.

Then in 1928 Daddy went into the service station business with Alma Nail and moved the family to Hagerman from Dexter. Our first home was the house now owned by Marjorie Luce on Argyle Street. Daddy later bought Alma out and continued to operate the Hagerman Service Station until 1945.

1930 found us moving to the Ray Stephens house where Billie Jean was born, in 1930. Then Daddy bought the George Losey home on west Argyle Street where Lawrence Ray was born in 1933.

Daddy was a true cattleman, living and breathing cattle, horses, ranching and all things of western flavor. At the big Lake Van rodeo in 1928, Daddy and Art Cazier got in the wild cow milking contest; Daddy was kicked in the nose, breaking it and so he carried the mark of it for the rest of his life.

Daddy leased the Frank Lation ranch east of Hagerman in 1934. Then in 1945, after selling the service station to Wayne Graham, they moved to the Adam Zimmerman ranch where they lived until 1954.

A fire destroyed everything they owned at the next ranch they lived on south of Fort Sumner. This catastrophe led to the purchase of the "Queen" ranch, in the Guadalupe Mountains and happiness prevailed for years until the death of our mother in 1961. Daddy stayed on the ranch until he sold out in February 1970. He died from a heart attack on May 5, 1970.

Earnest Bowen and Ede Harshey tell of the time in 1945 on V.J. Day when the whole town was elated over the victory of World War II. Earnest and Sadie Bowen, Lloyd and Ede Harshey, Jim and Jeannette Michelet, John and Nola Clark all went out to the Zimmerman ranch, wanting to share the good news with Perry and Jack, knowing that they would be welcomed. That's the way Perry and Jack were; always having that warm "Texas style" welcome for all of their many friends. Jack as usual prepared a bountiful supper and served liquid refreshments later on. They insisted on the group spending the night and after eating a big ranch style breakfast the next morning the group returned to Hagerman. Earnest recalls that this was the only time he was ever late to meet the passenger train in his forty-five years as depot agent in Hagerman. He also recalls that on the evening of celebrating after having the refreshments it was necessary for him to go outside to find a mesquite bush. A rattlesnake was in the mesquite and loudly protested the water works. Needless to say, Earnest got away from that mesquite bush and rattlesnake in record time.

Mother was a special kind of person, vibrant, vivacious and warm. A "good morning" from her was always accompanied with a sweet smile and a sparkle in her eyes.

Daddy served on the Hagerman Town Board, fire department and as a deputy sheriff under Perry Bean.

Jess Medlin married Jewell Barnett and he now lives in Truth or Consequences. Lillis Mae married Bob Conley; they live in Roswell and have two sons. Cork married Wanna B. Langenegger; they own and live in a house on their farm just north of the school and have three sons. Billie Jean married Dean Goff; they have three children and live at Lovington. Lawrence Ray married Betty Whitfield; they have three children and live in Roswell.

THE MARSHALL BAILEY FAMILY

Marshall Bailey and wife, Sabine Bailey, came to Hagerman from Des Moines, Iowa, in 1894. There were ten children: Laura, Alice, Nerio, Edwin, Bessie, Albert "Bert," Mae, Mable, Nellie, and Walter.

Mr. Bailey was engaged in raising stock, mainly hogs, and rough farming and came to Hagerman by way of a freight train. He belonged to the Christian Church. He homesteaded a farm southeast of Hagerman on which the lake now known as Tolliver Lake is located.

Bert, Mae, and Mable went to school here under Miss Blackstone.

Bert Bailey was the only one of the family who continued to reside in Hagerman. He married Miss Alline Williamson in 1909 and worked for the Hagerman Irrigation Company for many years until his death. Bert and Alline had two children, Mayola and James Sydney.

MY MEMORIES OF HAGERMAN
By C.A. Baker

On December 6, 1922, I became a citizen of Hagerman, New Mexico. My mother drove me thirty miles in a horse drawn buggy to Goldthwaite, Texas, where I could get a train and start toward Hagerman. I arrived in Clovis about eleven in the morning and from there to Roswell I almost smothered because that day there was a bad sandstorm. Ross White met me at the depot in Hagerman. In fact, Ross was responsible for my coming to New Mexico. I had to leave my home in central Texas for health reasons. I had asthma and it was hard to breathe in the low altitude I had come from.

I had gone to school with Horton and Ross White and their brother, known as Prof White. Prof wanted to have a good basketball team and I was a fair country ball player. The White boys had a place for me to stay out in the country with a bachelor named Howard Russell. When I arrived at his house I was told I could sleep upstairs. I went to look at the room. It was small and no one had been in it for a long time. Dirt and sand were about an inch thick on the bed and the floor. I raised the one window, threw the mattress and quilts out in the yard, shoveled out and swept and mopped the room. Then I walked to town and stayed with the Whites until my bedding was aired out. I stayed with Howard Russell until about Christmastime. I was getting homesick; seventeen years old and had never been away from home for long before.

At school one day Horton White asked me how I was doing. I told him "alright." He said, "Like hell you are. Ross and I will be out there next Saturday and move you to Prof's until we can find another place for you to stay. The first thing we know you'll be on a train leaving here." I stayed with Prof and his wife Mary until Christmas. I spent a good Christmas with friends who were farming in the Cottonwood area.

When I got back to Hagerman I moved out to the Felix Ranch where I milked two cows, night and morning, for my board and room. I was playing basketball then, and I remember well the first game that I played. It was at Hope, New Mexico. They had a fair team but we didn't have trouble beating them. We took a high school boy along with us and they talked him into refereeing. We told him to give them all the breaks possible. We did not have a basketball coach but Prof went with us to all of the games. After the game with Hope we went down to the hotel and were eating when we heard a commotion at the front door. There were about fifteen cowboys there saying they wanted the darned referee and they were going to show him that he couldn't come over there and beat their boys like that. The poor kid wanted to crawl under the table. Prof put on his old black hat and pulled it down on his head as far as it would go and looked as mean as he could (and he could look pretty mean). He was putting up a good argument when the Hope ball team came along and told the cowboys it had been a fair game and they left.

At the Felix ranch there was never a dull moment. I weighed 169 pounds when I moved there and in sixty days I weighed 180. We had whipped cream and other good food. The Williamson family was one of the nicest families I've ever known.

Cap Mossman was a great friend of Jim Williamson and he had 100 head of big Hereford bulls on the alfalfa at the ranch. Carl Paxton also had cattle on pasture there. He, too, stayed at the ranch. Sometime in February, 1923, the cattle had to be dipped and the only place to get this done was west of Lake Arthur at Bill Vermillion's. He had a dipping vat at his ranch. I stayed out of school to help Carl Paxton drive the cattle to the dipping vat, cross country, no fences. That morning when we were rounding up the cattle, my horse fell with me while crossing an irrigation ditch full of water. I got one foot wet and the weather was freezing.

When we got the cattle to Mr. Vermillion's ranch about two o'clock they had plenty to eat and corn whiskey. By this time I felt sick and had a high temperature. I took a few swallows of corn whiskey and decided to ride back to the Felix ranch. At one time I had to stop, tie my horse and lie down. I realized I had to get to the ranch if possible. Just before sundown I made it and Mrs. Williamson called Dr. Brown. I had pneumonia and did not know anything for two days. When I came to, Alline Bailey was at my bedside as my nurse. She had stayed there day and night and I really don't think I would have been alive today if she hadn't been with me.

After awhile I was able to be back in school and to play basketball. We had our district tournament in Roswell and after a struggle were eligible for the State Tournament in Albuquerque. We went to Albuquerque in Prof White's and Tollie West's Model T Fords. We got as far as Vaughn that day and ate at the Harvey House. From Vaughn to Albuquerque we were in a snowstorm and took turns riding on the running board, keeping the windshields wiped off so we could continue the trip. After playing some hard games we won the state tournament.

After the teams got back to Hagerman, the people of Hagerman and surrounding communities raised eighteen hundred dollars to send us to Chicago to the National Tournament. Prof and seven of the boys went to Chicago. I was not eligible to go because I had changed schools during the year. They lost their first game but I think all of them had the roof of their mouths blistered from looking up at so many tall buildings.

I spent the summer in Hagerman. A friend from central Texas, Albert McKandles, better known as Mac, came to attend school in Hagerman. Mac and I worked in the hay fields most of the time for Levi Barnett. I worked for Ben Jack West. I also worked for Elmer Graham and we filled hay barns that belonged to Roy Lochhead. It was hard, hot work.

R.N. Thomas decided to come to Hagerman and teach and coach our basketball team. When school started, Mac and I rented a room from Mrs. Noah West. Our room and a good breakfast cost $12.00 a month.

I carried two scuttles of coal upstairs to the telephone office every morning for $5.00 per month, swept out the bank every morning for $15.00 per month and worked at the C. and C. garage on Saturday for $10.00 per month. Some Saturdays I was away on ball trips. Mac set linotype for J.E. Wimberly at *The Messenger* office. We ate a hamburger for lunch and ate in the back of Teeds Grocery store some times at night for our evening meal. We were invited out to eat by some of the nicest people on earth, the people of Hagerman.

We had a good basketball team in 1924, won the district tournament and went on to win the state tournament.

J.E. Wimberly had a talk with Mac and me before graduation and asked us what we were going to do about a suit to wear for the graduation exercises. We told him we probably would not wear a suit. He took us to Tode Brenneman at the Model in Roswell and told him to fit us in suits and he would see that he got his money. I don't think he was ever sorry that he did this for us.

FELIPÉ BANUELLO
By Dorothy Devenport West

Ole' Felipé, as he was affectionally known, was one of the most colorful persons in town. He was from somewhere in Mexico and came to Hagerman as the gardener for the Roy Lochhead family but remained after the family left.

His garden was located west of the railroad track on the southside of Argyle. He had a real "green thumb" and his vegetables graced most of the dinner tables in town. He would peddle them from a little wagon that he pulled behind him.

He was partially deaf and you could hear his voice for blocks. Sometimes this would prove embarrassing for my mother as he didn't hesitate to describe to her, in full, any problems he might be having.

He usually wore three or four pairs of pants at one time. When he had a new pair these would be worn on the outside.

Ole' Felipé knew everyone in town and when he met them on the street he would say "hello." If they didn't speak (which was seldom) he would stop dead in his tracks and in a loud voice shout, "By Gawd - I said hello!"

He returned to his home in Mexico after he became too old to care for himself and he was missed by all who knew him.

THE LEVI BARNETTS
By Their Children

It occurred in the early 1900's, the place was Oklahoma Territory, Chickasaw Nation, that the Coctaw Indian tribe alloted land acreage to their "citizens by blood and intermarriage." Levi Barnett and his oldest son, Cecil, were granted their alloted acreage. The last (final) allotments were made in 1907. In 1915 when the health of our mother, Lottie, was in jeopardy the decision was made to move to a different climate. Thus some of the land was sold and the rest of the Oklahoma property was traded to W.Z. Thompson for his forty acre tract one mile west of Hagerman.

Levi, Lottie and three children, Cecil, Bernice and Basil, left Oklahoma by train and spent a few months in Southern Arizona. They left Duncan, Arizona, and traveled by Southern Pacific train via Lordsburg, New Mexico, to Pecos, Texas; then on to Hagerman by way of Carlsbad on a freight train, riding in the caboose. At Carlsbad they transferred to the Santa Fe passenger train. They arrived at Hagerman in 1915 at 1:00 o'clock in the morning and found lodging in the hotel operated by Mr. and Mrs. Walter H. Hamontree. The Hamontree's had a cafe and some rooms in the downstairs level and more rooms upstairs. Two of the Hamontree sons were moved out of their beds that night to give Cecil and Bernice a warm bed in which to sleep. They stayed at the hotel for a short period of time and then moved to the farm. The original house had burned while the trading transaction was being negotiated. They slept in a tent and Mom cooked in a little one-room house, called the bean house. The construction was started on the new house immediately. Mr. Hamontree helped with the finishing carpenter work on the house. By 1916 it was time for the birth of Jewell, so they moved into the new house although it was not finished, lacking the ceilings, the paint and the finishing of the walls. The house still stands in good condition on the home place.

On February 15, 1916, Jewell was delivered by Dr. Stallard.

In the trade with W.Z. Thompson Dad received, besides the forty acres, a wagon, a team of mares ("Coley and Maude") and a buggy. Thompson threw in a slightly used thirty-nine year old horse, "Old Prince." Shortly thereafter Dad walked into town to buy groceries with the last of the $40 cash that he had upon arrival in Hagerman. He commented before the group of men gathered in the Losey grocery store, operated by Ed Losey, that he needed to talk with the old banker about borrowing some money. Mr. George Losey stepped up to him and said, "By hell, I am that old banker, come to see me in the morning and we will do business." The transaction was completed the next day and was never forgotten.

On the original forty acres, the first year Dad had twenty-five acres of orchard, ten acres of alfalfa and five acres of beans. Later he bought twenty acres joining on the east, then eighty acres from Mr. Cahoon joining on the north. He also bought forty acres a half mile north of Hagerman. As the years went by the orchards were pulled out and more alfalfa, grain and cotton were planted. Most of the alfalfa was hauled by wagons and teams to the Lochhead mill in Hagerman. But some of it was baled on an "Auto Fedan" baler and later on an "Ann Arbor" baler. To bale the alfalfa required a large crew of men and many teams of horses.

Mark Boyce with his stationary thrasher thrashed the grain after it was cut and bundled with a broadcast binder. The straw stacks were great to play on. Herb Lang (Kid) helped Dad with much of the farm work and said that Mom always fed, abundantly, these large work crews as well as anyone who happened to be on the place at meal time.

By 1918 it would seem that Dad and Mom were more prosperous, for that year Dad bought a 1918 Overland four door sedan from Jess Williams in Roswell. He also traded

Levi.   *Lottie.*

Levi Barnett, 1884-1940

Lottie Ratliff Barnett, 1884-1973

    Cecil Homer Barnett, 1905-   ; married Flora Bowen
        Norman Cecil Barnett

    Bernice Leroy Barnett, 1910-   ; married Margaret Jackson (1)*-div.
                                          Ray Hulse (2)
        *Robert Leroy Barnett, *Joan Marie Pruitt, *Mary Margaret Fout,
        *Suzanne Cox, *Donald John Barnett

    Basil Archibald Barnett, 1913-   ; married Jessie Sartin (1)*-div.
                                           Abbie Austin (2)
        *Angeline Merritt, *Richard Irwin Barnett, *Lee Roy Barnett

    Jewell Marie Barnet, 1916-   ; married Jess Medlin-div.

    Gladys Juacile Barnett, 1917-   ; married Glynn Knoll
        Sylvia Ann Luce, Glynn Barnett Knoll, David Vance Knoll,
        James Harvey Knoll

    Vencil Ratliff Barnett, 1920-   ; married Bessie Mae Langenegger
        Kay Annette Moore, Mary Carolyn Anderson, Johnny Levi Barnett

milk cows for a model T pickup truck, a lovable horse named "George" and a Winchester 30-30 rifle. Dad used that rifle on many deer hunts. He loved to hunt as well as fish and was always happy and relaxed on these excursions.

By this time Juacile had arrived, and then Vencil arrived completing the happy family; thriving on love and respect, coming from revered parents and the family working together.

Dad bought ewes from the Runyans who lived on the Penasco in 1925. These sheep were driven from the Runyan ranch on the Penasco river to Hagerman. The ewes lambed out that spring with lots of help from all the family, and the lambs were sold in the late spring. The ewes were held until shearing time, sheared and then sold. One year was more than enough of that. Dad also fed pigs that he raised himself. He fed mostly his own grain to fatten the pigs but at times it was supplemented with car loads of Kansas corn to finish them. Some of the fats were shipped to livestock markets like Kansas City and Fort Worth, etc., but many of them were butchered by Dad and the boys and were loaded on the model T pickup and transported for marketing in Roswell.

Our Mom was a devout Baptist and we lovingly remember her going about the never ending work while cheerfully singing, sometimes just humming, her favorite hymns. We can still visualize her, bonnet on her head, tending her garden. The home garden was the only way, in those days, that our family could have fresh vegetables on the table. Forever the helpmate of Dad, she sold products from the milk cows and her turkeys to help carry the family through the hard times. Once when a Maytag washing machine salesman came along Dad insisted that Mom should have one. She grudgingly consented for the salesman to leave it for trial and then to decide if she wanted it. Not convinced that the machine could get her clothes clean enough for her immaculate taste, she continued to boil the white clothes in the old black pot and to use the rub board before putting them into the Maytag. But finally she was convinced that the machine really could get the clothes clean without the boiling and rubbing. She used that same Maytag for many years before she had an automatic washer.

Our Dad was a hard working progressive farmer, compassionate and gentle, yet he believed in discipline. He was civic minded having served sixteen years on the Hagerman school board, resigning to assume the office of County Commissioner. He also served on the Hagerman Irrigation Board eighteen years as well as the Cotton Growers Gin Association for four years.

Dad died in 1940 and Mom died in 1973. Both are buried at Hagerman.

Cecil married Flora Bowen in 1926. As a boy of fifteen he built his first radio which was enjoyed by all the family as well as many neighbors who came in the evenings to hear it. At that time there were only three radio broadcasting stations in the United States, Fort Worth being the closest one. Cecil earned the money for his radio parts by trapping skunks and selling the hides. He received a degree in Electrical Engineering from N.M.A.&M. College (N.M. State) and came immediately to Hagerman in the fall of 1928 to teach math and chemistry and taught through the spring of 1930; at which time he went to work for the A.T.&T. Co. He worked continuously for them until his retirement in 1967. They now live in Albuquerque.

Bernice married Margaret Jackson and they had five children, all born during the years that he farmed the school section known as the "O'Dell Place" just south of the "Barnett Place." He now lives with his wife, Ray, in Nevada. Basil married Jessie Sartin, and he now lives in Tennessee with his wife, Abbie. Jewell married Jess Medlin and she now lives in San Francisco and works for the A.T.&T. Co. Juancile married Glynn Knoll and they live in Hagerman. Vencil (V.R.) married Bessie Mae Langenegger and they own and live on the "Barnett Home Place."

GEORGE F. BAUM

George Baum's parents were from Germany and he was born in 1882 in Williamsburg, Ohio. In the early years he worked in the family's hotel as a waiter and kitchen helper.

George attended a technical school in Cincinnati, Ohio, at age sixteen. He became a draftsman and served four years with the Dayton Pattern Works where he received his degree as a highly recommended pattern maker in both wood and metal. He worked in an iron foundry and as a plumber, tinsmith, electrician and motion picture operator.

"Go West young man" beckoned and in 1910 he arrived in Elida, New Mexico. He spent several years working on the range doing all the things this job required plus adding surveying to his talents. His knowledge of machinery sent him to many areas in New Mexico and Texas, including Hagerman where he worked most of the time with Mark Boyce on the thrashing machines and other engines.

In 1927 he went to work for the Pecos Valley Milling Company as electrician and mechanic. George remained in Hagerman and was a "trouble shooter" for many businesses and farmers in the area until his health and advanced age limited his activity.

George never stopped studying. He received a degree from a correspondence course in electricity and later added one in radio, television and electronics. His recreation was gardening and reading such magazines as Radio Today, Electronic Industries and Refrigeration Engineer.

He died in 1974, just three months under 93 years of age, and is buried in Hagerman.

THE J. FRANK BAUSLIN FAMILY

Kansas lost a number of it's citizens to the Pecos Valley in the Territory of New Mexico around the turn of the century. One such family was the J. Frank Bauslin family who came to Hagerman in 1906. They bought a farm near the Felix River approximately one and a quarter miles west of town. The family consisted of Mr. Bauslin, his wife and a daughter, Helen.

Mr. Bauslin worked the farm, and when he had time from the farm, he worked in the Crisler Blacksmith shop. It is said that he could pound a horse shoe nail until it was red hot. On one occasion Mr. Bauslin and a friend, W.J. Alter, went to Capitan. It is not known what the circumstances were but it is believed their horses ran away and they walked all the way to Hagerman. Another time Mr. Bauslin swam across the Felix River when it was flooding.

The Bauslins were members and faithful attendants of the Methodist Church. Helen received her education in the Hagerman schools, graduating with the class of 1918. Helen married Oscar Bullock and lived in Roswell. Their only child, a son, Dixon Bullock, owns and operates the Bullock Jewelry Store which his father established.

Most old timers remember Mr. Bauslin for his fine singing voice and his willingness to use it. He was a member of a male quartet that sang at numerous functions. He also sang solos at church services and funerals.

Mr. and Mrs. Bauslin moved to Roswell where they purchased a home around 1940. Not long afterward Mrs. Bauslin passed away and Mr. Bauslin lived with the Bullocks until his death. Mr. and Mrs. Bullock, too, are deceased.

— Information furnished by Dixon Bullock.

THE LEWIS TRAVIS BEALER FAMILY
By Clifton "Dryke" Bealer

Lewis Travis Bealer and his wife, Lizzie Bealer, came to Hagerman with their family in 1923. They traveled by Model T Ford from Iowa Park, Texas, but, after a short time, they had to return to Texas because of the death of Lizzie's father.

In 1928 the family returned to Hagerman and went to work on the local farms. They located first on the John Langenegger farm in an adobe house.

Times were hard and money was difficult to get. Any "extra" money obtained could make a family feel rich. One time a Hollywood movie company was in the area making a movie at Red Bluff. None of the family became movie stars but the Bealer milk cow earned them an extra ten dollars by being in the movie.

The names of the children and who they married are as follows; Verna (Cliff Grimlan), Ellis (Kay Peterson), Lewis (Sally Worley), Clifton (Mary Tulk), Clyde (Wanda Hill), and Donald (Kathey Barnes).

Lewis and Lizzie moved to Bloomington, California, in 1945 and still live there. All the children live in California except Clifton and Mary who remained in Hagerman. They are the parents of three children, Don, Fronnie and Douglas.

E.L. BITNEY FAMILY
By Lewis Bitney

The E.L. Bitney family first came to the Hagerman community from Brock, Nebraska, in the spring of 1909, and settled on a farm one and a half miles southwest of Hagerman. Mr. Bitney had scouted the area previously in an urgent search for climatic relief of an asthmatic condition that had forced him to liquidate a profitable farming and cattle raising operation conducted jointly with his older brother Wesley on land which included their parents homestead. The family consisted of Elbert (Bert) and wife Margaret (Maggie), and a son Lewis, then about four years old. They first set up housekeeping in a one room tent house, where they lived while a permanent five room house was being built. This house has since burned down and been replaced.

Mr. Bitney was the second son of five children born to the Lewis Bitney family. Mr. Lewis Bitney was French. The name Bitney is anglicized from the French name Bitony and is unique to this family.

Mr. Bitney obtained permanent relief from his asthmatic afflication and sold the farm near Hagerman in the fall of 1911. He moved into Hagerman for the winter, where a second son, Raymond Victor, was born. That fall Mr. Bitney had the thrill of voting for New Mexico Territory to be made a state, which was accomplished in January, 1912. The following spring the family moved to Woodburn, Oregon, at the urging of a cousin of Mr. Bitney. Apparently the fall rains in that region was more than they had bargained for, as the family moved back to Brock, Nebraska, by the spring of 1913.

In the summer of 1921 it became definite that the purchaser of the Hagerman farm was not able to pay out, so it was repossessed and the family returned to it. Mr. and

Mrs. Bitney remained until their deaths.

The elder son, Lewis, graduated from Hagerman High School the following spring, and, after two years at home, went on to graduate from the University of Nebraska Lincoln Campus with a BS degree in Electrical Engineering in 1928. He spent his working years in the employ of electrical utilities, and when he retired in 1970, was planning engineer for Lincoln Electrical System in Lincoln, Nebraska. He continues to live in Lincoln where this account was written. While attending UN he became engaged to Esther Garner, and they were married in 1930. Only one child was born to this union, Gerald Victor, and he lives at Vacaville, California. He is employed as an engineer aid at nearby Travis AFB. Esther died suddenly of cerebral hemorrhage in 1970.

The younger son, Raymond, graduated from Hagerman High School in 1929, and then took airplane training at Love Field, Dallas, Texas. He was issued a pilots license in 1930. He had arranged financing to set up a flying service and was scouting for a suitable location when on September 19, 1930, he idly pulled on a propeller of a recently landed aircraft at Dennison, Texas. The engine fired and Raymond was thrown, causing his death. His body was buried in the family plot in Hagerman cemetery.

THE BLEDSOE FAMILIES
By Mrs. T.A. Bledsoe, Jr.

Albert Bledsoe and Rebecca Bledsoe came from Edina, Missouri, by train to Hydro, Oklahoma, in 1906 where they farmed for two years. In 1908 they moved to Elida, New Mexico, by covered wagon with their children. They homesteaded on land near Elida and Dora and it was at Elida that Albert first had a broom factory. In 1912 they moved to Hagerman by covered wagon and first lived on the Pomona Farms about three-quarters of a mile north and west of town. He established his broom factory in a building located on South Cambridge Street. Albert hauled his brooms by wagons and teams to Roswell and Carlsbad where he sold them.

The children of Albert and Rebecca Bledsoe were: Mamie, who married Dick Bull and moved to Missouri and died in 1944; Clara, who married Sam Wilson in California and died in 1966; Alda married E.G. Rudig and moved to Centralia, Washington, and died in 1967; Lillian married John Bible and lived in Dexter and died in 1959; Thomas Albert, Jr. married Dreta Williams.

Tommy and I, Dreta, married in Portales, New Mexico, in 1930. We farmed for one year in Dexter before moving to Hagerman in 1936 where we farmed a farm about one mile west of Hagerman. After one year on the first farm we bought the farm known as the "Bledsoe Place," one and a half miles west of Hagerman. We all lived in a three room house until we built our new home in 1947. In the three room house it was crowded with people, nine of us, and lots of love. We had grandmother Bledsoe living with us at the time.

We still own the farm and Mrs. Helms owns the house. All of our children are married and have their own homes and I now live in Roswell at 1008 N. Plains Park Drive.

Tommy worked at the Greendfield gin in Dexter until the farm was paid for and then quit his job. He took Charles Michelet's place on the Hagerman school board. After that he was elected and served in that position for twenty years.

Raymond married Barbara Hicks and they live in Mt. Grove, Missouri, with their three sons where Raymond farms.

Don married Betty Watford and they reside in Las Cruces with their three daughters. Don works for the Civil Service.

Dot and husband, Harrel Ford, live in Truth or Consequences and he works for the Border Patrol. They have one daughter and one son.

Tommy Jr. married Georgia Seeley and they have two sons. They live in Artesia where Tommy works for the Navajo Refinery Co.

Peggy and husband, Billy Hefner, are the parents of two sons and one daughter. They live in Roswell where Billy works for Transwestern Pipeline Co.

Ross married Val Haughtling and they live in Tucson where Ross works for the Border Patrol. They are the parents of one son.

Wanda Lee and Carolyn both died at an early age.

Thomas Albert, Jr. died in 1973 at the age of 71.

Tommy and I always said that Hagerman was a wonderful place to live and raise our family. The schools are the best and so are the churches. The most wonderful thing about Hagerman is the people. We always loved the people and the place that was home to us for so many years — Hagerman.

J.E. BLYTHE FAMILY

In 1910 my father and mother, Mr. and Mrs. J.E. Blythe, their three sons and two daughters and my mother's father and mother, Mr. and Mrs. Granville Kelton moved from Booneville, Mississippi, to Hagerman, New Mexico. My father had already purchased an alfalfa farm of 160 acres, three and a half miles northwest of town. A two-story white house had been built on the property. The place was soon landscaped and three large red hay barns added. Besides growing alfalfa my father raised a few fine horses which were exhibited at the Roswell County Fair, often winning blue ribbons.

My brothers rode their horses to school and my sister and I drove a horse and buggy. When the weather was cold, my grandfather heated bricks and wrapped them in heavy paper to keep our feet warm. This together with a heavy lap robe kept us comfortable on the long ride in the buggy. We had a real good old mare named Molly that knew the route as well as we did. One day on our way home from school we were letting Molly find her own way while we were reading the mail and newspapers we picked up at the post office. Suddenly old Molly stopped dead in her tracks, just in time to avoid being hit by the train at the crossing. That was the last time we ever put the reins over the dashboard and ignored what was going on around us.

Without fail on Sunday morning we hitched the team to the surrey and the entire family went to church in Hagerman. Quite often we drove to Roswell for shopping and other things, but this required a full day each way so we always spent a night or two at the Virginia Inn.

We will never forget the wonderful friends we made in Hagerman. Our father and mother couldn't possibly have picked a better place to raise their family. I left Hagerman in 1923 but will always have a warm feeling in my heart for Hagerman and will remember the song we sang in grammar school—"You ask what land I love the best, New Mexico, New Mexico."

— Florrie Blythe Mansfield

HAL BOGLE

Information furnished by Bill Bogle and friends

Just a "Mr." before the name of Hal Bogle does not seem like enough title for such a great man. To quote from an article written by Oscar Green: "Hal was one of the big men of the West, a builder. Not many of us know the extent of the empire he built and that stands as a tribute to his enterprise and wisdom. There was a joy in putting things together and making them grow and watching them work for Hal. I have seen him stop to pick up a feed sack to take care of it while he was spending tens of thousands to provide more jobs and food for people. He was a simple man, warm and unpretentious, as comfortable as an old shoe to be with."

Hal came to New Mexico from Tennessee for his health in 1917. After a short while he returned to Tennessee where he had owned property since he was seventeen. By 1919 his health was again bad and he decided to come to the Pecos Valley and bought a farm one mile north of Dexter. As soon as he recuperated from his illness he went to work as the manager of the Dexter Alfalfa Mill Company owned by Roy Lochhead.

In 1931 Hal bought the Felix Ranch and began to farm and buy mules. He knew the demand for mules in the Delta bottom land country of the South. They were being used to pull the stumps out of the swamp country. John Prather of Alamagordo, New Mexico and other ranchers sold the mules to Mr. Bogle. The mules were used and broken for about a year on the Felix Ranch and then shipped to the east.

Eventually Hal bought one half interest in the Pecos Valley Alfalfa Mill Co. and later a full interest in the mills. The company owned mills in Arizona, Ohio, Idaho, Oklahoma and Missouri.

When Mr. Bogle began to branch out by buying more farms, he was asked by Roy Lochhead why he was investing in old bankrupt farms. His answer was, "I'm already a lot worse than broke and if I can't make them pay I'll just go bankrupt."

Hal was a true, dignified, courteous Southern gentleman. No one ever came to his home without being offered a meal or his wonderful hospitality.

He was a first cattle feeder in New Mexico. His shrewdness in dealing with one cow was the same as in bargaining with thousands of cattle. Hal always realized our resources were not to be squandered but saved for future generations.

From Rev. Charles Fullinwider's sermon at Hal's funeral: "We owe so much to those who have been pioneers, who opened doors to new lands and new ventures."

"Mr." Hal had four sons, Bill, Jack, Jim and Pete. Bill resides in the Hagerman-Dexter area.

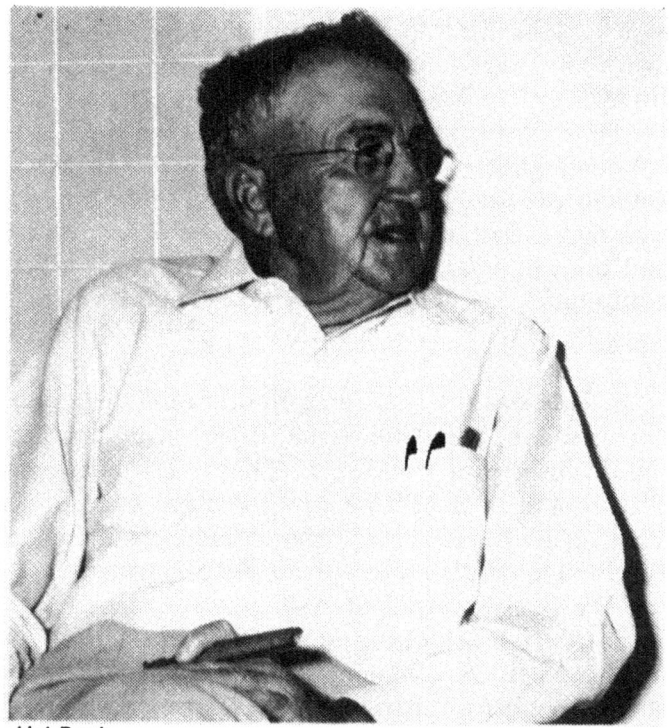

Hal Bogle.

MY MEMORIES OF HAGERMAN
By Elizabeth Bowen

In the summer of 1924, my brother, Curtis Baker, came home after his graduation to spend some time visiting. After hearing all about the wonderful people of Hagerman, and wishing I could go back with him, I really became quite excited over the possibility of making the trip. With our parents consent we took the train in Lubbock (my first train ride) and arrived in Hagerman that night at 9:20 o'clock. We were greeted by many young people, and I learned later that meeting the passenger train was the every night entertainment. They were all delighted to see Baker (he was called Baker by everyone, instead of Curtis). After meeting all his friends, I was especially excited over a very good friend of Baker's, John Bowen. He was in my opinion the best looking boy I had ever known.

We spent several nights with the Williamson Family. Each night we were following the trend of meeting with all our friends at the depot to wait for the train. I was always delighted to see and talk with everyone — especially John Bowen. During the school year I stayed with Alline and Bert Bailey, paying them the big sum of $20.00 per month for room and board. There will never be another couple as wonderful as the Baileys. My school year there was very enjoyable. There were so many nice teachers, and everybody was your friend. During the year I became engaged to John Bowen, and at the close of school I went back to Crosbyton, Texas. Johnnie visited us there and obtained permission from my parents for us to be married. We were married in 1926 in Portales. We lived in Hagerman where Johnnie worked as a barber. Part of that time I worked in Miller's

Grocery Store and also in People's Mercantile, which was owned by two wonderful people, Dub and Jane Andrus.

Shortly after our marriage, my Mother was killed by lightning. My two younger sisters, Verda and Ruby, visited us several times and seemed to enjoy being there. In 1930 we asked our Dad to let them come out to stay with us and finish high school. Verda graduated in 1932 and Ruby in 1933. It was so much pleasure for us to have them with us, and there was never a dull moment. We usually had an extra girl, Marteal Graham, and we enjoyed having her there so much. We never ran out of room for one more as they gave us so much joy. We rented a bedroom to a wonderful high school teacher, Miss Sylvia Gatignol. She taught English and Spanish and became a part of our fun family.

After the girls graduated they went back home for a while. Verda later married Bud Boggs in Artesia and Ruby married Paul Whitman of Dexter.

In 1934 our son Jim was born. He was, and always will be, a great joy to us. He now lives in Carlsbad after graduating from Denver University. He, and his wife Karen, presented us with five wonderful grandchildren.

In 1937 Johnnie became a member of the State Barber Board and traveled quite a lot until 1943. At this time he resigned and bought a shop in Carlsbad. That will always be our home, but we shall never forget our friends and the great joy of living in Hagerman.

THE W. E. BOWEN FAMILY

By the Bowen Family

On January 8, 1884, our mother, Louisa H. Boren, and our father, William Edwin Bowen, a school teacher, were married in Texas County, Missouri. After trying their luck at farming in Texas and working for the Copper Queen Mining Co. in Arizona they came to Hagerman in 1894. Dad became an employee of the Hagerman Irrigation Co. He began as a laborer and then became a ditch rider. In 1906 he was made superintendent of the company and held this position until his death in 1934.

Dad was one of the original stock holders in the First National Bank of Hagerman, organized Nov. 9, 1904, and remained a director until his death. For a time he was one of the town's volunteer firemen and was injured by an explosion. This later contributed to his death. He was a member of the Town Board and the Board of Education and for awhile president of this board. The Drainage Board of this District elected him secretary while he was a member. He was a faithful member of the First Christian Church where he served as an Elder. He belonged to the Masonic Lodge and the Independent Order of Odd Fellows in Hagerman.

The family had had two children before arriving in Hagerman, Eunice and one who had died in infancy. During the busy years in Hagerman six more children were added to the family: Opha, Ernest, Stanley, Volney, John, and the first twins born in Hagerman, Flora and Flossie. We were all active in school, church and community affairs and loved every minute of our growing-up years. The boys started working in fields at an early age and in their free time spent many happy hours fishing and swimming in the Felix River. They hunted small game which was plentiful, even throwing rocks at the quail and rabbits on the school grounds.

Eunice, Opha and Ernest started to school in the yellow brick school house which stands directly behind the Baptist Church facing east. Miss Hannah Blackstone was the teacher when Eunice started to school. Eunice married Charles Ballard of Roswell, New Mexico. Both are now deceased.

Opha, the second daughter was born the day before Eunice came home from school with what seemed to be a cold but which turned out to be whooping cough. The baby became sick too and there was no doctor available. Dad met the passenger train, boarded and asked if there was a doctor aboard. Fortunately there was and the train waited while the doctor attended the sick child. He bound her chest and provided medicine and advice. Opha was the singer and musician of the family. In later years she married Andrew Gibson. They had one son. She is now a widow, retired and living in Clovis, New Mexico.

Ernest, the oldest son, was born in Hagerman and is also the only child still living here. He attended the Business College in Chillicothe, Missouri, and went immediately to work for the Santa Fe Railroad. He worked most of fifty years as Station Agent and Telegrapher in Hagerman. He was interested in civic affairs, served on the Town Board for twenty-four years and has been a member of the Board of Directors of the Bank for twenty years. He married Sadie Beadle in 1919 and they had a son who died at the age of sixteen. Sadie was also active in civic affairs. She was one of the organizers of the Order of Rainbow for Girls in Hagerman. She was an Eastern Star member in Hagerman.

Volney went to Chillicothe Business College and returned to the Pecos Valley to become a station agent for the Santa Fe Railroad in Greenfield, Fort Sumner and Melrose, New Mexico. He married Rev. Hatfield's daughter, Ora, from Dexter. They have two daughters and a son and live in Clovis.

Johnnie will likely be best remembered for his sports activities in high school as the Captain of the basketball

W.E. Bowen.

Mrs. Luisa H. Bowen.

John L. Bowen.

Mrs. Eunice Ballard.

From l. to r.: Mrs. Flossie Johnson, Mrs. Flora Barnett, Volney Bowen, Mrs. Opha Gibson, Ernest Bowen.

team that won the State Championship in 1923. He married Elizabeth Baker and they have one son.

Of the twins, Flora was the first to marry. She became the wife of Cecil Barnett and they have one son.

Flossie married Ira Johnson and they have two children. After her husbands death in 1966 she continued to live in Clovis.

Louisa H., our dearly beloved mother, was a very busy woman totally dedicated to her home and family. She aided our dad and the children in many activities. In the early days neighbor helped neighbor when there was sickness or need. Mother was always available to help by sitting up at night nursing the sick or delivering babies as a midwife. One of the babies she delivered was a close friend of Ernest's, Harold Miller. She died in 1961 in Clovis and is buried next to Dad in the Masonic Cemetery of Hagerman.

Before we bring this family history to a close I, Ernest, would like to tell this incident that happened when I was a small boy. It must have been about 1908 or 1909. Dad told me one day that he was going up to the head of the canal and on to Roswell. He asked me to go with him. We spent the night in Roswell and heard William Jennings Bryan make one of his famous speeches. He was probably running for President at the time. We stayed at the El Capitan Hotel after putting our two horses and buggy in a livery stable. Then we went to the Court House lawn where they had bales of hay scattered around with two by twelve boards on them to make seats. We listened to what my dad said was a fine oration.

A few years after this I was working in the hay fields and had my leg broken. My dad came in one evening and carried me to a cot outside so that I could see Halley's Comet. It was a large comet with a long tail and it could be seen plainly. Dad said it would not be seen again for seventy-five years and that I might have a chance to see it again. It had better hurry.

Note: Ernest S. Bowen died August 26, 1975.

THE BUCK BOYCE FAMILY
By Alma Boyce Criddle

Our father, I. E. "Buck" Boyce, Sr., came to New Mexico in the winter of 1902. He first came out here with his oldest sister, Kate Clark, and her family.

Later Papa returned to Texas where he met our mother. They were married in Big Springs, Texas. Mama had been married before and her husband had died of typhoid fever leaving her with four small children. They were Viola Lee, Essie Mae, Elton Dudley and Allen Dulaney "Duke" Thompson.

Papa was farming near Coahoma, Texas, when he decided to move his family to Hagerman. He said that he wasn't enough of a preacher to raise crops by dry land farming.

In the spring of 1912, Papa, Mama, the Thompson children, Ike Ely and Nig (Rosa Mae) came to Hagerman in a covered wagon. Nig was a small baby and Mama said she cried after they arrived here as she missed the motion of the wagon.

Three more children were born to the family after they came here, Samuel Anderson, Francis Keener and Alma Sue.

Viola married Henry Kaiser and they had six children. Later she married West Rathbone and they had one daughter. At this time Viola is in a rest home in San Angelo, Texas, near two of her daughters.

Essie Mae (deceased) married Arthur B. Robinson and they had four children. Later she married Clyde Knight and they moved to California.

Elton (deceased) was married to Cecil Thompson and they had three sons.

Duke (deceased) married at Lordsburg and they had four children. Later, he married again in Wichita Falls, Texas. He and Helen had two children.

Ike was married to Vallie Nappier in Alamogordo, New Mexico. Their two children, Sue and Gerald, graduated from Hagerman High School. Vallie died in 1974.

Sam married Rachel Fletcher and they started their married life farming in Buffalo Valley, later moving to Roswell. At present they own and operate a grocery store in Dexter, New Mexico. They have one son.

Slick married Vernese Davis and they have two sons, Gary and Francis K. Jr. "Cisco." Slick has been postmaster in Hagerman since 1965 and Vernese has been employed at the bank for over thirty years.

I married Charlie Criddle (deceased) and we had nine children. After I retired from the postoffice in El Paso, Texas, I moved back to Hagerman.

Mama was a member of Eastern Star, the Woman's Club, L. C. Club and the Presbyterian Missionary-Aid Society. Mama and Papa were members of the Presbyterian Church and at one time Papa sang in the choir.

Papa farmed, baled hay, worked for the Hagerman Irrigation Co. and the Lochhead Alfalfa Mill. He also drove a schoolbus and had his own truck for hauling hay, grain, etc., from this area to parts of Texas and New Mexico.

When Papa was working for the alfalfa mill he had a team of horses trained to come home at noon for a drink of water. They would then walk back to the mill and wait until they were needed to move wagons or spot boxcars. At night they would come home and wait at the corral until someone opened the gate.

Some of the people I remember best were Grandpa and Grandma Smith who always had homemade cookies for us, and in their front room they had a cuckoo clock that fascinated me. Also, Teed Devenport whose cigar always looked the same length to me, Belle and Richmond Ham in the drugstore and L. W. Garner at the grocery store because he always gave us a box of chocolates at Christmas and I think they were the best.

I used to sit around and listen to Papa, Jim King and other oldtimers talk about when they first came to the valley. I remember Papa telling of working in a livery stable for a grouchy old man. One night he and some of his friends decided to play a joke on the old man. They quietly led all the horses from the stable and turned them loose in a pasture, then replaced them in the stalls with some wild donkeys. The man had the habit of going in before good daylight and patting the horses on the rump to move them over so he could feed them. That morning feeding time was much livelier than usual! Papa and his friends had a fast round-up to return the horses.

Growing up in Hagerman held many memories of Fourth of July picnics, rodeos and dances at Lake Van. We would swim anywhere that had enough water; one of my favorites was a spot just below the big dam on the Felix River.

HARLAN BOYCE REMINISCES

A few years ago Harlan Boyce was reminiscing about his youth in the Hagerman area. It seems that he had gone to the mountains with Charlie Tanner in Charlie's car. On the way back, about 35 miles from the nearest town, the steering gear broke and there was no way to guide the car. Harlan and Charlie discussed the problem. Rather than walk, it was decided that Harlan should sit a-straddle the right front fender and kick the front of the revolving tire with his right heel to make the car move to the left. A kick with the left heel gave the opposite steering. With Charlie at the throttle Harlan had many thrills! To make a long story short, they arrived in town safely by using this method.

A True "Yarn" of Mary Mason's As Spun To Her Nephew

About 1917 Harlan Boyce and his wife, Jessie, were living in a small house in Buffalo Valley. Mary Mason, Harlan's sister, had been to call on them. When the three decided to go to Hagerman they chose to ford the Pecos. They were riding in a light single buggy with the "gals" in the seat and Harlan standing on the small platform behind them. When they entered the Pecos they saw it was "up a little" and by the time they reached mid-stream water was wetting their shoe soles. At that spot the single tree broke! Harlan said, "Whoa Nellie!" She stopped. He then leaned over and spoke and spoke again. "Whoa, Nellie, Whoa"; patted the horse gently on the hip; grasped the very root of her tail firmly with both hands and said, "Get up, Nell!" She pulled them out as Harlan held firmly to the root of her tail. Temporary repairs were made and they drove on to Hagerman without further incident.

— Written by Harlan Walworth Boyce, son of Harlan Boyce.

MARK BOYCE

Mark Boyce, son of Rufus Boyce, came to Hagerman, New Mexico, on January 25, 1908, from Middletown, Des Moines County, Iowa.

Mr. Boyce believes his Hart Parr was the first gas tractor ever to come to New Mexico. He did a great deal of breaking of sod with it. Later he did threshing all up and down the Pecos Valley for years. He believes he was the second man to do threshing here. Mr. Jim Cowles likely was first. Mr. Cowles had a Hutter wooden case separator and two steam tractors when Mr. Boyce arrived with the Hart Parr.

Mr. Boyce threshed all kinds of small grain, wheat, oats, barley, milo maize and kaffir corn. The main crop he threshed was alfalfa seed.

A former customer of Mr. Boyce said, "One had to be prepared with many teams and men because Boyce could really run a lot of crops through the machine in a hurry." At least six to ten teams and wagons were required to get the crops to the machine to be threshed. Also, four to six men were standing by to pitch it on the wagons. Two grain wagons were used, one to be loading up while the other unloaded the threshed grain. When alfalfa was threshed an expert sack sewer was required.

The highlight of the early threshing days was the big dinners that the women served to the threshing crews.

This could not be concluded without mentioning Pat Summers, who worked for Mr. Boyce for several years as separator man. He sat on top of the machine and saw to it that it was fed regularly, and he also watched for any foreign materials such as mesquite roots and boards. Once in a while a pitch fork got loose from one of the feeders and if Pat wasn't there all this could run through the machine and tear it up. Mr. Boyce was a very efficient operator and loved his work. He died in Hagerman in September of 1973.

— Contributed by Mrs. Grace Hart.

Mark Boyce's Thresher. This threshing machine was assembled by Mark Boyce and George Baum. The two men gathered parts from various places and assembled it. The machine was in operation from about 1914 until 1925.

The Hart Parr machine owned by Mark Boyce.

RUFUS T. BOYCE FAMILY
By Mary Boyce Mason

Rufus T. Boyce and his wife Mary Carter Boyce came to Hagerman in the spring of 1908 by train. Their children were Marcus Boyce, deceased, who married Grace Cunningham; Allen P. Boyce, deceased; Wayne Boyce, deceased; Harlan Boyce, deceased; Mary Boyce married Cassius G. Mason, deceased, and now resides in Hagerman; Grace Boyce married Bill Hart, deceased, and resides in Hagerman; John Boyce, deceased; Esther M. Boyce married Clifton L. Morgan, deceased, and lives in Hagerman.

Mr. Boyce was a farmer, a Republican and a Presbyterian. He was born in Fairhaven, Ohio, but moved with his parents to Burlington, Iowa, when he was quite young. He lived there until the spring of 1908 when he sold his land, timberland and most of his dairy herd, rented a boxcar, loaded it full with stock, furniture and everything he needed to take to New Mexico. He came by rail over the Santa Fe to Hagerman and his family followed a little later by train.

On a previous prospecting trip he purchased land east of Hagerman in what is called Buffalo Valley. He installed a pumping plant to pump water out of the Pecos River for irrigation of what was to be an alfalfa and small grain farm and orchard.

He bought a big Hart-Parr tractor and thrashing machine to thrash grain and seeds through the country.

Some of the land joined the big Turkey Track Ranch and, with no fences established as yet, his prize Jersey bull was shot and killed by the ranch people.

The stock and horses and Jersey cattle did not do well on the salt grass pasture and salty water so Mr. Boyce sold off most of the stock that survived. Wind blew so hard at times that chickens lost most of their feathers and snakes bit the dogs. Drinking water was hauled from Hagerman twelve miles away, going by the bridge. It was still a long way even if you could ford the river which was a risky business.

Children left one by one, some liked New Mexico, others didn't.

Later, Mr. Boyce bought a house in town (the old brick schoolhouse) and lived there until he passed away in 1923. He is buried in the Hagerman cemetery. He loved the land of his adoption regardless of losing a small fortune in the big adventure.

After Mr. Boyce's death, Mrs. Boyce and the younger children went back to Iowa. She lived to be 98 years old. Some will remember Mr. Boyce as the justice of the peace in Hagerman, who was affectionately called "Judge."

Harlan

Wayne

Mark

Rufus

Mary

John

Mrs. Rufus Boyce

Esther

Grace

Allen

THE D.A. BRADLEY FAMILY

By Sam Bradley and Bonnie Bell Phillips

D.A. (Dock) Bradley and Edna Bradley came to Hagerman in August of 1917. They homesteaded on a section of land located on top of the Caprock about 35 miles east of Hagerman. We moved from Fluvanna, Texas, in a covered wagon in April of 1917 to the homestead, stayed there for about four months before moving into the town of Hagerman in our covered wagon. We made two or three trips to Hagerman for supplies during our stay at the homestead.

Our first home in Hagerman was a house on Perth street about two blocks east of Kemp Lumber Co. Our neighbors were the Buck Boyce family. Then we moved to a farm, two and three-quarters miles northwest of Hagerman where our neighbors were the Ed Lanes. Later, about 1920, we moved to the Losey place, about a half mile southwest of town, and our close neighbor and friends here were the Levi Barnetts. We lived in the Hagerman area until about 1925 before moving to a place on the Cottonwood (six miles west of Lake Arthur).

The reason that we left our homestead and moved to Hagerman was that the farmers were in need of extra men and teams on their farms. In those early days homesteaders were required to live a specified amount of time on their claims in order to be granted legal title as owners. So this amount of time the homesteaders worked on the farms counted as having lived on their homesteads.

There were three of us children when we came to Hagerman; Sam, Claude (Hoot), and Bonnie Bell. In 1923 a son, Maurice Johnson, was born while we were living on the Losey place. He was killed in 1941 while horseback riding. Sam married Mary Jo Morgan in 1932 in Carlsbad, New Mexico. Claude married Etheleen Pottor in 1938 in Roswell. Bonnie Bell married Owen Phillips in Roswell in 1936.

Mother and Dad were both very active in the Presbyterian Church, Ladies Aid, Masonic and Eastern Star. Dad died in 1963. Mother is now 88 years old and is living at Sunset Villa Nursing Home in Roswell, New Mexico.

THE BRAMBLETT FAMILIES
By Marvin Bramblett

Nix Bramblett was born in Alabama in 1881. He and his wife, Addie, and four sons came to New Mexico about 1916 from Coryell County, Texas. The four sons, Leo, Feno, Omer and Joe, were all born in Texas. A fifth son, Vernon, and a daughter, Kitty Beth, were born in New Mexico.

Nix Bramblett, my grandfather, was a blacksmith by trade and he worked in the blacksmith shop presently owned by Leonard George on North Cambridge street, as well as in a blacksmith shop in Dexter in the 1920's. Nix was a brother to Jim Bramblett who lived in Hagerman with his family from 1916 until his death in 1956. Grandfather, Nix, died in 1932 in Texas. Grandmother died in California in 1973.

My father, Leo, was the oldest child of Nix and Addie Bramblett and he lived around Hagerman until 1943. He married my mother, Mattie Fletcher, in 1927. She was a sister to Rachel Boyce, Penix and Rosco Fletcher. My father worked on the O'Dell farm, a half mile southwest of Hagerman, at the time of their marriage and he took his bride to live in the house just south of the big O'Dell home (this O'Dell home stood on the northeast corner of the school section and has been razed). I was born in this small house in 1928. Then in 1930 my sister, Modene, was born in the big house — the O'Dell home. My father and mother took my sister and me to Texas shortly before my mother died in 1932 at Dimmitt, Texas. My father brought his two very small children, Modene and me, back to Hagerman to be near his people and the Fletchers. Grandmother Fletcher had much to do with the rearing of Modene and me.

I recall the hard times of the depression years although I wasn't so very old. My father would hunt cottontail rabbits in the sand hills east of the Pecos river. He sold them for 10¢ per dozen.

Father married Hattie Howard of Hagerman in 1940. They moved to Carlsbad in 1943 where he worked in the potash mines until his death in 1958. They had five children.

I married Beth in Texas where I finished school and returned to New Mexico in 1952 and have been engaged in farming northeast of Dexter since then. We have three children.

Modene Shepard has lived in Carlsbad, New Mexico, for some years and has three daughters.

Feno, the second son of Nix and Addie Bramblett, married Sally Pilley of Hagerman in 1929. Feno worked in the C & C Garage a number of years before moving to California in 1942 where he died in 1958. His family was active in the Assembly of God Church in Hagerman. They had four daughters. The two older girls, Doris and Wilma, spent most of their school years in Hagerman.

Omer, the third son, married Birdie Downs of Lake Arthur. They lived around the Hagerman area, operated a saw mill in the Sacramento Mountains in the late 30's and early 40's, worked in the potash mines at Carlsbad and had a dairy farm in Arkansas at the time of his death in 1958.

The two younger sons, Joe and Vernon, did not live in the Hagerman area as much as the older boys. Joe lives in California, is married and has one daughter. Vernon farms in Oklahoma where he and his wife had two sons. Kitty Beth, the daughter, went to school in Hagerman, graduated from high school in Artesia, and now lives in Virginia.

THE JIM BRAMBLETTS
By Georgia Bramblett Fluitt

My father, James N. Bramblett, his wife, Sallie Mae, and two children came to New Mexico in a covered wagon from Arkansas. We located near Lovington first and stayed there for about a year before moving to Hagerman. We made the move from Arkansas trying to find the promised land that my father's brother, Ed Bramblett, had told about.

The year that we arrived it was very dry and it was discouraging. We lived in a half dugout, burned cow chips for fuel and ate lots of beans. We were very poor. Our first home in Hagerman was on Manchester Street, owned by Pete Losey. We only lived there for a very short time and paid $6.00 per month for rent, water furnished. Then my father bought their home, just north of the Losey house, in 1917 and continued to live there until his death in 1956. Mother lived in the home after his death until 1961 and then sold the house and moved to California with me.

My parents liked Hagerman and seemed to always enjoy living there. They both did just about any kind of work that they found to do. My father worked in the fields and orchards a lot.

My mother was a Baptist for a good part of her life and then in the mid-thirties we became associated with the Assembly of God Church. My mother died in November of 1965.

I had one brother, Forrest V. Bramblett, who was killed in an automobile accident in 1929.

I have two sons; James Forrest Kerwin and Richard T. Kerwin both living in California. I live with my husband, Olen E. Fluitt, in Modesta, California.

THE BROOKSHIER FAMILY
By June Brookshier Usrey

Papa, George Walton Brookshier, born in 1873, was a descendant of Jesse Brookshier, a settler in Rowan County, North Carolina, about 1790. Mama, Magnolia Tuttle Brookshier, born in 1877, was a descendant of Capt. John Rucker who came from England to Jamestown, Virginia, in 1699. Both of my parents were born near Ruckerville, Kentucky, so named for the family ancestor.

After my parents married, Papa farmed near Winchester, Kentucky, and later moved to Lexington, Kentucky. Virgil, Gay, Frank and Boutcher were born here in Lexington.

When Mama was about thirty years old, she became ill from a lung disease which was prevalent in Kentucky in those years. The doctor told Papa if he wanted to save her, to move out west where the climate was hot and dry. Many families came to New Mexico under these same conditions. This was a sad decision for Papa to make as they all loved their home, their friends and Papa's business was good. Nevertheless, all property was sold and the family boarded the train for the West. Papa had read many stories of the West and wanted a ranch of his own.

The train trip to New Mexico took almost a week and the family arrived in Kenna, New Mexico. They lived in a dugout until a house could be built. It was difficult for the family to get used to the hot, dry weather but Mama improved rapidly in the climate.

After experiencing a terrible prairie fire the family traded for a combination variety and millinery shop in Roswell. Later they traded the businesses for a homestead about six miles south of Roswell. It was here that Kirk was born.

A year or so later the family moved to Hagerman for a short time, living near the town on the highway. While here, Gay recalls a trip they made to Tahoka, Texas, to see cotton. Cotton was not grown in the Pecos Valley during those years.

Mama and Papa bought a farm near Artesia a short time later. This is where I was born. Mama liked this home and didn't want to move again, but Papa thought he could make better money on a larger farm so they moved to the Rudig farm, just west of Hagerman near the Felix River. I don't remember this farm except the two-story white house and the stairs coming down into the kitchen.

During the years that we lived in the Hagerman area, the High School had winning basketball teams. Boutcher played on these teams. He later played on the basketball and football teams at the New Mexico Military Institute in Roswell where he was attending school. Frank had to stay out of school to help Papa in the Hagerman years so he attended the high school which was in operation at the New Mexico A.&M. College (now known as New Mexico State University). Later, Frank attended Arizona State University in Tucson as well as Boutcher. Frank then attended Northwestern University near Chicago while Boutcher attended Wake Forest College in North Carolina. Kirk was a top basketball player and attended Old Center College in Kentucky. My brothers still get together for important athletic contests such as Olympics or world championship events.

About 1923 the family decided to move back to Roswell and live in town, though they still owned the ranch south of town. Mama and Papa both loved Kentucky, but Papa grew to love the West and was very happy here. Mama never forgot Kentucky and never grew as fond of the West as Papa.

Virgil married Floy Muncy and had two children. He died in 1925.

Gay married Nevil Muncy. They have two daughters. Gay and Nevil live in Artesia.

Frank married Florence Mehlhop, niece of F.L. Mehlhop of Dexter. They live in Maxwell, New Mexico and have no children.

Boutcher lives in Batesburg, South Carolina. He married Celeste Angelea and they have no children.

Kirk married Clara Belle McPherson and lives in Safford, Arizona. They have three children.

June married Crawford Usrey of Sullivan, Indiana, and lives in Roswell. They have no children.

THE BROWN FAMILIES
By Louise Brown Sleeper & Frances Brown Hall

In 1914 Jacob Vedder Brown came to the Pecos Valley with his parents from Galveston, Texas. His Father was born in Richmond, Virginia in 1840, and educated at Virginia Military Institute. He entered the Confederate Army of America, serving with honor and was made Captain in Anderson's Brigade of Lee's Army of Virginia. He was wounded at the second battle of Bull Run. He married Miss Grace King Vedder in Galveston after the war was over. She was born in New York State and educated at the Boston Conservatory of Music. Through her mother's family she was descended from Rufus King, whose name appears on the Declaration of Independence. Another ancestor was William Rufus King, who was elected Vice-President of the United States under the Administration of Franklin Pierce.

While in Texas Captain Brown served as a senator in the State Legislature and a Judge. Having survived two destructive hurricanes, seeing houses, bodies, and all possessions floating by their home, Hagerman was a haven to them. One of their eight children, Milton Brown, Jr. resided in Hagerman. He was Manager of the Kemp Lumber Company but in a short time he moved to Texico with his wife, Agnes, and four daughters, Agnes K., Grace, Malcolm and Frances.

Vedder was then made Manager of Kemp Lumber Company. His Father, having been injured in the flood of 1900 in Galveston, had become totally paralized so a house was rented across the street from Kemps so Vedder could help his mother with his care. Captain Brown died in 1918. Vedder never neglected his mother and supported her until her death in 1930. Although Vedder was never able to enjoy many of the activities of the young people, he kept the young ladies happy with his humor and compliments. He married Louise Michelet in 1922.

The Kemp Lumber Company was a large business, with two large lumber sheds, a coal bin, warehouse and the main store containing household wares, nails, bolts, glass, stoves and anything the farmers needed. He never refused to help a farmer if he needed repairs, day or night. The office was a part of this main building.

Vedder resigned this position in 1944 and enjoyed the farms, raising livestock, cattle, chickens, horses and hogs. The chickens furnished the high school youngsters their chicken fries on the Felix River which was not far from the house. One dark night a disturbing noise was heard in the chicken house so Vedder and his nephew ran for their shot guns and went to the chicken house for the "big catch." As they arrived at the chicken house door a white faced bull came charging out, almost running over the two. Their fright spared us a lot of bull.

In 1952 Vedder died leaving his wife, Louise, two sons, Louis Vedder, seventeen; Milton J., thirteen and a daughter, Priscilla Rose, twelve. Vedder was a true southern gentleman, a devoted father, admired and loved by everyone. He was widely known for his original, comical words of conversation. Priscilla died in 1955. Milton J. was killed in an airplane accident leaving his wife, Mary Evans Brown, and two children. Louis Vedder and wife, Ruth Evans Brown, and their son and daughter enjoy farming.

HENRY M. BROWN M.D.
By Marian Brown Stewart

From doctoring for the Inland Steel Mills of East Chicago, Indiana, to farming in New Mexico was not the radical change it would seem, for Doctor Brown was born a farmer and remained a farmer at heart.

He was born on a farm in Bonus, Illinois, in 1868, attended Northwestern University and Rush Medical College.

In 1896 Dr. Brown married Olive Frances Foss and acquired a family of four daughters by 1903. He then was ready to quit practice.

Farming was in his blood so what could be more natural that he find himself a full fledged farmer in New Mexico.

A few short years and the bubble burst when the Felix dam washed out and a thriving farm was turned back to dry land. Taking his loss in stride he hung out his shingle and became again "Dr. Brown," community doctor.

"Community" became quite an elastic term as he found himself driving days at a time in all directions serving his patients well into the 1920s.

Retiring to Colorado Springs for his final years, he died in 1947 and is at rest in the community he served so well.

Other early day docters were:
Dr. Shelley
Dr. W.W. Rhyan
Dr. E.C. Thorne
Dr. M.M. Brayshaw

Dr. G.E. Shoemaker
Dr. Miller
Dr. Stallard
  Early day veterinarians were:
Dr. Crawford
Dr. Jones
Dr. E.G. Lathrop

Dr. Henry M. Brown.

THE BURCK FAMILY
By Mary E. Tollett

Hannah Potter Teague Burck, a widow with five children—William, Katie, Mary Ellen, Joseph and Louis Reginald—arrived in New Mexico from Llano County, Texas, in 1892. They came to New Mexico by covered wagon and lost one of their horses while fording the Pecos River. The family located at McKittrick Springs west of what is now Carlsbad, New Mexico, and moved to Hagerman two years later.

Grandma Burck, as she was known to the residents of Hagerman, worked hard to supplement the family income. She was a trained midwife and served the community well in the absence of a doctor. She made her own lye soap in a big iron pot and did the family laundry on a rub board.

William and Louis Reginald were the only children who remained in Hagerman.

William Burck, the eldest son, worked on alfalfa ranches where cattle were fed out for market and also farmed. He married Mary Walter and had a family of six children before moving back to Texas in the early 1900's. He passed away in 1952 in Santa Fe, New Mexico. Myrtle Burck, William's eldest child, remained in Hagerman with her grandmother, Hannah P. Burck, and attended the Hagerman schools. She married G.E. Jones and had one son. She later married Mr. Whittle, and she and her son are both living in Austin, Texas. The only other surviving child of William and Mary Burck is a daughter, Willie Hill. She has two daughters and lives in Sacramento, California.

Louis Reginald Burck (1881-1941) attended school in Hagerman when Hannah Blackstone (Mrs. Harry Cowan) was a teacher. When a boy, he helped fill the family larder with wild game. As shells were scarce and expensive, he packed his own, and after shooting game, he retrieved the shot to use another day.

Louis was a charter member of the Hagerman Methodist Church. He was a believing and practicing Christian.

During his early life he engaged in irrigation construction work. He served as town marshall in the early days of Hagerman and was a strict believer in the theory that it was not necessary to shoot anyone in order to "bring him in," and he never did. He used to tell of how the cowboys would come to town on Saturday night and "liven" things up. They would open both the back and front doors of a business house and gallop through the building.

Louis Reginald Burck married Mary Edna James in 1911, and they became parents of four children—Louis James, William Joseph, Mary Edna, and Hannah Jane.

After marriage Louis was active in farming and was one of the first to grow cotton. He enrolled and excelled in a school for cotton grading, and as a result he became one of the top cotton buyers for certain Texas companies in the early 1930's.

Edna was a member of the Methodist Church, a charter member of the Hagerman Epworth League and active in all areas of the church and community. She had served as a substitute teacher in Hagerman and Greenfield before marriage and did private tutoring following her husband's death.

Edna had a keen interest in writing and soon after arriving in Hagerman she started writing Hagerman News for various papers in the area. Although her desire to write a novel was not fulfilled, she did write articles and stories which were published in magazines.

Edna moved to Sudan, Texas, in 1953 and continued to be active in the church and to write for that area's newspapers until she suffered a stroke in 1967 dying two years later.

Louis James Burck graduated from Hagerman High School in 1929. He married Mary Marguerite Watford in 1930. Marguerite was the daughter of Rev. Angus E. Watford and Ruby Watford. (Reverend Watford was pastor of the Methodist Church of Hagerman in the early 1930's.) James farmed in Hagerman and lived on his grandfather James's "Red Bluff Farm." He enlisted in the Navy during World War II. After the war he moved his family to Espanola, New Mexico. Later he bought his own orchard at Rinconado, New Mexico. James and Marguerite were parents of one son and four daughters. James died suddenly in 1968 following a heart attack. Marguerite now lives in San Juan, New Mexico, to be near her children.

William Joseph Burck graduated from Hagerman High School in 1930 and later enrolled at Texas Tech where he received his BS degree in Horticulture in 1941. In 1936 he married Gladys Menefee, daughter of Mr. and Mrs. J.P. Menefee, and they are the parents of one son and three daughters. In 1948 he was employed by the Arabian American Oil Company as an agriculture advisor to King Ibn Saud's Al Kharj project. After returning to the United States he settled at Langhorne, Pennsylvania, where he is an environmental consultant and landscape contractor. He is a Director in the National Association of Landscape Contractors.

Mary Edna Burck graduated from Hagerman High School in 1935, received her BA Degree from New Mexico Highlands and MEd from Texas Tech in 1956 and has taught school in Sudan, Texas, for twenty-seven years. She was selected as "Teacher of the Year" by the Texas Business Education Association District XVII in 1974. She married Marvin H. Tollett in 1938. They are parents of a son and a daughter. Marvin is the manager of a grain elevator in Sudan, Texas.

Hannah Jane Burck graduated from Hagerman High School in 1940 and did secretarial work in Roswell and Albuquerque for several years. She married Cornelius Kooiman, Jr. in 1945. He is employed in the engineering division of North American Aircraft. They live in San Pedro, California, and are yacht enthusiasts. They are parents of a son and a daughter. Hannah has been employed as a secretary in the Palos Verdes Peninsula Middle School for twelve years.

Childhood memories of the Louis Burck children include hunting rabbits east of the Pecos River, the apple cider Daddy made from the good sweet apples raised on the farm now owned by the Fred Evans family, the annual Methodist Sunday School picnic held at the E.A. Paddock grove each summer, swimming in the Felix River and wading and playing in the quicksand of the Pecos River and picnics at the syphon.

UNCLE GEORGE BUTLER AND THE PRITCHARD FAMILY

By Stuart Pritchard and Winifred Butler Pritchard

Back in the early twenties, when I was a very small boy, my grandfather, "Uncle George" Butler, was termed the "best known man in Hagerman" by the Hagerman *Messenger*. The *Messenger* printed an article about him which recounted his life in considerable detail and confirmed to us in the C.C. Pritchard family what a very talented and unusual person he was. Parts of that newspaper article follow:

Uncle George Butler is the best known man about Hagerman. He has lived in New Mexico eighteen years and has grown to be a very old man, his eyesight is very poor, nevertheless he believes so much in Hagerman that he consented to tell people about it. He does not think there is any place equal to the Pecos Valley and more particularly to Hagerman.

Uncle George has spent his life in the printing and newspaper business. He was born in southwest Missouri and when yet a young boy went to Albany, New York. He managed to get a position in a small printing shop and later was employed by the State Printing Office.

Within a comparatively short time he went to work with the Menonite Publishing Company of Elkhart, Indiana, and served as superintendent of that plant for four years.

It was while with this house that Mr. Butler made the first tablet in use in the United States. At his suggestion this Menonite Publishing Co. founded a tablet factory. Using his artistic talents, he designed covers for the tablets, the most noteworthy was the "Big Chief" which is still in use today.

Uncle George made the first cuts and cartons for Kellogg and Post cereals.

Mr. Butler left Elkhart in 1910 and came to New Mexico for his wife's health. Two of their four children, Winifred and Chester, came with them. They first settled in Lake Arthur where he homesteaded. Soon after, he became editor of the Lake Arthur newspaper.

The daughter, Winifred, recalls those years: "I married in 1912 and went to Iowa, then later to Kansas. My mother's health worsened so my husband, C.C. Pritchard, and I came back to be near her.

We also took up a homestead near my father's, about three miles south of Hagerman. My parents' house was on one side of the road and ours was on the other side about a mile apart.

My mother died in the spring of 1916. Shortly after, my father moved in with us and lived with our family the rest of his life. He was a favorite of our growing family and a most welcome addition.

I would like to recount a very sad incident which occurred prior to his departure from his home.

One day I placed my son, Dick, just eighteen months old, and my four month old daughter, Helen, in the buggy to go down to father's place to do the washing. I very carefully locked all the doors so that Dick could not get out. Father came to the house and as he left neither of us thought to lock the door. In a little while I heard Dick screaming. Father and I rushed to him and found he had been bitten by a rattlesnake. I picked him up, ran to the house, grabbed a paring knife that I had used to cut the soap, cut where the snake had bitten and sucked the blood. My father had jumped on his horse and rode as fast as he could to the Washington Ranch to the nearest phone to call Dr. Brown. The doctor came and did what he could but the boy was very sick. After a day or so the doctor thought he would have to amputate the leg but I pleaded for him to wait as long as possible. I prayed and prayed and the good Lord heard my prayers and answered. Next morning the doctor came and said, 'He's going to be all right.' Dick walks with a slight limp but his life was spared.

The Pritchards moved to Hagerman in 1918.

Mr. Butler was one of the best boosters this valley ever had. He wrote articles for papers and had great faith in the medicinal value of the Hagerman Mineral Wells. He lived with the Pritchards when they moved to town to send the children to school.

He was a prime mover in the building of the swimming pool for the children of the town.

He was interested and worked at getting the Mineral Wells apartments and bath houses.

One time when he went to visit his son, Chet, in Denver he became ill. The doctors didn't seem to think there was much they could do for him. So he said that if he was going to die he wanted to come home to die. They put him in an ambulance with a nurse and attendants and brought him home. The Pritchards were living in the house at Inverness and Cambridge (the Casabonne house). As the nurse was leaving Mrs. Pritchard asked her if there wasn't some medicine for her father. She said, "No, he probably won't live but a day or so." But she also said to give him as much liquid as possible.

After a short time there was a knock at the door. It was Kirby Hughes, asking if there was any thing he could do. Mrs. Pritchard asked him if he could bring some water from the Mineral Wells. Every morning and evening he brought a bucket of water. Mr. Butler drank as much as he could and he recovered. Always afterward he credited Hagerman water with saving his life. He called it "the fountain of life."

The Pritchards were the parents of six children. In addition to Dick and Helen there were Mary, now Mrs. Wallace Wilson of Roswell; Jean, Mrs. W.L. Card, Fort Stockton, Texas; Stuart of Roswell and Constance, Port Townsend, Washington. Helen was married to Max Riley (deceased) and she lives in Roswell. Dick is married and lives in California.

Besides being an artist Mr. Butler was a musician. He played the violin and often a group would get together and make sweet music. Chet Butler inherited his fathers musical talent as he played the violin and almost every other instrument, especially the piano. He could hear a tune and sit down and play it.

Chet served in the Navy during the first World War. He and his wife, Blondell, are parents of two girls and one boy. They live in Denver where he worked for years as auditor at Denver University.

Mrs. Pritchard remembers the years in Hagerman as some of the happiest years of her life. They left Hagerman in 1926. Her father passed away about six years later. Her husband also is deceased. She still lives in Roswell and at age of eighty-six is alert and happy.

THE JOHN F. CAMPBELL FAMILY

By Fletcher Campbell

The John F. Campbell family came to Texico, New Mexico in 1920 from Texas. The family consisted of John Felix Campbell, his wife, Kay, and four married sons, John W., Roy A., Rufus G. and Fletcher B.

In 1923 John, his wife, Zade, their two sons, Olen and Ray, and their daughter, Laverne, moved to Hagerman in a truck. He came to work for the Roy Lochhead Alfalfa Mill and the gin. He served as Justice of the Peace in Hagerman in 1928. The family were members of the Methodist Church and were always active in civic and social affairs. Mrs. Campbell passed away in 1931 and Mr. Campbell passed away in 1947.

In 1925 Rufus, his wife, Myrtle, and their two daughters, Marie and Kara Lee, moved to Loving, New Mexico, by covered wagon. He ran the gin at Loving for one year and then they moved to Hagerman. He and his brother John built and operated a garage and filling station. It stood on the corner of Argyle and Oxford streets. They operated it until 1928 when Rufus went back to ginning and John worked for the Johnston Lodewick Oil Co. In 1934 John and his family moved to Las Cruces where he owned and operated a dry cleaning shop until his death in 1973.

In 1929 Rufus and his father were partners in farming. Rufus later bought and operated a farm west of Hagerman. Another daughter, Marlea Ruth, was born in 1930. Rufus operated the gin in the fall of each year. He lost his left arm in the gin saws which ended his ginning career. Mrs. Myrtle Campbell died in 1947. Rufus operated his farm until the 1960's when he sold out and moved to Texas where he still lives. The Rufus Campbell family were members of the Methodist Church and were active in community affairs.

In 1927 Fletcher B., his wife, Lucille, and their two little sons, Clifford and Eugene, moved to Hagerman by train from Jacksonville, Texas. He came to operate the Lake Arthur gin which he ran for several years. In 1928 their first daughter, Glennice, was born and in 1931 another daughter, Virginia, was born and completed the family. Fletcher operated the Lake Arthur, Cottonwood and Hagerman gins for many years. In 1943 an accident at the gin, which broke his left leg, ended his ginning career. He was a carpenter for many years and has been a substitute mail carrier since 1946. The Campbell family are members of the Methodist Church. Mr. and Mrs. Campbell still live in their home in Hagerman.

Clifford Campbell married Eulalia Gregory who is Assistant Postmistress at the Hagerman Post Office. They have one son, one daughter and five grandchildren. He and his wife reside in Hagerman. He works as a carpenter. He and his father have built hundreds of barns and houses in the Pecos Valley. They are of the Baptist faith. Gene Campbell was married to Clara Pate. They had one son, one daughter and two grandsons. Gene was very active in civic affairs and was scoutmaster for many years. He owned and operated a furniture store and plumbing business in Hagerman until moving to Roswell in 1971. He owned and operated the Campbell Plumbing Co. until his death on April 8, 1975, three weeks before his 48th birthday.

Glennice married John Collis. They have three sons, four daughters and seven grandchildren. John is retired from the U.S. Air Force. He worked for a Flying Service in Roswell until an airplane accident in 1971. The Collis family are active members of the Methodist Church.

Virginia is married to Lynn Owens. They have one son, two daughters and one grandson. They live in Pecos, Texas, where he is manager of the Brown Pipe and Supply Co. They are of the Baptist faith.

JACK AND J.P. (PETE) CASABONNE

Both Jack and J.P. Casabonne were born in Lescom, France; J.P. in 1883 and Jack in 1890. There were five boys in the family. One son, Julien, stayed in France with his parents and lost his life in World War I. The rest came to the United States. Paul was the first to come. He came to Hope, New Mexico, where other Frenchmen he knew had already settled.

It was compulsory to serve in the French army from age eighteen to twenty-one. John and Jack came to the United States before having to serve their time. Pete served his three years for a penny a day. He came to the United States at age twenty-one unable to speak or write English. He wanted to go to Hope, New Mexico, where his brothers and other Frenchmen were. When he was let off the train at Alamagordo, New Mexico, he was unable to communicate and he got on the next train and ended up in California at a French settlement in San Francisco. He later returned to New Mexico by way of Pecos, Texas. When he arrived in Carlsbad it was the Fourth of July and a big celebration was being held. The noise of gunfire frightened him and he went to his hotel room and stayed, believing there was an uprising or war. The next day when all was quiet he continued his journey.

John and Jack did not have the difficulty of communication. John had studied English and had learned to read and write enough for them to get by.

They all got jobs herding sheep as this is what they were most familiar with from their country.

John and Jack went to Wyoming to work and Pete stayed in New Mexico.

They had already lost their brother Paul who had become ill while herding and did not have help. As shepherds they often spent weeks alone on the range with their herd. When Paul was found with a ruptured appendix it was too late.

Pete first learned to speak Spanish from the Spanish herders. Realizing he was making no progress in English, he took a job herding sheep from Vaughn to the Capitan Mountains to the Pecos river with English-speaking men. He earned $100 a month and his food. The herders slept wherever they stopped with the herd for the night. In all kinds of weather they slept outside, sometimes awakening under a blanket of snow and ice. All was open range then and they had dogs to help with their herds at night and to warn them of varmints.

After a few years of herding and saving their money Pete and Jack and two other men bought a ranch west of Hope, New Mexico. This was known as The Big 4 Ranch. While operating this business Pete met Blanche Michelet who was teaching school at Hope. They were married in 1918. They had four children; Johnny, Marie C., Paul and Helen.

Jack was called to serve in the United States Army. He was stationed in California and taught troops about France and how to manage if sent there. After his tour of duty was over he met Rose Michelet at Pete and Blanche's home. Jack and Rose were married in 1920. They had one son, George.

The children of both families were raised in Hagerman.

Jack and Pete split with the Big 4 and went into partnership ranching. Eventually they dissolved their partnership and each had his own ranch. Both were self-taught in reading and writing English and both were loyal United States citizens. They were generous contributors to the support of the community, church and many other worthy causes. Neither ever returned to his homeland.

The curve that is about one mile north of the Felix River bridge is knows as "Casabonne curve." The old homes of both Jack and Pete Casabonne still stand where they used to live.

CLARK-ATKINSON FAMILIES
By Perla Morgan Clark

When New Mexico was being settled, Robert E. Lee Clark often went on cattle drives helping take stock over there from Texas. Lee Clark and his wife, the former Rebecca Katherine Boyce, and their children, Mary, Aaron and John, lived on a farm near London, Texas. When the doctors advised a change of climate for his wife, Lee decided to sell his farm and move his family to the Pecos Valley in southeastern New Mexico.

Hitching four horses (a wheel team and a lead team) to a spring wagon and trailing a wagon with supplies and camping equipment, he was followed by the family driving a team to a "hack." They were accompanied by Ike Ely (Buck) Boyce and Homer Bethel who helped drive the Clark and Atkinson stock. They left the stock at the Atkinson Brothers Ranch near Sterling City, Texas, until spring and crossed the Texas-New Mexico line on Christmas Eve, 1902, having been six months making the journey. The Clarks homesteaded five miles southwest of Hagerman.

Later James Brown Atkinson, his wife (the former Lula Storey) and their family located north of the Clark home across the Felix River. Their oldest daughter Margaret taught the country school near their home. Their younger children, Lou Mae, Dixie and Charles and Aaron and John Clark, attended school there. The Clark boys rode their pony "Big Enough" to and fro from home, while Mary stayed with the Atkinsons during the week and rode with Belle Atkinson to school at Hagerman. One of Mary's favorite teachers was Mrs. Harry Cowan. After the Atkinson family moved back to Texas Mary and her brothers drove the pony to a buggy to school at Hagerman until the Clarks moved to town in 1906.

Oscar Atkinson and Mary Clark were married in 1907 in the Clark home and left to make their home in Texas.

Aaron graduated from the Hagerman High School in 1913; John graduated in 1914. They worked on farms and helped their parents in the hotel. Aaron hauled freight from Hagerman to ranches between there and Lovington until he began working with Mr. Garrison for the Midland Bridge and Construction Company out of Kansas City. He helped during the building of the bridges crossing the Felix and Pecos Rivers. He was working for B.H. Wixom on the farm when he enlisted in the Armed Forces in June, 1918. John was working for Kemp Lumber Company when he enlisted a few weeks later.

After their sons left for training camps Lee and Kate moved to a farm near Knickerbocker, Texas, to be near their daughter Mary and her family.

Both Aaron and John were stationed in France when the Armistice was signed and returned to Hagerman in 1919. John again worked for Kemp Lumber Company until he moved to Texas later that year. Aaron went back to work for B.H. Wixom and later for T.D. Devenport at his grocery and market.

Aaron T. Clark and Perla Irene Morgan were married in 1920 in the Morgan home and lived on the Rose-hedge farm. They were members of the First Presbyterian Church and active in children's and young people's work. Later they moved into the Van Arsdal rent house in the southeast part of town.

James Robert (Jim Bob) Clark was born in 1921.

In 1921 Robert E. Lee Clark passed away at the Mulberry Ranch near Sterling City, Texas, and was buried in the Hagerman Cemetery beside his brother John.

Aaron rented land for several years, until he bought a forty-acre irrigated farm from J.P. Morgan, and they made their home there north of town.

Aaron and Perla moved to Sterling City, Texas, in December of 1933. J.P. Morgan took Perla over to their new home in his automobile, but Aaron and Jim Bob went with the team and wagon trailing the Model T Ford. (Thus, after thirty-one years, Aaron left Hagerman the same way he arrived.)

Jim Bob married Elizabeth Long of Englewood, Colorado, while serving in the Army during World War II. They have two sons and a daughter.

THE JOHN W. COFFEE FAMILY

By Elizabeth Coffee Ruminson

My mother was Dorothy McCormick Coffee.

My father, John W. Coffee, rented a farm for several years in the East Grand Plains area east of Roswell. Some time later he swapped his holdings for a livery stable on Virginia Avenue in Roswell, New Mexico. From there he took us briefly to a ranch south of Lake Arthur and eventually returned to homestead a farm about four miles west of Hagerman.

There were five of us youngsters on this farm in 1918 following World War I. Oldest was Audrey, then Lawrence, myself (Elizabeth), Helen and John, Jr. We all attended Hagerman schools, went to Hagerman churches and most remained there until 1941 when we all migrated to California.

A few years earlier, while my family was still residing in the Hagerman area, I was studying to become a registered nurse in California. It was there I met and married Dr. W. Walter Ruminson, a wonderful guy who has since become a famous surgeon. Rummy and I have five children.

My older sister, Audrey, married Arthur Willheim, who was a farmer. They resided in Hagerman until 1941. They moved to California where they became Medical Technicians. They had two daughters. Audrey passed away in 1968.

My sister Helen married John Margaretich. They live near Long Beach, California, and he owns and operates a catering truck.

My older brother, Lawrence, married Mary Frakes and to them were born two girls. They moved to Pendleton, Oregon, in 1947 and have since resided there where he has worked in the Harris Pine Mills.

My brother, John H., married Joyce Walker. John also owns and operates his own catering truck. They live near Helen. There are two boys and one girl in John's family.

My mother, Dorothy McCormick Coffee, died in 1954, while my father, John W. Coffee, Sr., lived until 1968.

HISTORY OF THE CHARLES WALLACE COLE FAMILY
By Grace Cole-Greer

As I recall my mother telling, most all property in Ireland was owned by English landlords and rented to the Irish farmers on long time leases. Grandfather McKinstry operated a fair size farm on a 100 year lease, but with a large family and nearly all boys, there wasn't much room for expansion. Therefore, the thoughts of the United States and it's vast amount of land was a drawing card to come to the States.

Grandfather was well thought of by both rich and poor in the old country. The story is told that during the Ireland famine of the 1800's he would take a load of oats, which he had stored in his grainery, to the mill and get them ground, then dole it out by buckets or pans full to the waiting line of starving poor folks, Protestant and Catholic alike, who knew he would help them out.

In order to make up his mind concerning immigration to the United States, James McKinstry and two of his boys, Thomas and William, came to the States to look over the possibilities. There were relatives in Illinois who offered them farming land to rent. The two boys in their teens found work as bellhops for a railroad company in Chicago — the Illinois Central, I think.

James McKinstry returned to Ireland to close out his farm work there and bring the rest of his family, consisting of a wife and seven children, to the states. They landed in Philadelphia on the 10th of April, 1888. They continued their journey to Illinois.

Elizabeth, who was sixteen, found work at a boarding house in Chicago for $3.00 a week plus room and board and remitted most of her earnings to her parents to help them get started in America. She kept this job a little over a year and then went home to help her mother on the farm. Tom also gave up his work at the railroad and returned to the farm, but William continued with railroad work both in Chicago and in Savannah, Georgia, then again in Chicago until he retired as Controller of the Illinois Central Railroad in his late years. He and his wife returned to Savannah, Georgia, which was Aunt Mary's home town, to retire. She had been his secretary while he was in the railroad business in Georgia.

Of the McKinstry family, Elizabeth was the first to get married. After returning home from Chicago, she met a young man, Charles W. Cole, who had been a school teacher in a little country school near Onarga. She used to tell of the first time they met. She had pulled off her shoes and hose to mop the kitchen floor. As she went out the back door to throw out the mop water Charlie Cole drove into the yard and caught her without her shoes and hose in her bare feet. That was very humiliating to her in those days!

Charles and Elizabeth (or Lizzie as she was called then) were married on Christmas Day, 1890. The first year or so of their married life they lived in Marquette, Michigan, where Charles worked with a brother as a bricklayer and plasterer. Winnie was born in Marquette, Michigan, and the rest of us children in Illinois.

Since a number of the McKinstry family had migrated to the Pecos Valley, Grandfather, Grandmother, Jim, Sam, Harrison, Adeline, and Edith to Hagerman and John and his wife, Alma Woodruff, to Roswell, there was an incentive for the Cole family to come to New Mexico also. At that time John was a land agent, selling land to tourists as they came to the Valley. Grandfather and family had come mainly on account of Aunt Adeline's health. She had contracted tuberculosis. She did get better for a year or two but later caught a cold which brought it back on severely, and she died.

My father, Charles Cole, came to New Mexico before bringing his family. While here he bought the eighty acre piece of land joining the McKinstry farm on the east, three miles northwest of Hagerman. He built a small red barn on the place, laid a wide board floor in part of it and that was the mansion for the family until our home was built the next winter. The little red barn still stands on the Menoud farm. Grandfather and Grandmother Wallace Cole also came with their daughter, Myrta, who was sick with tuberculosis and lived for a while in a lean-to on the red barn, until they could find a house to live in.

My father came back to Illinois, closed out his farm dealings, had a sale and placed his wife, Elizabeth, and four children on the train for New Mexico. They were accompanied by her brother, Harrison McKinstry, who had evidently returned to Illinois on business. On our way to Hagerman, probably after leaving Kansas City, Uncle Harrison had wandered into another car on the train and was talking to some party heading south also when a young lady thought she recognized the voice. She got up and looked around and, sure enough, it was her brother Harrison. She was Aunt Edith, who was returning from school in Nebraska. Quite a happy time followed with her moving to the car with the rest of the family. We arrived in Hagerman in February of 1907. My father followed by freight car, bringing our furniture and belongings, enough lumber to build our new home and "Old Polly," the horse we youngsters drove to school until Ramona and Leon finished the 9th grade in our little Seventh Day Adventist church school. They then went to Keene, Texas, to finish the academy.

I was only three years old when we came, so do not remember a great deal about it. However, I've heard the family recall how they left Illinois in very cold weather, and, upon arriving in the good old Pecos Valley, they didn't even need to wear their coats. This seemed unbelievable to them.

Our farm was just a strip of unbroken raw land, so the spring and summer was spent in getting it into farm crops. During that fall and winter my father, with the help of neighbors and perhaps a hired man, built our home.

About three years later this farm was sold to J.E. Blythe. We lived in town for part of a year until a transaction was closed with Jacques Michelet for his farm north of the Felix River and near the mouth of the Pecos River.

Since my father was a bricklayer and plasterer by trade, there were many chimneys and fireplaces in and around Hagerman that were built by him. Also neighbors would dig large holes in their yards and he would plaster them with cement to make large cisterns for them to either catch rain water in or haul good drinking water to be placed in them. There were also two houses made of tile that I know he built. One was the C.W. Curry farm home, and the other was the Jacques Michelet home. It is the house near Rose Casabonne's home.

Of the children, Winifred or Winnie, as she was known, passed away at a rest home in Colorado. Leon married a school sweetheart, Edna Menne. They worked at various denominational work for two or three years until they decided to come back to Hagerman to help Dad farm. At that time my father owned some land east of the old Pecos River bridge, and they lived on that place. After the bridge collapsed with a herd of cattle crossing it, it was rather inconvenient to go south to the present Pecos bridge and then back north to the home farm with a team of horses, just to exchange some farm implement. Therefore, my dad sold that place to A.F. Deason and bought the place known as the old "Pegg" place which was the farm with the cement house north of the Felix River and joining the railroad.

Leon became ill and died in 1930 of what was finally discovered to be Addison's disease. It was probably caused from an injury he received when a team of horses ran away, and he ran in front to try to stop them. He was knocked down and rolled over and over beneath the wagon. Leon and Edna had three girls.

Ramona and her husband, H.E. Blackwelder, spent two or three years as missionaries in Cuba after their marriage. On account of Ramona's health, they returned to the States, and he engaged in farming both in New Mexico and California at various times. They had five children. It was about a month after the birth of the last child that Ramona passed away in 1935.

I am the youngest and only one left of the Cole family of Hagerman. My profession was either schoolteacher or bookkeeper. I have taught in the commercial department in the Dexter, Hondo, and Hagerman High Schools. During World War II, when they couldn't find another bookkeeper I worked for seven years as one, for the Farmers Co-op Gin at Hagerman. I married Ernest Greer in 1938 and we lived on one of the Cole farms and operated them with our own land. We had no children of our own, but in 1953 we had the opportunity to adopt a sweet little baby girl. Ernest farmed until he had brain surgery in March of 1961 after which he was unable to do the farm work.

We have retired to the little town of Menard, Texas, but it still seems like coming home when we come back to the town of Hagerman.

HARRY COWAN FAMILY

Among the earliest families that came to this area before 1900 were a widow, Mrs. Mary Cowan, and her six children. They came from Knoxville, Iowa, in 1895 for health reasons. Two sisters later died of tuberculosis. Harry, age twenty-three, and two younger sisters drove to New Mexico in a covered wagon joining other wagons on the way. The rest of the family came later by train.

Harry said the first money he made in Hagerman was taking easterners with his fast team and buggy to overtake antelope for them to shoot. He and a friend went into Old Mexico to work for a time and he was in Cloudcroft to ride the first train load of lumber taken out of that area. He also worked as foreman for John Chisum before settling down to farming. He and his brother, James, farmed south of town on the land that the members of the family homesteaded. Harry remained in Hagerman until his death in 1956. During this time he was very active in the development of this area. This included the Methodist Church and the canal company. He served one term as County Commissioner, was a member of the school board for a number of years, served during World War I on the County Draft Board and for many years as superintendent of the Methodist Sunday School.

Jim Cowan, deceased, said he "worked at everything but tending bar, preaching, and teaching school" and spent his last years in Ruidoso. As a young man he served as town clerk, town marshal, and was in charge of the water works after the system was installed. He also owned a livery stable with Frank Anderson and later with A.A. Bailey. He married Hallie Robinson and they had three children. He went to Roswell from Hagerman where he was employed by the New Mexico Military Institute for many years. A sister, Susie Cowan, married Mr. Langford of the Langford-Sanford business partnership.

Mr. and Mrs. Harry Cowan, wedding picture.

Mrs. Mary Cowan's house.

Harry Cowan was married to Hannah Elizabeth Blackstone who was the first school teacher in Hagerman. She came to Hagerman early in 1895 from Kansas. Her sister's family, the A.D. Strattons, were already here and she followed as soon as her school in Kansas was out. They came as a result of a seven-year drought in Kansas but returned after four years of hard times farming east of Hagerman. Besides teaching in Hagerman, Hannah also taught at South Springs and boarded at the Jim Chisum ranch house. She got to her school either by horseback or on a bicycle following cow trails. In all she taught seven years in the area. The Harry Cowans had two daughters, Mabel, deceased, and Dorothea, who is now Mrs. J.A. Johnson, and resides with her husband on the farm south of town that her father's family homesteaded.

THE H.J. CUMPSTEN FAMILY

By Helen Cumpsten Curry

Many times I have heard it said that preachers' kids are the meanest kids in town. I take exception to that. Maybe people expect too much of them and, also, preachers' kids do not want to be too different from other kids. The Cumpsten kids were no exception. We had happy childhoods even though we were as "poor as a church mouse" in material things. We were rich in having wonderful parents to teach us by word and example.

Our father, Henry Joseph Cumpsten, was born in New Orleans, Louisiana. He was called Harry most of his life. His parents were Scotch Presbyterians and through their teaching it was not surprising that he became a minister of the gospel.

He attended Southwestern Presbyterian University in Clarksville, Tennessee, graduating in 1892 with excellent grades. On the day that he was ordained by the Presbytery in New Orleans our father received a call from the First Presbyterian Church of McComb, Mississippi. It was there he met and married our mother, Helen B. Sinclair.

Their first three children, Harry, Robert and Ruth, were born in McComb. Later the family moved to Learned, Mississippi, and it was there that I was born.

Our father was afflicted with asthma and doctors advised the drier climate of the west. In 1906 the family came to Carlsbad where daddy was the pastor of the Presbyterian Church. After a few years we moved to Midland, Texas, and then to Thurber, Texas. While at Thurber Daddy became ill with pleurisy, so as soon as he was able, we returned to Carlsbad, where he spent some time in the hospital. As soon as he was well enough to do his work we moved to Lake Arthur, since there was no vacancy in the Carlsbad church. Daddy served the churches at Lake Arthur, Dayton and Lakewood.

A vacancy occurred in the Hagerman and Dexter churches due to the death of their minister. We moved to Hagerman in May 1912, as soon as the Lake Arthur school was out. J.W. Parks, an elder in the church, sent a wagon and team to bring the household goods from Lake Arthur. Harry and Robert came on the wagon and the rest of us came on the train. The house we moved into was on North Cambridge, north of the present high school. Our neighbors to the south were the Wimberlys and to the north, the Parks family.

Daddy preached in Dexter and Hagerman on alternate Sundays. He rode to Dexter in the caboose of the local freight train, going on Saturday afternoon and returning on Monday. Sometimes he would go on to Orchard Park and East Grand Plains for afternoon and evening services.

Two well remembered occurrences in 1913 were the addition of William Raynal to the family, and the start of a manse for the minister's family. It was to be located just south of the church building on Cambridge Street. We moved into the manse in 1914.

The first year we were in Hagerman, Harry and Robert rode bicycles up the railroad track, crossing the Felix River on the railroad bridge, to attend school in Dexter. This was because the superintendent J.E. Conder, had been superintendent in Lake Arthur and had become a good friend of the family.

The next year we all attended the Hagerman school and became involved in school activities. Harry and Robert played in the school and the town bands. During the years that Professor Kelsey was here as superintendent, the band would play while the other students marched around the school yard. My brothers played baseball and basketball (all basketball games were played outside). Sometimes the wind would blow, but who cared?

Our daddy was very fond of sports and at one time during his younger years he managed a baseball team. I must have inherited my interest in baseball from him.

During the summer months the boys worked on farms helping with haying, picking apples or whatever there was to do. They worked for A.C. Harter who owned Meadow Crest Farms. A few times Mrs. Harter invited me out to spend the day. I will never forget those days.

As we were growing up we made many friends. The Wimberlys and Parks, being our first neighbors, were our first and long-time friends. After moving into the manse we had other neighbors and friends including the Osbornes, the Bush family, the Pardees, the Pritchards and when the Harry Cowan family moved to town they became our neighbors and friends. Mabel Cowan and I became inseparable. Then she went to college and later to Silver City to teach but we kept in touch. Dorothea Cowan Johnson is still living here and I count her as one of my dearest friends.

After we moved from the manse we lived in different neighborhoods but always had fine neighbors. The Woodmases, the Noah Wests and the Grahams, to name a few.

When World War I was declared both boys, having graduated from high school, enlisted in the army, as did many other Hagerman boys. Harry, Robert, Guy West and George and Vergil Parks were put in the same band and were together all during their time of service. On one occasion, while they were stationed in a camp in Louisville, Kentucky, their band had the honor of playing with John Philip Sousa's band.

1918 was a year indelibly stamped in our memories. In February our sister, Ruth, became ill and the diagnosis was tuberculosis. She was a senior that year and was able to go to her graduation by being carried up the stairs and sitting in an easy chair near the stage in the auditorium.

In June Daddy took her to Albuquerque by train to the Presbyterian Sanatarium. She was there two months but did not improve, so Daddy brought her home the first of August. Two days later our Daddy died of a cerebral hemorrhage. Three months later Ruth passed away. The boys were discharged from the army in December, much to the relief of my mother and me.

Mother and the boys bought the Walton-Samford Meat Market which they operated a few years. After selling out

Harry and Robert did carpenter work and mother did sewing, baked cakes for parties, kept children and later clerked in the Woodmas Store.

Then Robert went to Las Vegas where he joined an orchestra and worked as brakeman on the Santa Fe Railroad. He came back in 1922 for my graduation and to marry his high school sweetheart, Alta Morgan.

During our growing-up years most of our activities centered around the church. Sunday School, worship services and prayer meetings were all a part of our lives. Sometimes the churches would combine to hold revival meetings. One such meeting was held in the Wool and Hide Building which became known as "The Glory Barn." Many members were added to the church rolls as a result of that meeting. In the summertime open air meetings were held in the evening with different churches participating. Some times they were held at the schoolyard with the minister preaching from the school steps. Other times they were held downtown using the bandstand as a pulpit.

All of us worked in the church as Sunday School superintendent, or teachers; we sang in the choir and

Rev. Henry Joseph Cumpsten.

Helen Sinclair (Mrs. H.J.) Cumpsten.

mother and I were active in women's work. All three of my brothers are ordained elders. I served as pianist at times and worked with the children in Vacation Bible School.

Music was another interest we all shared. We would play and sing, sometimes just the family and other times with friends. Ruth had a good alto voice and she and Alta Morgan, who sang soprano, would sing duets at school affairs as well as church services.

O.R. Gable was superintendent of schools during the war years. He wrote and published a song, "True to My Soldier Boy," which was introduced by Ruth and Alta. Their picture appeared on the cover.

When the boys were in the army they sent a soldier suit to Raynal, who was then about four years old. We taught him to sing "It's a Long Way to Tipperary." When dressed in his uniform he would stand up and sing the song, much to the enjoyment of every one who heard him. A Mr. Ed Losey had a store on the northeast corner of Cambridge and Argyle Streets. Every time he saw Raynal in town, he would call him over and have him sing. Then he would give him candy, and since I was born with a "sweet tooth," I made sure Raynal went to town quite often.

After Robert (better known as Bob) and Alta were married they lived in Las Vegas, New Mexico, for two or three years, and it was there that their son, Bobby, was born. After their return to Hagerman, their daughter, Polly, was born. A second daughter died in infancy while they were living in Vaughn. Returning to Hagerman Bob became postmaster and just before retiring saw his dream of a new post office building come true. During World War II Bob was in the service for a time and Alta served as postmistress. She later worked for the First National Bank for many years. Their son and daughter are both married with children of their own. Bobby lives in Loveland, Colorado, and Polly lives in Dallas, Texas. After retiring Bob and Alta bought a home in Lincoln where they lived several years, then moved to Carlsbad. Alta passed away in 1974. Bob will continue to live in his home for awhile, then will take an apartment in the Landsun Home.

Harry worked at various jobs, farming, carpenter work and painting until he found employment with the Santa Fe

Railroad as signal maintainer. While stationed at Mountainair he met and married Helen Van Kirk, a teacher in the school there. They spent several years in Vaughn before returning to Hagerman where they lived for many years. He did carpenter work and she taught in the Lake Arthur school. They have now taken up residence in a cottage at the Presbyterian Retirement Village near Dallas.

After graduating from high school I attended the Las Vegas Normal School for one year and received a first grade teaching certificate. The next year, since I had not obtained a teaching position, I went back to high school for typing and shorthand. The next two years I was employed as a teacher in the Hagerman School. Since the board did not employ married teachers at that time, I gave up my teaching career to marry Bayard W. Curry.

Our two daughters are Mabel Nail and Helen Ruth Reynolds. Mabel and her husband Jack live in Hagerman. Mabel has worked for the First National Bank for a number of years. Helen Ruth and her husband live in Oklahoma on a farm. She teaches in a nearby school. Jack and Mabel are the parents of two children, a son, and a daughter.

Raynal also finished high school in Hagerman, then went to Coyne Electrical School in Chicago. On his return he worked with Bob until he went to work at the C & C Garage in 1935. Later he worked for Auto Supply Company in Roswell as traveling salesman. Presently he is employed by Farm and Livestock Supply Co. His wife, the former Mary Alice Rabb of Roswell, works in a doctor's office in Roswell. Their only child, Peggy Jane, lives with her husband and two sons in California.

We were and are interested in Hagerman, the church, the school and all projects for the betterment of the community. We hope we have contributed in some small way toward that goal.

THE CHARLES W. CURRY FAMILY
By Bayard, Julia and Margaret

"All Aboard," called the conductor. The train whistle blew and the train started to move. Our mother, Leona Hebbard Curry, and six of us children, Bayard, Helen, Albert, Alva Lloyd (Ted), Vinton and Frank were on the way to a new home in a new land. We had lived in Illinois on a farm. Our father was coming on a freight train with the household goods and horses. The year was 1906.

Dad had been down here looking over the country and he had bought a farm, but it had no house on it so he rented another farm that had a house.

We arrived in Hagerman after a long hard trip. We went to a boarding house on the northeast corner of Argyle and Winchester streets. About a week later Dad arrived, and we went to the rented farm to start our farming operations. The farm was the one where Richard Harshey now lives about three quarters of a mile north of the Felix River bridge.

We had been living there two or three months when one day there was a knock on the door. The man at the door said he had bought the farm and was to have immediate possession.

Dad was in no financial condition to build a house then, but he got enough lumber to build a three or four room house for us to live in. It was later used for a chicken house and horse barn. It was on the farm Dad had bought about a half mile west of the rented farm. We hauled water from a hydrant at the house on the road half a mile west. It was piped from a well on the Felix Ranch. Sometimes we got water at Greenfield.

The Charles W. Curry family. Front row, l. to r.: Leona, C.W., Bayard. Second row: Margaret, Julia, Lula. Back row: Vinton, Ted (Alva), Helen, Albert, Frank.

Julia and Lulu were born in that little house. The children walked to school at Greenfield until the new school house was built in Hagerman.

In 1910 the big house of cement blocks was constructed. All of us that were big enough to help did so. Dad and Charlie Cole were the real builders.

Margaret and Clarice Elizabeth were born in the big house. Clarice died at the age of three months.

We were Methodists and attended church regularly and did whatever we could for the church. Church picnics and Epworth League parties were always enjoyed. Many times young people would gather at our house for a Sunday afternoon visit.

Our neighbors were the Michelets, the E.J. Mason family across the road, and south of us were the Holmans, Campbells, Lanes and McCoys.

We had orchards and alfalfa as well as summer wheat and other crops.

Dad and Ernest McCoy bought an Auto Fedan hay baler and did custom baling. As each of us boys got big enough we joined the crew. Later Bayard worked for Jim Williamson on the Felix Ranch. Helen and Albert worked for the Lanes at times.

All of the children graduated from the Hagerman High School. When World War I began Bayard enlisted in the army. After he was discharged he went to an automotive school and then went into the repair business in Hagerman. He married Helen Cumpsten and two daughters were born to them. He is the only one of the Currys still living in Hagerman.

Helen, Albert, Vinton and Lulu all entered the teaching profession and made it their careers. Helen passed away in Roswell in 1973. She was a teacher and school principal there for many years until her retirement.

Albert was married to Jennie George. They were the parents of a son and daughter. He was on the staff at New Mexico State University for forty years. He died in 1969.

Vinton married Verna West. He taught in the University at Boulder, Colorado, for many years and was a Certified Public Accountant. He is now retired and lives on Mercer Island, Washington.

Lulu spent her entire teaching career in the schools of Silver City. She was married to Tracy Egbert until his death several years ago. She is now retired and living in Silver City.

Alva Lloyd (Ted) worked for the Santa Fe Railroad, first as telegrapher and later as depot agent. He married Ethel West and they had a son. Ted died in 1967.

Frank taught for several years before going into the ministry. He served Methodist Churches in New Mexico and Texas. His wife was formerly Valera Menefee. They make their home in Artesia. He also is retired.

Julia taught school a year or so before marrying Morton F. Thomas. They are the parents of a son and daughter. They are retired and now live in Roswell.

Margaret was married to Coy Knoll and they had two daughters. Coy was killed in a plane crash. Some time later Margaret became the wife of Dacus Parker and they were the parents of a son. Dacus is also deceased. Margaret lives in Roswell where she is in charge of the womens dormitory at ENMU-Roswell.

Our father was active in civic affairs and was in charge of the Alfalfa Growers Association office for several years. He was one of several farmers who built the storage and loading barn at Russell Spur. He served as County Commissioner and was one of the organizers of the Farmers' Gin Company. He was secretary-treasurer and managed the gin office for a good many years. He also served on the school board.

Our mother was active in Womans Club, Missionary Society, Thursday Club and Garden Club.

Dad died in 1941 and Mother died in 1959.

THE DAVIS FAMILY
By Leona Davis

We lived in Tamaha, Oklahoma, and decided to move to Hagerman, New Mexico. Dewey Davis' brother, Jewel Davis, and his wife were living there. They had been living in Hagerman for two years and were farming on the Pecos River.

We gathered our crops and traveled by train, arriving in Hagerman on Christmas Eve in 1922. Orlie Brock, a friend of ours, had the old Star Cafe. We had our Christmas dinner there and spent the night as they had rooms over the cafe. Dewey, myself (his wife), Vernese (our daughter), Emma Davis (his mother) and his brother, Charlie, and Charlie's wife, Stella, were in the group.

We stayed with Jewel Davis and his wife, Lola, for a few days, then Mr. Pritchard let us move into his old ranch-house, located between Hagerman and Lake Arthur. We then moved to a house in Hagerman, known by old-timers as the little brick schoolhouse. Later we moved to a house at 106 S. Manchester. Here we met Mother Devenport, her daughter, Iola Lemon, Clay Lemon, and Ida Bea (their daughter). They were to remain good friends over the years.

Mrs. Devenport's son, Teed, had a grocery and meat market where we were able to buy a good steak for 25¢ a pound. I also remember going to Mr. Heitman's apple orchard. He would let people have the apples that had fallen to the ground.

Vernese started her first year of school at what we know now as the Christian Church building. Mrs. Stella B. Palmer was the teacher.

Dewey Davis became ill and passed away in 1928. Later I married Dave Davis and we had a daughter, Ditta Mae.

Vernese married Francis "Slick" Boyce.

Ditta Mae married William F. McCullough. They were parents of two sons and two daughters; Jim, Bill, Barbara and Lois Jean. Ditta Mae has served as Clerk for the Town of Hagerman since 1964.

THE ALPHA DEASON FAMILY

By Leona Deason Mayberry

Alpha F. Deason and Nora A. Connell were married in Roswell, New Mexico, in 1917. They later moved to Hagerman (about 1918). They purchased a farm northeast of town near what we know as Red Bluff. They were the parents of five children, Aline and Lorene (twins), Ruth, Leona and Alice.

Ruth passed away at the age of nine years and Lorene passed away when she was two years old.

Aline is married to Rine Van Essen and they live in Wapote, Washington. They have three children, Bill, Lyle and Judy.

Leona married Thurman Mayberry and they continue to make their home in Hagerman. Thurman has been with the maintenance department of the local schools for twenty-five years. Leona is employed by the Hagerman Branch of the First National Bank of Roswell. They are parents of two sons, Ronnie, and Don.

Alice is married to Jim Alsup. He is employed by the Santa Fe Railroad and served as station agent in Hagerman for a short time. They now live in Artesia, New Mexico, and have two children, Larry and Cindy.

The Deason children had a unique way of catching the school bus. Their father strung a pulley across the Pecos River and attached an open cart, large enough to carry about four children. This ride was a real treat for any visitors, but the Deason family didn't always find it so much fun, especially when the river was running full or overflowing.

THE TOM DERRICK FAMILY
By the Derrick Children

Robert Thomas Derrick was born October 27, 1877, in Salina, Kansas and several years later moved to Woodward, Oklahoma. In 1900 our cowboy father, with the help of Ed Conner, drove a herd of horses to the Tobe Odum ranch (Calumet Ranch) east of Dexter. He hired on with Tobe and worked for awhile until one day when Tobe ordered Tom to kill a Mexican for him, Daddy refused to do the killing and was fired on the spot.

Three years later, about 1903, Daddy was driving a herd of cattle near Carlsbad in search of water, when he came upon a covered wagon camped. This turned out to be our Daddy's first meeting with our mother, Thelma America (Maggie) Walker, and her family. Our Mother was standing by the side of the covered wagon combing her long dark hair and our Daddy fell in love with the beautiful young girl, even though he had to depart and did not find her again for three years. He made the statement that he had been looking for her all this time because he had lost his heart to her at that first sight. He found her in 1906 near Lake Arthur, where her family had settled, and they were immediately married in Roswell on July 3 by Judge Brice. Judge Brice was then a very young judge and they were the first couple he married.

After their marriage they settled at Cedar Point. The oldest brother, Millard Lewis, was born at this ranch on May 31, 1907.

About 1912 they filed on and homesteaded a 320 acre tract of land east of the Buffalo Valley farms. They later bought more land to add to this original 320 acres. The law allowed them to run as many cattle as they had water for; water was the determining factor.

The Derrick Ranch bordered the Turkey Track Ranch and was about five miles north of the Neigh Styles Ranch. The Turkey Track Ranch was owned and managed, at this time, by Cap Mossman. The Turkey Track had no liking for the homesteaders because they took up the grass land and the precious water that the large Turkey Track ranch had been using. Even though the homesteaders were legal holders of their land and water under federal law, Cap Mossman tried in many ways to persuade them to move on. First he tried to buy them out, but not many sold. Then stronger action was taken by the Turkey Track crew. There were many arguments, disputes and armed confrontations although there never was any proven deaths from gunfire. Likely, both factions, the "big outfit" and the homesteaders, felt that their actions were valid.

We, the children of Tom and Thelma (Maggie) Derrick, recall the incidence that happened in the early 1920's at a roundup on the Neigh Styles ranch (known now as the Bill Merritt ranch) about fourteen miles southeast of Hagerman. The roundup cowboys, all friends and neighbors, were Neigh Styles, Efe Griffith, Ben Smith and our father. The Turkey Track wagon was camped about one and a half miles east of the Styles house — the work wagon outfits from the large ranch wouldn't think of working or neighboring with the smaller outfits. The well armed Turkey Track bunch came riding, "Hell bent for election," over the hill to where the Styles' roundup was going on. Neigh tried to make it to his house for a gun — all of his crew were unarmed. The Turkey Track bunch were coming up on him fast — our father quickly rode in to intercept, spoke, but there was no answer. All riders rode on at breakneck speed after Neigh. The Turkey Track ramrod, Ed, kept yelling at Neigh to stop — Neigh finally did stop and rode back to meet his pursuers. Daddy (always acting as the peacemaker) quickly rode in between the two outfits and said, "DON'T SHOOT." Neigh, calling the bluff, said to Ed, "Pull off your gun and get down off your horse if you want a real fight." Ed, backing down, said, "Ah-h-h, I don't want to get all beat up." But the fracas wasn't yet over for that day. The two outfits continued to argue with Neigh and Art almost getting into a big fight. Ed pulled his gun on Neigh but Daddy stepped in between them, possibly stopping a killing.

Guns made men act brave but likely these men had been given orders to harass and try scaring the homesteaders out and not to kill. But Tom Derrick didn't scare. Earnest Langenegger says that Tom didn't back down from any man and would do more to help a neighbor than he would do for himself.

Nevertheless the homesteaders stayed!

Another time the Turkey Track ramrod sent word to Daddy that they were going to tear the fence down that Earnest and John Langenegger had built for him. Daddy stood guard up on the hill with his rifle all that day. But they never came — just another bluff!

Then word came from the "big outfit" that the homesteaders were not to work cattle without Turkey Track men present to watch. Daddy, John Walker (brother-in-law) and Joe Winkler all said, "Well now, we are going to work cattle tomorrow — be there." They did gather the cattle the next day but the Turkey Track bunch didn't show. Once more it was just a bluff!

And still Daddy and Mother stayed — Daddy until his death in June of 1947. Mother lived on the ranch for about 15 more years after Daddy died before she went to live with her daughters until her death in March of 1974. Both are buried in the Hagerman cemetery. They were members of the Hagerman Church of Christ. They were active in P.T.A. work and Daddy served on the Lake Arthur school board for eight or ten years. He was also very influential in persuading his many friends to vote for his favorite candidate at election time.

W.W. Walker, father of Thelma America Derrick, died at the age of 49 and was the first person to be buried in the present Hagerman cemetery on June 15, 1903.

We all have fond memories of our growing-up days on the ranch. In the early 1920's we went to school, by horseback or sometimes in the buggy, to the little schoolhouse in Buffalo Valley. Grace Harvey taught us one or two years. She rode to school by horseback from the Lane ranch, located between Lake Arthur and Buffalo Valley. Later on Wade Lane taught us some.

Aside from the love of our ranch home and close-knit family, one of our greatest pleasures in life was playing basketball. During our high school days we Derrick kids, boys and girls, received many honors in athletics.

We, Slick and Curly, played basketball in Hagerman our freshman year of high school. Then the Roswell coach became interested in us as basketball players, so we were offered board, room and jobs for our spending money, if we would come to Roswell for school and basketball. Six weeks of that city life was more than enough for us, so we quit and came home. Later we played with the Hagerman "Poison Five" independent team, coached by a great coach, Tucker Collins.

All of us Derrick kids had a short stint in the Hagerman school before the Lake Arthur school bus line extended to us. We all graduated and played basketball at the Lake Arthur high school.

The model T school bus that we rode to school in was really something else to remember. The compartment in which we rode was built on seperate from the cab, and we, therefore, loaded from the rear of the bus. Instead of windows the bus had curtains that were forever flapping in the wind and allowing the dust and dirt to cover and stifle us. Sam says that he thinks the reason we never learned very much in school was because our lungs were full of dust and dirt, and we couldn't breathe properly by the time we reached the school. Another time, in route to school in freezing weather, the school bus froze up and lost all of its radiator water. Slick found his boot to be right handy, and just about the only thing available, to dip water out of the Pecos River to fill the radiator.

Millard married Ruby Parnell and they had one child. He now lives with his wife, Rena, in Artesia. They have one son. Joyce Andrews, daughter of Millard and Ruby, lives in Hagerman.

James William (Curly) married Anna Mary Lattion and they live at Mayhill. They have two sons.

Tommy Lee (Slick) first married Helen Hunter, then Lois Johns. Both wives are dead.

Robert Samuel (Sam) married Mary Graham and they had one daughter. He now lives in Hagerman with his wife Dale.

Mattie married Roy Hammons and they had two children. She now lives in Artesia with her husband Clyde Rasor.

Ola Bea married V.L. (Tommy) Thompson and they live in Roswell. They have three sons.

Laura married Henry Heath and they have one son and reside in Artesia.

Buddy married Elizabeth Merritt and they live in Artesia and have four children.

THE DEVENPORTS
By Dorothy Devenport West

The William Devenport family arrived in Roswell in May, 1903, from Martin, Oklahoma. William and his wife, Ardelier Newberry Devenport, were parents of six children. The boys were John, Wade, Clarence and T.D. The daughters were Viola and Iola.

The oldest son, John, had come to Roswell earlier and the rest of the family came because of the father's illness. However, he died shortly after they arrived. John never lived in the Hagerman area.

The family remained in Roswell for about a year. The girls attended the old Central School and the boys worked at various jobs. Wade and T.D. helped put in the first sidewalks in Roswell and also helped build the old Roswell Hotel that was located close to the railroad depot.

After leaving Roswell, they lived for a short time at Spring Mound Valley, near Dexter. Mother Devenport decided to file on a claim located three miles east of Lake Arthur. The mother and girls lived on the claim and the boys worked at a variety of jobs. T.D. worked as "straw boss" for Jim Williamson at the Felix Ranch. He would ride horseback each weekend to Lake Arthur to see his family.

In 1910 the family moved to a house in the 300 block of Perth Street in Hagerman. Later, Mother Devenport moved to 104 S. Manchester, where she remained until she was unable to live alone. She died in 1945 at age ninety.

Wade (1882-1949) married Hazel Glass of Lake Arthur in 1909 and in a short time moved to Cleburne, Texas. He never lived in Hagerman for any length of time after this. In 1919 he married Winnie Belle Blalock. She died in Miami, Florida, in 1937. They had two daughters and a son.

In 1943 Wade's youngest daughter, Juanita, came from Miami to visit her relatives and attend school. She married

Jack Langenegger (youngest son of Ernest Langenegger) in 1944. They have continued to live in Hagerman. Jack is a farmer and they are both very active in many organizations and the church. They have a son and a daughter.

Clarence (1884-1962) married Etta Pitt whose family ranched on the Caprock, east of Hagerman. The two oldest of their four children were born in Hagerman. Clarence worked for the Wool and Hide Company and later for the alfalfa mill. They moved to the Melrose and House, New Mexico, area.

Viola (1891-1965) married Will Newman in 1911. They ranched in Texas and New Mexico, settling later at Silverton, Texas. They had one adopted son.

Iola (1884-   ) married H. Clay Lemon in 1917 and remained in Hagerman.

The Devenports were faithful members of the Church of Christ and helped organize the first Church of Christ in Hagerman.

T.D. DEVENPORT FAMILY

T.D. "Teed" (1886-1963) sold his horse to obtain money to go in the restaurant business. His first cafe was at the corner of Oxford and Argyle. The building had a second story that contained beds. He rented these to the cowboys who were in town overnight. Ernest Langenegger swears that he would rent them to seven men at one time and they would have to sleep crosswise.

The cafe was almost a family business as his sister, Iola, worked with him and his mother would bake a dozen (or more) pies each day for him to sell. Iola remembers it as a very busy time with long hours. They would open before six a.m., and it was often after midnight before they could close. They baked their own bread and spent many hours making sandwiches, etc., for different meetings in town. She remembers one Fourth of July celebration at the Washington Ranch. Many people had booths. Teed sold pink lemonade from a stock-watering tank (new, I hope). She helped him and they did such a thriving business the tank had to be refilled.

Teed remained a fixture on Argyle from this time until his death in 1963. He had a grocery store, butcher shop and soda fountain on the north side of the street for many years, later moving everything, but the grocery store, across the street and adding a short-order cafe. He also started handling the first refrigerators to be sold in town, later adding radios, etc. The last fifteen years were spent in the appliance business.

Teed and Perditia "Ditta" Morgan (1891-1965) were married in 1922. They rented a house, south of town, for a couple of years, then built their first home, an adobe, on West Argyle. Later, they built another home, just across the driveway from the first and remained there the rest of their lives.

Ditta was very active in the community and church. She taught Sunday School, Bible School, worked with groups of young married women, baby clinics and the Red Cross. Though she did not always tell people what they wanted to hear, they knew they could come to her for help.

The Girl Scouts occupied a great deal of her time for almost thirty years. She obtained for Hagerman one of the first charters in the state. Many wonderful people worked as leaders on the advisory board or supported them with their money. In the early years, her father, Jim Morgan, often joined the outings. They had many memorable experiences. One time on a trip to the newly opened Carlsbad Caverns, one of the girls became ill and had to be brought to the surface in the big bucket.

In later years, for several summers, Hagerman Scouts had their own camps in the mountains. Jim Michelet, a wonderful civic-minded man, would take off a week from his busy farming operation, furnish a truck, act as driver and guide and put up with thirty giggling girls.

Teed and Ditta had one child, Dorothy Sue. She graduated from Baylor University School of Nursing and married Robert West (son of Tollie and Edith West) in 1946.

T.D. Devenport, in Teed's Confectionery, 1942.

THE FRED H. EVANS FAMILY
By Mr. and Mrs. A.V. Evans

Fred Evans was stricken by malaria. The doctors in Oklahoma advised him to go to a dry climate. New Mexico was well known as a healthful place, and, since his older brother, Luther, was living here, Hagerman seemed the logical place to relocate.

He and his wife, Leota, sold all their household goods, livestock and farm equipment before leaving Oklahoma. Traveling by train Mr. Evans with his four sons, Aubrey, George, Robley and Ellsworth, arrived at Hagerman on Thanksgiving Day, 1914.

In order to have a place ready for housekeeping when his wife and daughters, Faye, Lillian and Waunita, arrived in a few weeks, he bought the household furnishings of the Gimry family, who were going elsewhere.

Although the farming methods and crops were not those to which he was accustomed, Mr. Evans chose to farm in New Mexico. As his health improved, he rented land whereever it was available.

His avocation was hunting. During the first years here he kept greyhounds, training the dogs to hunt and kill coyotes. Each hunting season he brought home ducks and quail until Mrs. Evans would almost refuse to prepare and cook them.

Deer hunting was the high sport of the year. In the fall he and neighborhood friends went to the mountains by team and wagon to hunt. In later years his sons hunted deer with him. Usually there was venison on the Evans' dinner table for several weeks following the deer hunting season.

Mrs. Evans seemed never to tire of telling her children and grandchildren about her childhood in Missouri. Her father, W.E. Collins, was a first cousin of General Robert E. Lee, and she often told and retold stories of the Civil War.

Mr. and Mrs. Evans were the parents of two other sons, Leroy and Evan, who were born in New Mexico.

In 1921, before the day of "miracle drugs," at the age of twelve, Robley passed away because of an attack of appendicitis. This was a sad blow to the Evans family.

Mr. and Mrs. Evans belonged to the First Christian Church. They attended services there as long as the church in Hagerman was active.

After having rented farms for a number of years, Mr. Evans acquired several pieces of property of his own. He and his family made their permanent home on Highway 285 (alternate) at the farm the early settlers knew as the Harry Cowan place on "Cottonwood Row."

Leota Evans passed away in 1961. Her husband, Fred, passed away in 1971, just three weeks before his ninety-fifth birthday, having lived many years more than he had expected when he came to Hagerman in 1914.

THE A.V. EVANS FAMILY
By Alta G. Evans

Aubrey, the eldest of Fred and Leota Evans' family, began his farming career early. He did a man's work from the time he came to New Mexico.

There were apples to be picked and boxes to be made in which to ship them. Using a pitch fork he loaded many a mill wagon with hay to be hauled to the Hagerman Alfalfa Mill.

However, Aubrey went to church socials, the Chautauqua or whatever was the local amusement. On special occasions he drove his Dad's Dodge touring car on the condition that he would not drive faster than twenty-five miles an hour.

On one such occasion he was hurrying home after he and "Miss Alta" had been to the movies. As he made the last corner, Bang! He thought "Oh no, not a flat tire! What will Dad say?" He decided the only thing to do was to get out the pump and try to fix it. As he walked around the car he heard a suspicious noise in the tall grass. He discovered his friend and neighbor, Lewis Bitney, shot gun in hand and exploding with laughter. Lewis must have been the original practical joker. Lewis was a student at the University of Nebraska, Aubrey thought he might enjoy college life, too, but after one winter at the University of Nebraska he decided to come back to the farm.

In the spring of 1927 Alta Gehman and Aubrey were married. They became the parents of eight lovely daughters: Pauline, Mrs. J.C. Wyman Jr.; Frances, Mrs. J. Winstead Laymance; Hazel Ann, Mrs. Hazel Stuart; Lois Rae, Mrs. T.R. Allen; Mary, (Milton Brown deceased) Mrs. Charles Weisleder; Ruth, Mrs. L.V. Brown; Carol, Mrs. Robert E. Scott. None of the girls live in Hagerman.

Aubrey and Alta have been content with farm life, making their home on the old Brayshaw place where the doctor had built a house and set out an orchard in 1900.

THE L.E. EVANS FAMILY
By Alta G. Evans

The first of the Evans family to come to Hagerman from Oklahoma were Mr. and Mrs. L.E. Evans and their four daughters. Mrs. Maude Evans had a homestead several miles southwest of Hagerman. However, the family made their home two miles west of Hagerman on the north side of the road which is now known as State Road 339.

Luther Evans had an orchard with many kinds of fruit trees including nectarines.

The three older daughters were grown young ladies when they came. Fern and Lucile had a photo studio in Roswell. Ruby did office work. All three girls married local men. Fern became Mrs. Jim Wheaton and lived at Lake Van. Lucile's husband was Earl Boyd. He lost his life in the flu epidemic that swept through the training camps of World War I. Ruby married Charles Wyatt, who served with Battery A. After the war the Evans daughters and their families settled elsewhere.

Eloise, the youngest daughter attended grade school in Hagerman and often rode a burro to school. The burro was slow and stubborn and often caused her to be late. Those of us who walked were envious of a burro to ride.

Mr. Evans was an educated man of that time, being interested in many things. Nevertheless, the newfangled automobiles were hard to handle even for a man as intelligent as Luther Evans. One of their most disconcerting habits being that they would not stop when the driver hallooed, "Whoa."

The L.E. Evans family attended the Baptist church. Mr. Evans was Sunday School superintendent there for several years. He was also a member of the community male quartet. Other members of this quartet were E.A. Paddock, B.F. Gehman and J.F. Bauslin.

In 1916 L.E. Evans decided to return to Oklahoma. When disposing of his property here, he sold a piece of land on the hill to the town of Hagerman. There is where the town drilled a well for its first water system. In times of emergency the town still uses water from the hill wells.

THE J.M. FLETCHER FAMILY

By Rachel Fletcher Boyce

We moved to Lake Arthur, New Mexico, in 1923 from Hot Springs, Arkansas, for my father's health.

My father, J.M. Fletcher, and an older brother, Fred, and his son, J.J., came about a month before the rest of the family. He rented the E.L. Selby farm about four miles north of Lake Arthur and sent for the rest of the family.

Mother, Hattie Craft Fletcher, six children, ranging in age from twenty-one to seven years, and our pet dog, "Copper," came by train. We were on the train three days and nights. Some of us had never ridden a train before and that in itself was quite an experience, besides coming to such a different country.

We had never seen a jack rabbit, horned toad, sandstorm, cowboy and many other new things we found in New Mexico. However, we did miss the trees and woodlands of Arkansas and were quite homesick for awhile.

We entered school in Lake Arthur our first year in New Mexico. We attended the Lake Arthur Methodist Church.

Our first neighbors there were the Arthur Russell and Calvin Graham families.

From the Selby farm we moved to the Washington Ranch south of Hagerman in 1924. Our neighbors there were the J.W. Wiggins, H.A. White, Carl Hanson and Louis Bitney families.

We grew up in Hagerman and attended school and church there. Some of the stores and businesses I remember were the A.N. Miller store where we bought groceries, W.P. Woodmas Dry Goods and Teed Devenport's Cafe.

One of the most interesting things to us at the time was seeing the ranchers ship cattle all year round and sheep in the fall. The Washington Ranch, now owned and operated by Leroy Miles, was a shipping point with railroad siding, stockpens and scales. After the ranchers had brought their sheep into the pens, the buyers would come in to ship them. Since we didn't know what a cowboy looked like, it was very interesting to see them work the livestock.

Another interesting thing was to live in a house made of dirt, adobe, since we had never seen anything like that. The forty-two stall barn that used to house the saddle horses was also built of adobe. Also, we enjoyed the apple orchards and the honey here.

With a sick father, we really had our share of problems, but, with a good ambitious, hardworking, young mother, we always made it.

After our father passed away in 1932 during the Depression, we moved to the Buffalo Valley Farm, then owned by Mrs. Helen Gilroy and managed by Kenneth Servatious. Penix and Rosco were teen-agers at the time but had to do the farming. Grady had his own crop but still lived with us. Later, in 1935, Penix and Rosco bought the Marie Losey Stewart farm and moved from Buffalo Valley.

Grady married the former Theola Friddle, neice of the late Mrs. Elton Lankford. They have one daughter and two grandchildren. They lived in Denver for several years and, upon retirement, moved to Roswell to make their home.

Velmer married Corinne Bobo, sister of Mrs. W.R. Goodwin. They, too, have one daughter and two grandsons. They are retired and live in Oklahoma City.

Mattie married Leo Bramblett of Hagerman. Both are deceased. They were the parents of Marvin Bramblett, a Dexter farmer and Modene Shepard, Carlsbad.

Rachel was the only Fletcher to marry a native Hagermanite and native New Mexican. She married Sam Boyce, son of Mr. & Mrs. "Buck" Boyce. They have one son and two grandchildren. They have operated a grocery store in Dexter for the past twenty-four years.

Penix is married to the former Lois Bivens. They have four daughters, a son and one grandson.

Rosco married the former Eileen Rapp of Roswell. They have one daughter and a grandson.

Both Penix and Rosco are now Dexter farmers.

Our mother passed away in 1970 at the age of eighty-four.

I am very thankful for the years we spent in Hagerman.

THE O.J. FORD FAMILY
By O.J. Ford

My wife, Mae, son Joe (age eight months) and I arrived in Hagerman in 1928 via Santa Fe train. There were no vacant houses in town, or at least that is what we were told by every one who had a rent house. We wondered if they were not afraid to rent to a couple of "seedy" looking "Okies." Anyway we caught a ride to Roswell where we stayed for a week. Finally Ernie and Sadie Bowen took pity on us and rented us a room in their home, where we stayed until we moved into the house where John and Nola Clark now live at 304 West Argyle.

I came to Hagerman to take a job as manager of a cotton gin and stayed at the same location for thirty-one years as manager of the Farmers Co-Op Association, retiring in 1965.

Times were pretty hard in those days; we built a new gin in Dexter in 1933 and paid 25¢ per hour for carpenters and had all the help we needed. We turned people away every day who were looking for work. I have seen St. Mid. 1⅛" staple cotton sell for 5¢ per pound and cotton seed for $6.00 per ton. The charges for ginning was 30¢ per hundred (seed cotton) and $1.90 for bagging and ties, a total of about $6.00 per bale. If the seed did not pay the ginning, we just took the seed. All cotton was brought to the gin by wagon and teams. Our gin had a steam boiler and big whistle, and that whistle caused many run-aways. I believe the first farm tractor in the Hagerman area was owned by N.S. West and the name of it was "Du-All."

Things and times were not all bad. I have seen (in later years) land that produced three bales of cotton per acre and around seven tons of hay per year, with prices up to 45¢ per pound for cotton and $55.00 per ton for hay.

Our lives were blessed in 1931 by the arrival of a baby daughter, Ruth Ann. We now had a son and a daughter and we were busy and happy trying to make a living and a home for our family. Both "kiddos" graduated from Hagerman high school and then E.N.M.U. at Portales. Joe married Jane Mayberry of Hagerman and Ruth married Mickey McGuire from Hope, New Mexico.

Now for just a few of the unusual things that happened during the forty-five years that we lived at Hagerman.

On August 16, 1931, an earthquake was felt. It was severe enough to rattle the dishes and swing the lights which hung from the ceilings on cords. It also caused the bedsteads to move a few inches on the floor. No damage was reported.

On February 5, 1933, the thermometer read 40° below zero. This reading was recorded on the U.S. weather station in Hagerman and was supervised by Dr. I.B. McCormick. Practically all the large cottonwood trees, which were numerous, were killed. It was fortunate that there was no wind, otherwise many head of cattle would have been lost.

On October 2, 1954, there was a flood on the Felix River that hit the Hagerman community about 2 a.m. No warning had been given, and, due to the early morning hour, everybody who lived along the river was asleep when the water arrived. Consequently, eleven people were swept away and drowned. Seven people lived in a farm house on the Fife farm, an eighth of a mile south of the Felix bridge, close to the river; five of these people were drowned. The other victims were farm workers who had come to the vicinity to pick cotton. This was the worst flood on the Felix River while I lived there.

Being in public business in Hagerman for forty-five years, I made many friends and perhaps a few enemies; but if enemies, I'm sorry because I always tried to do the best that I could. Some of the best friends we ever had still live there.

As for civic and religious activities, I served on the school board for about eighteen or twenty years. We were active members of the First Baptist Church all the time that we were there.

Hagerman has been good to us, and no matter where we may be, we shall always think of Hagerman as home!

THE A.N. FRANKLIN FAMILY

As told to Helen Curry by Mrs. Franklin

Annis N. Franklin, his wife, Ethel Daugherty Franklin, and three small children left Holiday, Texas (five miles from Wichita Falls), to come to the oil fields near Artesia, New Mexico. The year was 1925.

They came in a covered wagon with three horses, two to pull the wagon and one to lead. They changed off from time to time each horse taking turns at pulling. The trip took twenty-three days.

They camped out each night and often they shot rabbits or ducks to help out with the food. At one stop Mr. Franklin had only three shells left for the 22 rifle. He took three shots at a rabbit and missed three times. Mrs. Franklin had picked up some coal along a railroad track to make a fire. Mr. Franklin picked up a piece of coal and hit the rabbit and killed it so they did not miss their supper that night.

The family arrived at Dexter one evening and camped out there. They spent their last fifteen cents in Dexter. In the morning they started for Artesia, but, when they reached Hagerman, Mr. Franklin went into the Miller store and asked if they knew of any one who needed help. Mr. Miller called Mr. Hammonds in Buffalo Valley and was told to send them out.

They went out to Buffalo Valley and remained there eleven years. Four more children were added to the family. The children are David, Mary, Pete, Lottie, Paul, J.D. and Earnest. The Franklins lost two sons in World War II. David died on the death march in the Philippines. Earnest went down in a plane which crashed in the Philippines.

During the time the family lived in Buffalo Valley, Mrs. Franklin tells of the killing of a rattlesnake under their house. She said it was over five feet in length and very large around because it had eaten so many pack rats. After the snake was killed the men coiled it in a five gallon bucket which it filled to the top.

After the older children were big enough to care for the younger ones, Mrs. Franklin, who said she liked to do farm work, went out to the fields and worked like a man and drew a man's pay. Phil Stowe was manager of the Valley farms at the time. After leaving Buffalo Valley the family moved to one of Bill Langenegger's farms, where they worked several years.

All of the children attended school in Hagerman. Twenty-three years ago Mr. and Mrs. Franklin came to Hagerman where they bought a lot at 505 W. Kansas Street and built a house. They did all of the work except for $100.00 worth they hired done.

When Mr. Franklin's health failed he was in the Veteran's Hospital in Albuquerque for some time before his death in 1970. Mr. Franklin was a veteran of World War I. He was a loyal and faithful member of the Eastside Church of Christ in Hagerman. Whenever there was any repair needed to the church or yard, Mr. Franklin did it.

Mrs. Franklin still lives in her home here, and she is always busy. She says busy people live longer.

Paul married Zora Mae Barton and makes his home here. They have two children. He is a pilot and flies a crop spraying plane. J.D. married Anna Mae Brewer, lives in Hagerman and has two children. He works for Mark Caraway at Stockmen's Well and Supply Co. in Roswell. He used to participate in rodeos and was winner many times. He now enjoys skeet shooting. Mary is married to Jody Troublefield and they are the parents of two children, one of whom, Don, also lives here. Mary and her husband travel quite a bit but own a home in Hagerman. Pete married Helen York. They have four children. He lives and works on the Langenegger Ranch northeast of Dexter. Lottie's home is in Alabama.

LAWRENCE AND LELA GARNER

By John Garner

Lawrence Wigginton Garner arrived in Hagerman as a bachelor from Pembroke, Kentucky, in 1903. He had operated a general store and was a tobacco farmer in Kentucky. He could never remember the date he arrived in Hagerman and always had to ask Tom Banks who was on the same train the day he arrived. He finally wrote the date in the family Bible.

He first worked for Stanford and Langford general store, located on the corner now occupied by Hagerman Service Station. Later he became dry goods manager for the Joyce-Pruit Company and held this position until the building was destroyed by fire in 1915.

Mary Lela Mullis arrived in Hagerman by train with the Duke R. Mullis family from Arkansas in 1906. Lela and Lawrence Garner were married in 1912. They had two sons, William Lawrence Garner who died in 1916 and John Duke Garner who still lives in Hagerman.

After the Joyce-Pruit fire the Garners moved to Portales where Mr. Garner worked for the Joyce-Pruit Company until 1920. He and his brother Byrd D. Garner bought the Picacho Trading Post and Hotel. Lawrence was the Picacho postmaster for five years.

In 1924 the Garners moved back to Hagerman and purchased the Baldridge store. In 1925 they bought the A.N. Miller general merchandise store and operated this business until retirement in 1944.

Lawrence Garner is well remembered by people who traded with him in his general store. As he walked around the store filling a bill of groceries he usually had a sly little

Mrs. L.W. Garner

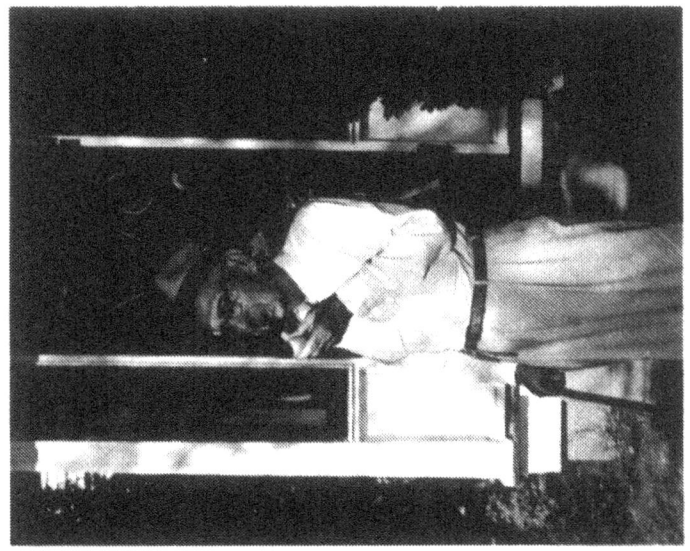

Mr. L.W. Garner

grin and hummed a happy tune, sometimes asking the customer if he didn't want to "spend that other nickel." His customers left the store with a smile on their faces, too. He carried accounts as long as a year for the farmers and ranchers and others. Many could not have stayed in their own business had he not let them have this credit. When a bill was paid at the end of six months or a year, Mr. Garner always gave a gift to the patron, a pocket knife, a vase or dishes and there was always a small brown bag of candy to take home to the children. A new rolling pin was given to each new bride in Hagerman. Women of the community brought their eggs, butter and other commodities for trade in the store. In the spring the children of the town left early in the mornings to gather the wild asparagus that grew on the ditches around Hagerman. The asparagus was tied in a small bundle and taken to Mr. Garner's store and they received a nickel a bunch or took the 5¢ out in trade for candy or gum.

Lela Garner was one of the jolliest people in town. She, too, smiled often and always had a cute story to tell about herself or someone else that made friends laugh. On picnics and outings she was more fun than the gathering itself and the friends she was with had their day made perfect by Lela's good sense of humor.

The Garners were members of the First Presbyterian Church. He was a member of the Masonic Lodge, IOOF and served on the Hagerman town board.

John Duke Garner married Jewell Maye Gates of Waco, Texas, in 1941. They returned to Hagerman in 1946. Jewell is a teacher in the Hagerman school. John worked in the First National Bank until 1958 when he affiliated with the Keeth Gas Company, Inc. They have two children.

THE B.F. GEHMAN FAMILY
By Alta G. Evans

B.F. Gehman brought his wife, Lydia, and daughter, Alta, to Hagerman in 1911. The forty acres of land he had bought in 1906 were now under irrigation from the Hagerman Canal. The young orchard was growing and things were prospering in this community. Now seemed the time to make the decisive move from school teaching in Kansas to farming in New Mexico.

He came on the freight train with the household furniture, the farm equipment and his horses. His family, my mother and I, came a week or so later on the passenger train.

We arrived just after dark on Dec. 20, 1911. My father was waiting at the depot with our trusty old driving horse hitched to the buggy.

It had been a long journey to unknown surroundings. As we passed the barn where the horses were stabled, it was reassuring to hear them nicker to "Babe," the buggy horse.

Our first Hagerman home was the house at 605 W. Kansas. We lived there through the cold weather while the barn and chicken house were being built on the farm.

We had come from a much colder climate, but here in the middle of the winter one of our neighbors always wore a sunbonnet when she went to the store or post office. Then it seemed strange. To see Mrs. Anna Lang in her sun bonnet came to be one of my cherished memories.

When we moved to the farm when the weather was warmer we were one mile due west of the schoolhouse. As many families did in those early years, we lived in the new hen house with a tent making a pleasant bedroom. Mr.

Chedester was the trusted carpenter of this area, having built many houses here. He was building a home for us.

The building of the house which she had planned was the all consuming interest for my mother. To me the drilling of the well was the most intriguing. Each day I watched the machine and men at work. When they brought up the water and I was allowed to carry a dipperful of it into the house for my mother, that was the most exciting and proudest moment of my life. There have been many outstanding times in my life, but that was the first.

With the windmill turning and a big wooden tank to hold the water, a garden naturally came next. Not to have a garden was unthinkable to anyone from eastern Kansas. The soil was virgin, the water fresh and the garden grew.

Our nearest neighbors were the Bauslins, whose farm joined ours on the west. Just west of them on the hill were the Alters. At that time Mr. Alter had a cheese making factory there. When the cucumbers and other things from the garden were plentiful, one of my chores was to carry fresh vegetables to our neighbors.

I liked best of all to go to Bauslin's house. Helen, their daughter, had a collection of dolls. Mrs. Bauslin had many treasures which I spent hours examining. The cookie jar was usually full, but, if it wasn't, I could always have a snack of puffed wheat with a sweet dressing over it that no one but Mrs. Bauslin knew how to make.

Mr. Bauslin was our village blacksmith — "he stands under a spreading chestnut tree?" No, he stands under a spreading cottonwood tree. Then I wondered, did Longfellow's smithy keep peppermint candy in his pocket as did Mr. Bauslin?

Mother planted a rose garden near the house in the corner just between the front and back porches. She often had roses to give away. One summer afternoon Anna Bell Hamilton and her beau, John Langenegger, stopped by. Anna Bell was distressed by the many ants in the path which quickly covered her ankles. However she was happy to have a bouquet of roses. A few days later on hearing that John and Anna Bell were married, mother speculated that perhaps the roses had added a bit to her wedding day.

My parents were members of the Methodist Church. They supported all of the church activities. For many years the church was the center of our social life. The friends we made there have been dear ones through all the years.

Lydia Gehman passed away in 1920. Ben F. Gehman left us in 1940. Both were taken to Olathe, Kansas, there to rest side by side in the family burial plot.

The B.F. Gehman house.

DEMETRO GONZALES FAMILY

By Lutecia Gonzales Barela

I came to Hagerman with my parents in 1924. I was one year old and we came in a covered wagon from Arabela, Lincoln County, New Mexico. We came to live on a piece of land my father had traded for land in Arabela. My father, with some help, made our house out of adobe. My parents farmed nine acres of land until my father's death in 1954. I lived on this farm until I married.

My father's name was Demetro Gonzales and my mother's name was Rebecca Gonzales. I have two brothers, Jay Gonzales and Ermino Gonzales. I have three sisters, Felia Montoya, Elvira Sanchez and Beatrice Gonzales. Beatrice was working for Mrs. Jim McKinstry when we came in 1924 and she continued to work for her for many years. Beatrice still lives and works in Hagerman and is a faithful member of the local Spanish Assembly of God Church.

When we got here, my father and Jay started their first job (bailing hay) with Mr. Heitman, father of Fred Heitman. My parents also picked cotton for Sam McKinstry.

I started school with my brother, Ermino, when I was eight years old, with the aid of Mrs. Ditta Devenport, who helped many people. We were the only Spanish children in school at that time and it was very hard. Many of the other children did not like us. Ermino would go home day after day with his shirt torn off of his back. When "Prof" White learned of this, he put a stop to it.

I remember being very scared, I did not understand English and when they wanted me to go to another room I was afraid they were taking me somewhere to beat me up. Now, my daughter-in-law, Mary Barela, works as an aide in kindergarten at school. I'm glad it is easier for young children today.

I have good memories, too. Our neighbors, the Belyeus, were wonderful. All the children played together, and they helped us get over our fear of school. I often wonder what happened to them. Also, I remember Mr. Garner in his grocery store. He was always humming as he worked. After we bought our groceries he would give us a sack of candy. My sack lasted a long time as I ate only one piece a day.

In 1937 I married Tom Barela in Hagerman. He came here from Cottonwood where he worked for the Pearson Brothers. He has worked in this area ever since. He owns his own truck for hay hauling, etc.

I worked in the school cafeteria, off and on, for fourteen years while most of my children were in school.

We have eight children (two girls and six boys): Tom Barela, Jr., lives in Hagerman and owns his own trucks; Godfrey Barela lives in Denver City, Texas, and is the minister of the First Assembly of God Church in Seminole; Amelia Barela, a graduate of Latin American Bible College of El Paso, a missionary in Mexico and now in Detroit, Michigan; Nora Gamboa, a secretary at NMSU in Las Cruces, New Mexico; Lionel Barela, a graduate with honors from ENMU, — Portales, has Masters Degree and works for an accounting firm in Laredo, Texas; Henry Barela works in Hagerman area; Ernest Barela attends ENMU — Roswell refrigeration school and Bobby Barela, still at home, and attending the Hagerman schools.

Though I was frightened as a child, I am happy to say, most of my schoolmates became my friends and our children and our grandchildren play and work together.

THE W.R. GOODWIN FAMILY
By Ruth Goodwin

We moved to Hagerman in 1928 from Elkins, New Mexico, where Will worked for the railroad. Our oldest son, Wallace, had been boarding out in Roswell in order to be able to attend high school, and he was very unhappy to be parted from his family. So we decided to move to a new location that had a high school. Hagerman was our choice because of the much talked about fine orchards.

We first located on Morgan Street and lived there in the same house for forty-three and a half years before I moved to my little house at 205 Cambridge in 1972.

Will worked at the alfalfa mill for awhile before he became janitor for the school. He worked for the school system for nineteen years, having resigned when his health broke. He had room in his heart to love all those school children and so many people (then school children) have told me that Will was a special friend to them, always having time to listen to their troubles. The school teachers and the school children gave Will a party and a nice gift of a radio when he retired. William R. Goodwin died in June of 1963.

All four of our children graduated from Hagerman high school. They were an industrious bunch, always helping out by doing odd jobs like delivering papers, picking and chopping cotton.

Wallace W. attended Draughns Business College in Abeline, Texas. He then worked as a salesman for Shaw Machinery Co. for several years before he served for four years in the "Sea Bees." Later he bought his own shop and home in Tyler, Texas. He married Mollie Joe Hill in Abeline and they adopted a daughter, Mollie Ruth. Wallace died of cancer in 1966.

Vera attended West Texas State College at Canyon, Texas, Highland University at Las Vegas, New Mexico, and The University of Arizona at Tucson, Arizona. She married Byron Gress and she lives in San Bernardino, California, where she operates a dance studio.

George attended the Socorro School of Mines at Socorro, New Mexico, and the A & M College at Stillwater, Oklahoma. He also served for four years in the "Sea Bees" and married Ann Styles. They live in Artesia where George works for the Central Valley Electric Coop. George and Ann have three children, Tommy, Eddie and Patty.

Helen received her training at the Roswell Business College. She married Bill Langenegger, farmer and rancher, and they have three daughters, Jeaneen, Lana Ruth and Alice Kathleen. They live at Hagerman.

We are Baptists by faith and are willing workers in the church.

I recall that trip in our covered wagon from Tell, Texas, to Elkins in December of 1916. We had two children at that time, Wallace and Vera. It was dreadfully cold and we were all pretty miserable. Will and his half brother who traveled with us walked to keep warm. We stopped at a camp house near Caprock to cook and decided to heat some bricks to place in the wagon under our feet to help keep the children and me warm. After we had traveled on our way for awhile, Will came to the wagon and said, "Ruth it seems I smell something burning." I told him, "No, everything is fine in here and we are all nice and warm." The third time he came to the wagon to check on us he just began pulling the quilts out and they quickly flamed up when the air hit them. Of course big holes were burned in three of them but enough was saved that I could patch them when we arrived at our homestead on January 1, 1917. We disposed of the bricks right there as soon as we had the fire out. Our covered wagon was a fourteen foot frame. We had all of our household goods in the bottom compartment of the wagon and two beds made on the floor of the wagon and this is where the children and I rode, directly over the household goods and sitting on the beds.

It was a memorable and happy occasion when Bill and Helen had open house for Will and me on our Golden Wedding Anniversary in 1959. Will and I were married in Iowa Park, Texas, in 1909.

THE CALVIN GRAHAMS
By William J. Graham

Soon after they were married my parents, Calvin Graham and his wife, Jackie Mae Graham, came to Hagerman in 1900. They traveled in a covered wagon from Young County, Texas. They were attracted to Hagerman after hearing that this was a new country with many opportunities.

They first located, and lived for about one year, on a forty acre tract of land that they bought between the railroad tracks and Highway 285. The house in which they lived on the forty acre tract was on the north side of W. Argyle Street.

After this first year they traded the Hagerman property for homestead property southwest of Hagerman, finished proving up on the homestead right and received a patent on it. This was the Graham home until they sold it in 1946 when Daddy's health began to fail and they moved to town. The canal ran through the southeast corner of the property and on this small acreage Daddy grew some feed crops and apples. He was a rancher having owned a twenty-one section ranch west of Hagerman for many years, better known, perhaps, as the "Breeb Hurst Ranch."

My parents were hardy pioneers and respected citizens who contributed to the development of our community in its earlier years. Daddy served on the board of Directors of the Bank for many years, having retired in 1947.

Daddy died in 1950 and mother died in 1967.

They had three children, John W. born in 1906 and died in 1932. Mary Josephine was born in 1914, married Sam Derrick and they had one child, Vivian Louise. Mary died in 1961. I, William J., married Zilpha Taylor and we have three children, William C., Mary V. and Connie L. We live at Hagerman.

W.E. GRAHAM FAMILY

William Elmer Graham and Willetta Mae Ridgley Graham came to Hagerman in November, 1913, from Logan, Kansas.

Mr. Graham bought W.E. King's dray and beautiful Percheron team of horses. Later he operated a truck line.

Their children were William Wayne, who remained in Hagerman for many years. He was married to Berthyl (Boots) Tayes. He served as mayor of Hagerman at one time and was owner and operator of the Conoco Station. When he sold out he bought a station near Dexter and now lives in Roswell.

Irma married L.H. Humphries and lives in Oklahoma City.

Marteal is the wife of Glaze Sacra and lives in Roswell.

Vedder L. is married and makes his home in Roswell.

Willis B. married Laverne Watson and resides in Roswell. Gladys married Kenneth LaFleur and they are in Oklahoma City. Leland F. is single and lives with his mother in Hagerman.

THE GREER FAMILY
Information from their children

Weatherstun S. Greer who was born in Tennessee in 1832 and his wife, Lydia Stubbs Greer, a native of Alabama, born in 1834, came to Hagerman accompanied by their son, James W. Greer, in 1903. They came from Savoy, Texas.

Weatherstun S. Greer had been a Captain of Company D, First Tennessee Cavalry, Confederate States of America. He died in 1909 and his wife died in Hagerman in 1918.

The family came first to Elida where they filed on a claim. They put down a well but the water was so salty that they moved on to Hagerman. They bought land from J.J. Hagerman, located about one and three-quarters of a mile due west of the school house.

James (Jim) Greer was married in the family home to Minerva Mae Kidd from Sherman, Texas, in 1904. They were the parents of nine children, seven of whom survive. Arvil died at the age of five and Vernon was killed in action on Biak Island in 1945 during World War II. The others are Laura Mae Quinn, Bend, Oregon; Olivia Boren, Spring Valley, California; Ernest, Menard, Texas; Edward, Centralia, Missouri; Milton, Riverside, California; Weatherston S. (who spells his name with an o rather than a u as his grandfather) and Bertha Flores, both of Hagerman.

Mr. Jim Greer dug the first grave in the present Hagerman cemetery for W.W. Walker. He also helped build the canal but he was mainly a farmer. In 1925 Mr. Greer moved the family to the Cottonwood community to farm the Malone farm. They returned to Hagerman in 1929 and continued to farm until Mr. Greer retired. They moved into town and lived at S. Indiana and W. Morgan Streets. Jim Greer died in 1959 and Mrs. Greer passed away in 1973.

The following paragraph was added by Helen Curry:

The Greer family were Seventh Day Adventists and were loyal to their church by attendance and support. Their friends were many, not only among their church people but people of other faiths. They were and are an asset to their respective communities.

THE WILEY GRIZZLE FAMILY

In 1928 Mr. and Mrs. Wiley Grizzle of Roswell purchased a farm about five miles northwest of Hagerman. At this time the Grizzles had Gerald, Harold, and Oscar Allison, stepsons of Mr. Grizzle, also Wiley Jr., Ollie Mae, and Mary. Shortly after arriving in Hagerman, Jim was born and later twin daughters who died shortly after birth.

When the Grizzle family arrived in Hagerman they had a Model T truck (about a 1922 model), a 1922 Buick Sedan, very little money, but they had a dream of making a better life for their growing family. The land they bought was native pasture land, and Mr. Grizzle drilled a well for irrigation and broke the land for crops. About two years later, the Grizzles bought another plot of land which joined their land, again drilling an irrigation well and breaking it for cultivation. Later they bought a farm southeast of Hagerman drilling about six irrigation wells on this property.

The early years in Hagerman were spent improving their land, drilling irrigation wells for the neighbors and doing back-breaking work which produced abundant crops. Some of the first crops grown by Mr. Grizzle were cotton, corn, maize and later alfalfa. Also the Grizzles fed out sheep and cattle to supplement the family income. Mr. Grizzle was a pioneer in the field of drilling shallow wells for irrigation, and he seemed to possess a sixth sense when it came to knowing where water could be found.

The Allison and Grizzle children attended the Presbyterian Church and the Hagerman schools. Harold and Oscar graduated from Hagerman High School while the family lived there. Before Hagerman had school buses, Mr.

Grizzle loaded the car with his children and some of the neighbor children, driving them to school, actually one of the first school buses in Hagerman. Some of the neighbor children which he picked up were Elizabeth McKinstry, daughter of the Harrison McKinstrys, the Tom Andrews children, and the Bill Richardson children.

Harold and Oscar recall one day while attending Hagerman High School when two Lake Arthur boys came to school looking for trouble. These boys thought this would be easy to do as only Mr. Welborne, then the mathematics teacher, was on duty, and he was no match in size for these strapping young men. But they underestimated Mr. Welborne and suddenly one of the young men found himself on the floor. Following this unexpected flurry, the young men decided this was not the place to be and executed a hasty retreat. This incident made Mr. Welborne something of a hero among the students and certainly eliminated many discipline problems, because who could challange such strength?

In 1938 the Grizzles sold their Hagerman property and bought another native pasture plot of land close to Roswell in the East Grand Plains Community. The family again improved this farm, and Mr. Grizzle and all of his boys built a three-bedroom home for the family where they lived for a number of years. Although the Grizzle family no longer lived in Hagerman, the children kept in close contact with their Hagerman friends and two of the boys (Harold and Oscar) later married Hagerman girls.

Mr. Grizzle and his family continued buying and improving land. Son Jim and stepsons Gerald, Harold and Oscar, have all continued this family tradition of buying and improving land with irrigation.

Mr. Grizzle died in 1973 in Ft. Sumner and Mrs. Grizzle continues to live there. Shortly before Mr. Grizzle's death, the couple celebrated their fiftieth wedding anniversary.

In 1936 Gerald Allison married Ethel Lenore Wells of Roswell, and they have five grown children. They live in Muleshoe, Texas.

Harold Allison married Jean McKinstry of Hagerman in 1944, and they also live in Muleshoe. They had five children, one son is now deceased.

In 1948 Oscar Allison married Sammy McKinstry Hewitt of Hagerman, and they live in Muleshoe. They have four grown children.

Wiley Grizzle, Jr. was a fighter pilot during World War II and was killed in action over Germany in 1945.

Ollie Mae Grizzle married George Didlake of the East Grand Plains Community in 1946, and they have four children. They now live on Palos Verdes Peninsula, California.

In 1946 Mary Grizzle married F.A. Andreas of Yakima, Washington, and they now live in Ft. Sumner. They have three grown children.

Jim Grizzle married Verona Warner of Muleshoe in 1951, and they have four children. They also live in Ft. Sumner.

THE ZACH HAM FAMILY
By Rosa Jane Lacy

Zach J. and Rosa Lee Ham left south Texas for New Mexico in 1913. They were rice farmers and had lost heavily in the 1913 flood. Zach said that he never wanted to live in flooded areas again and he figured New Mexico would be high and dry.

They traveled by train to Midland, Texas, and from there to Lovington in a covered wagon. Later they homesteaded a section of land about twenty miles east of Hagerman. In 1917 they moved to Hagerman for the children to attend school.

Zach worked at the alfalfa mill there. Later he did farm labor and eventually farmed for himself. In those days apple orchards were everywhere. Later the apple orchards were pulled out because it cost too much to smudge to keep the apples from freezing. In the '20's cotton and alfalfa were the main crops.

Six of the Ham children are still living. Margot Hugueley, the youngest daughter, passed away in 1974. Rosa passed away in 1926. Zach lived to be eighty-four years of age. He passed away in 1966. The Ham family moved to California in the early '30's.

Sadie, who married Orley Brock, lives in Sheridan, Oregon. Emma Lee Bower lives in Monterey, California. Rosa Jane Lacy is living in Fresno, California. Debs Ham owns a cattle ranch in Yamhill, Oregon. Katherine married Quentin Watson. They live near Emma Lee at Pacific Grove, California. Violet Winters, one of the youngest daughters, also lives in Pacific Grove, California.

We had a happy childhood living in Hagerman. Folks in the southwestern United States have always been friendly. There are many happy memories of the years spent there. I especially remember how happy everyone was when World War I was over. They rang the bells in the old firehouse. It was a privilege to have lived and grown up in such a nice town as Hagerman.

JIM HAMMONS FAMILY

In 1924 an old truck bounced into what is now the Hagerman area. The truck carried Jim and Ella Mae Hammons and nine of the Hammons children.

They settled in Buffalo Valley in a house that has since burned to the ground. Jim and the boys worked for Bill Waldrip on land owned by the First National Bank of Roswell. The girls and younger boys attended school in Lake Arthur, New Mexico.

The next year, 1925, Jim became manager in place of Bill Waldrip. Ella Mae passed away in the fall of 1926. The family then resided on what was called the Floto place.

Jim died in 1968 at the age of eighty-nine. Only one of the children, Roy, stayed in the Pecos Valley. He now lives in the Artesia area.

THE RICHMOND HAMS FAMILY

W.A. Hams and wife moved from Michigan to Lake Arthur in 1905. Their son, Richmond, joined them in 1906 for a short time then returned to Michigan to complete his education. In 1910 he was married. He and his wife Belle were the parents of one daughter, Viola Belle. In 1920 they returned to Lake Arthur and in 1921 came to Hagerman when he bought a drug store from George Sasser.

There was only one house in Hagerman with a bath and as soon as it was available Mr. Hams rented it. Until then all their baths were taken in Everett Latimer's barber shop.

In a year or so Hams homesteaded on a place about a mile and a half east of town. After living there a number of years they sold the place and went back to Lake Arthur. But not for long. When they returned they bought a concrete house in west Hagerman at 604 W. Kansas Street.

While living on the homestead they had cows and chickens. One year there was a big snow storm and when they started home to do the chores they got only as far as the Methodist Church. They backed the old Ford to Lampton's Blacksmith Shop and put the car in out of the weather. The next morning Sheb Russell came by on a horse and Mrs. Hams rode out with him to do chores.

Viola remembers another time when a terrible dust storm was blowing. Her mother had gone on to prepare supper and when the others got there Mrs. Hams was in bed with her head covered with a blanket under an inch or so of sand. Everything in the house was full of sand, even the supper.

The Hams bought the Van Arsdol dairy and delivered milk all over town.

Viola wrote, "The best times, at least the fun times, were the years in the drug store. During the time of our state champion basketball teams, a lot of people would gather in the drug store to hear the results as they came over the wire to Ernie Bowen and were telephoned by him to the store."

In 1946 Mr. Hams sold the drug store to E.C. Smith and the family moved to Ignacio, Colorado.

Viola and Frankie Davis were married and have a son, "Smokey" Davis.

— Information from Viola Davis Lipscomb.

CARL R. HANSON
By Allen and Nadine Hanson

When he was a boy of just fourteen years Carl R. Hanson came to the United States from Sweden where he was born in 1872. He became a citizen of the U.S. in 1893 at the age of twenty-one.

Carl and his wife, Olive, moved to Hagerman in 1918 from Esterday, Minnesota, with their six children, Nina, Viola, Joe, Carl, Harold and Allen. They came to the land of sunshine to escape the extreme cold winters of Minnesota.

When they came to Hagerman they bought their farm and always lived there in the white house one-half mile west of the Hagerman school. It was known as the Hanson place. The farm is now owned by Langenegger's. They raised apples and alfalfa hay on the farm. From about 1924 to 1928 they were engaged in the apple packing and shipping business with N.S. West. One year they shipped out of Hagerman sixty-seven rail box car loads of apples to Texas and Oklahoma.

Olive Hanson was born in Minnesota and died in 1960 in California. She was a schoolteacher as a young girl.

As a young man Carl worked in clearing the forests in Minnesota for lumber and the land for farming. Before moving to Hagerman the Hanson's had a farm and a cheese factory. Carl died in 1955 in California.

Harold lives in Hagerman and we live in Roswell.

THE M.E. HARSHEY FAMILY

By Ede McKinstry Harshey

Marzealous Edward Harshey loaded a railroad box car with livestock, household goods, all their belongings, and even Roy and Clarence, the two older children, at Jacksonville, Illinois, in 1894 to come to New Mexico. In the car he brought lumber from Illinois to build the house that I still live in. It was built that year. It sits on a foundation of flat rocks that were hauled from the Pecos River.

Mrs. Harshey (Abbie) stayed in Jacksonville until the house was completed then she, Olive and Lloyd came to New Mexico. Dewey, Frances, and Charlie were born in this state.

Mr. Harshey homesteaded the farm and it has been in the family all these years.

When Clarence and Roy were teenagers they left home. Clarence went to Amarillo where he later married a Texas girl. They were the parents of two children. Roy went to Canada where he married. He was the father of five children, and still resides in Canada.

All seven of the Harshey children attended the Hagerman school. Olive graduated in the second graduating class. She married Roger Durand of Dexter and they have lived most of their married life in Artesia. They have one daughter, Abbie Terry.

Mrs. Harshey passed away in May, 1916, as a result of pneumonia. At that time Lloyd, Frances, and Charlie were still at home.

Lloyd enlisted August 5, 1918, in World War I. He was in service overseas until about June 20, 1919 when he was discharged at Ft. Bliss, Texas, and came back to Hagerman.

The Harshey family. Seated, l. to r.: Dewey Harshey, Marzeleous Edward Harshey, Charley Harshey, Abbie. Standing, l. to r.: Roy Harshey, Olive Harshey (Durand), Clarence Harshey, Lloyd Harshey. A girl soon to be born, Frances Harshey (Pearson), completed the family.

Lloyd and I, Elizabeth Ede McKinstry, were married by C.C. Hill of Roswell in a home wedding July 1, 1920. We immediately went to the Harshey farm which Lloyd was farming.

Our first child was a red haired daughter who did not live. Lloyd Edgar, Richard, Clarence and Betty Lou made up our family. Betty Lou was killed in an airplane accident with Jim Michelet on one of New Mexico's windy, dusty days in 1950. Rita McAllister and Loveta Williamson were with them but they survived the crash.

Mr. Harshey and Frances moved to Hagerman. Dewey had gone to Clovis to do railroad work. But Mr. Harshey became homesick for the old home so he and Frances moved back. Lloyd was doing the farming but we moved to the J.E. Blythe place, which my mother had bought, and which Lloyd was farming also.

Mr. Harshey became ill in 1925 so he and Frances came to our home. When he passed away in November Frances went to Artesia to live with her sister, Olive, and attended school there until she graduated.

We bought the Harshey home place in 1925 and several years later we bought the northeast forty acres of the J.E. Blythe place.

Charlie and Lloyd had always been together so Charlie continued to live with us until his death in 1927.

Frances married Ralph Pearson and lived on the Cottonwood. They had two children, Raymond and Abbie Frances.

Our oldest son, Lloyd Edgar, married Adaline Coleman of Dexter. They have four children and have lived in Alamogordo for several years. Richard and Clarence farm and feed livestock in the Hagarman area. Richard married Helen Keeth and they have three children. Clarence married Judy Lang and they have three children.

In the last fifty-five years I have seen the automatic washer displace the wash board, the kerosene lamp replaced by the electric pole lamp and the horse and buggy set aside for the Model T, the Chevy, and the Apollo space ship to the moon.

JOHN I. HINKLE

John I. Hinkle left Clinton, Missouri, in 1906 to accept the position of cashier in the Hagerman National Bank. He and his brother, James, were stockholders of the bank. He was twice elected prosecuting attorney of Franklin county in Missouri, and left a short time of his term unfinished to come to Hagerman.

Mr. Hinkle attended Central College at Fayette, graduating in the law department of the State University. He was a man of high character and won the confidence and esteem of the people of Hagerman.

Mr. and Mrs. Hinkle expressed themselves as being delighted to return to Hagerman and advance the material and other interests of Hagerman and vicinity. They resided in the Hotel Hagerman until they moved to a house west of the railroad, now the home of Mrs. W.M. Tulk.

John I. Hinkle's brother, James, was a member of the New Mexico senate and served as mayor of Roswell, New Mexico. He was governor of New Mexico in 1923-1924.

— The information for most of this article was found in the October 26, 1906 *Messenger*.

THE L.E. HINRICHSEN FAMILY
By Mrs. L.E. Hinrichsen

Lester E. Hinrichsen came to Artesia, New Mexico, with his parents, Mr. and Mrs. F.W. Hinrichsen, in 1909 in an immigrant train from Kearney, Nebraska. He was born in Mokena, Illinois in 1894, moving to Glidden, Iowa, when a small boy, then later to Nebraska.

Lester's father, of Artesia, helped erect the cement markers designating the Ozark Trail in various towns of the valley. The marker on Lake Arthur's main street is the only one still standing.

In 1916 Lester met Miss Doyle Womble in Wildorado, Texas, whom he married in 1920, after spending one year on the Mexican border and over two years in the army in France during World War I. He served in a convoy of U.S. Government trucks, driving truck #1, which took supplies into Old Mexico from Columbus, New Mexico, for the U.S. troops after the Pancho Villa uprising. He and two other young men were the first volunteers from Artesia for military service in 1917.

The Hinrichsen's spent their first month of married life on a claim fourteen miles southwest of Artesia, where he built a dirt reservoir for another claim holder. They lived in a "claim shack" with a dirt floor. Doyle laughs now when she tells about scrubbing the floor twice a week by sprinkling dish water on it. While the floor dried she went out on the prairie and picked up the next few days' "fuel" for heat and cooking. They hauled water from the nearest neighbor, six miles away.

They made their home the first six years on Lower Cottonwood, a farming community north of Artesia. While there, Hinrichsen, Tom Terry and Quincy Vaughn moved a church from a Negro community, Blackdom, west of Hagerman, to Cottonwood, which became a Methodist Church. Lester was the first Sunday School Superintendent and Doyle played an old pump organ until the church bought a piano.

The Hinrichsen's two older daughters, Doris and Alphadeen, were born while they lived on Cottonwood.

In 1927 they bought a farm a quarter of a mile east of the city limits of Hagerman, where they made their home for several years. Their first Hagerman farm home was the west half of a large two story house. A family by the name of Meeks, long-time friends, lived in the east half. After the first year the large house was torn down and two smaller ones were built, one for each of the two families. The Hinrichsens located their house on the "west 40" in a former apple orchard, pulling out two apple trees in order to build. Behind the barn was an Arkansas Black apple tree which produced fruit that kept well until March of the next year.

Their daughter, Eleanor, was born after they moved to Hagerman. The three girls started in the first grade and attended the Hagerman Schools through graduation.

After farming several years Lester worked at the Farmers Co-op Gin, where he kept books. Later on he took up the carpenter trade which he had learned from his father. He built numerous houses in and near Hagerman, even some at L.F.D. and Roswell. He remodeled many more houses and either repaired part of the house or some piece of furniture in a majority of the houses of the community. During World War II, when building materials were scarce for private use, he went into the woodmill shops at Walker Air Force Base, Roswell. Later he received a promotion and was transferred to Holloman Air Base, Alamogordo, New Mexico, where the family made their home for over two years.

Upon returning to Hagerman the Hinrichsens remodeled their farm home and lived there until 1950. They sold the farm to Vale Stewart and built a home on South Cambridge where Doyle still resides. She says she can't give up this home as Lester built the house and a large part of the furniture.

Their three daughters married and live away from Hagerman. Doris married A.C. White Jr., a newspaper publisher, currently owner and editor of the DeBaca County News at Ft. Sumner, New Mexico. Alphadeen married an airman, M/Sgt. B.F. Arnett, now a retiree after having served two years each in Alaska and France, and several years in the United States. They live in Folsom, California. Eleanor is married to E.M. Hill Jr., of Roswell, where he owns and operates a Standard gas station. She is an officer in the First National Bank of Roswell.

The Hinrichsens have seven grandchildren who are married and nine great-grandchildren with two more "on the way."

After suffering a heart attack Lester was semi-retired, doing only shop work, making cabinets and furniture. He loved wood — his favorite being walnut. He learned to live with his heart condition for several years but succumbed to the malady in 1968.

The Hinrichsens acquired a wheat and grain farm near Hereford, Texas, in the late 40s. Doyle still oversees the operation of it. She was for most of the time a homemaker. She gave some music lessons and worked in the Methodist Church as a Sunday School teacher, pianist and in the Women's Organization. She served on the various levels of W.S.C.S. work, attending their School of Missions eleven years consecutively at the Methodist Camp in Sacramento, New Mexico. She is now a retiree working with her hobbies — crocheting, flower arranging, making ojos and other handicrafts from junk such as bottles, driftwood, etc. She enjoys participating in the activities at the Hagerman Joy Center. For the last four years she has done volunteer work at Villa Solano School for the retarded. She helps the boys do embroidery work. Doyle never had a social security number until she became a Senior Citizen and has never had a driver's license.

C.O. HOLLOWAY

Chalmer O. Holloway, Sr. came to Roswell from Missouri for his health in 1905. He was originally from Indiana. Olive Hadder arrived in Roswell in 1906 coming from East Texas where she lived for a short time. Originally she was from Alabama. Both came to Roswell by immigrant train then called the "Hagerman Line."

They were married on May 17, 1916, in Roswell. Before marriage Olive Holloway taught school at Berrendo, Lake Arthur and East Grand Plains.

After they were married they rented a farm on the Cottonwood for one year, then in 1917 they moved to Hagerman and farmed what is now known as the north end of Howard Menefee's place then owned by the Occidental Insurance Co. While farming at this farm Mr. Holloway had one of the first tractors in the Valley. The Holloways moved from there to up state New York in 1919 where that winter they encountered too much snow. That spring they moved to Phoenix, Arizona, stayed a year and then moved back to Hagerman and rented the Rich Carter place.

The next year he rented the Ben Fife place south of the Felix Bridge. In 1928 he purchased the existing farm known as the Holloway Place where they lived until their death.

Mr. Holloway died in 1960 and Mrs. Holloway in 1969.

In 1933 Mark Dockey, Jiles Barron, Weatherston Greer and the C.O. Holloway's homesteaded east of Hagerman. The Greer and Holloway families still own this property.

They had two children, one died in infancy and the other, C.O., Jr., married Katie Page of Phoenix, Arizona. They now live in Roswell where he is a building contractor. They have three children.

Mr. Holloway was a Past Master of Felix Lodge #29 AM & FM and a Past Patron of Harmony Chapter #17 OES, an elder and treasurer in the Christian Church until it was disbanded. Mrs. Holloway was a Past Matron and was secretary of Harmony Chapter #17 OES for approximately forty-four years. She was a member of the First Christian Church and later attended the Presbyterian Church where she was a Sunday School teacher and active in many women's organizations.

THE CHARLES G. HOW FAMILY

By Charles Glendon How

My father, Charles Gilmore; my mother, Nellie Ware How, and I came to Hagerman by automobile in 1916. We moved from Collinsville, Oklahoma, because of my father's health.

One of the first memories I have of New Mexico is a covered wagon trip to the mountains west of Hagerman with the L.E. Evans family. We cooked over an open fire with a dutch oven.

Soon afterward we purchased the first farm east of the cemetery. From here I rode a horse to school. A school bus was unheard of then. At recess we played "Run Sheep Run" and "One and a Half." No teacher was ever bothered about bruising our young egos. The all time "champion" was a Miss Thacker, who would paddle you for clearing your throat.

My trapping career ended abruptly when I trapped and skinned a skunk and went to school. It was in the winter time and when I came inside the school room and hit the warm air, R.N. Thomas wasn't long in suggesting that I should leave.

Our food preparation was crude by present standards. We cooked on a kerosene stove and used a frame placed in the window covered by damp canvas and cooled by evaporation to keep our food fresh. Occasionally, a man would butcher a calf and peddle the meat from a wagon. We hunted quail and ducks over by the Pecos River, and, after our turn to irrigate from the canal water, we frequently found fish in the ditches.

No one ever locked their doors and a man's handshake was considered as binding as a written contract.

My father said that there were two things that couldn't be beat in Hagerman — the climate and the people. We grew alfalfa and my father was President of the Hay Growers Association for several years. He was also interested in organizing a Farmers Co-Op.

THE ROSS AND JOSIE JACOBS FAMILY
By Kern Jacobs

Ross and Josie Jacobs, pioneer residents of the Hagerman area, arrived in 1915 by train from Arkansas, with fifteen cents and three children, Carmen, Cecille and Kern. The family settled on a farm in the area west of Hagerman and worked long hours to make a living as farmers. Three more children were born into the Jacobs family in Hagerman, June, Wallace and Cleta Glee.

The Jacobs had moved to Hagerman for health reasons and it seemed a very good move as they both lived to late seventys and eightys. They had a good life in the community. They were members of the Methodist Church. Raising six children, making a living, church activities and all the children attending Hagerman school kept the family busy.

An outing was something unusual, but a well remembered one was made during the early years. The original family of five made a trip by covered wagon to what is now Fort Sumner. As the three children played behind the wagon they were urged by their mother to "get in the wagon quickly, we are coming into a herd of buffalo." The family had planned to homestead in this newer land but soon returned to Hagerman.

A close and hard working family, they never lacked for food, necessities and a well rounded life filled with love. As the saying goes, "we were poor, but didn't know it then."

Both Ross and Josie are deceased, as well as the oldest daughter, Carmen. Carmen had one daughter, Mrs. Larry (Jackie) Hess, now living in Roswell.

Cecille married a Hagerman boy, Elton Thompson. They resided in the area and finally in Artesia. After Elton's death, Cecille remained there. They had three sons, William N., born in Hagerman, who married Gaye Lair of Roswell and resides in Roswell now managing his cleaning establishment. They have two daughters. The third son, James, born in Roswell, also resides in Roswell with his wife, Ann, and four children. James is with the First National Bank. The second son, Robert D. also born in Roswell, lives in Albuquerque with his wife, Patti. They have a daughter and a son.

Kern married Grace Paddock (daughter of an early day Hagerman superintendent, D.A. Paddock, 1908-1910) who came to Hagerman as an elementary teacher in the 1930's. They have one daughter, Norma Jo, who married Richard Graves III. Richard's parents, Richard Graves II and Julia Ferrell, were also former Hagerman residents. Norma and Richard reside in Houston with their three children. Kern and Grace live in Roswell where Kern is part-owner and pharmacist of Cathey-Jacobs Pharmacy.

June Burch, a widow, resides in Artesia. She has two children, Wanda June Booker and Dr. Hugh Burch. Wanda and husband, Reese, have three children. Hugh and wife, Patty, have five children. Both families live in Oklahoma City.

Wallace Ray married Roma Bible of Dexter and they have farmed for many years in Bowie, Arizona. Their children are two sons, John Ray and Glen Kern. John lives with his wife, Sandra, and three children in San Simon, Arizona. Glen lives with his wife, Cathy, in Midland, Michigan, where Cathy teaches and Glen is finishing his education.

Cleta married Buddy Worsham in Roswell. They now live in Oklahoma City where Buddy is with the F.A.A. They have two daughters, Elizabeth Kay and Patricia.

Ross and Josie left five living children, eleven grandchildren and twenty-two great-grandchildren.

HUGO JACOBSON-JIM MICHELET FAMILIES
By Jeannette Jacobson Michelet

C.H. (Hugo) Jacobson came to Hagerman from Salina, Kansas, in May of 1918. He was in the real estate business there, and at one time his father-in-law, Mr. John A. Nelson, had traded a hotel in Kansas for a farm-ranch about six miles southwest of Hagerman. Mr. Jacobson took charge of the ranch until such a time as it could be disposed of. Mrs. Jacobson came out from Salina in September of 1918. The ranch was stocked with registered Hereford cattle, and there was a small orchard on the farm part of the ranch, together with some alfalfa and grain and, later, cotton. Mrs. Jacobson was active in the Presbyterian Church and Eastern Star. Mr. Jacobson served as Elder of the Presbyterian Church.

In May of 1919, Mr. and Mrs. Nelson came out to Hagerman from Salina bringing the Jacobson's youngest daughter, Jeannette. Jeannette graduated from Hagerman High School and claimed to have driven the first school bus in Hagerman. She had a Dodge touring car and would pick up the various children along the route to school. The car was usually full. Some of the children were from the Jacobs, Phillips and other families along the way.

Jeannette married Jim Michelet, the oldest son of a pioneer family. Jim and his brother Charles were members of the Old Battery "A" in Roswell and served on the border under Col. de Bremond during the Pancho Villa raids. Following their service, they returned to Hagerman and graduated from Hagerman High. After graduation Jim enlisted in the Army and served during World War I. Upon his return he leased the Tanner garage and ran that for some time. After his marriage to Jeannette, he started farming. He, together with W.J. Alter, bought a large farm across the Pecos River and later bought the adjacent farm land. In 1939 Jim bought the old Floto farm and the Lang farm and then bought Mr. Alter's partnership in the original farm. Jim was active in all civic affairs, serving on the Town Board and the AAA for Chaves County during the World War II years. He helped organize and served as President of the Farmer's Co-op of Hagerman. He was a member of the Presbyterian Church, serving as a Trustee for many years. He spent many hours working with the Girl Scouts and the Order of Rainbow for Girls.

Mrs. Michelet is active in many organizations, having served the American Legion Auxiliary as State President. She and Jim were charter members when the local American Legion Post No. 43 and its Auxiliary were formed in 1922. In Eight and Forty, a subsidiary of the American Legion Auxiliary, she served as State and National President. She serves the Presbyterian Church as organist and has been a Trustee, Elder and Clerk of the Session.

Jim Michelet started flying in the late 1940's and was a member of the Flying Farmers and came to his death in a crash of his plane in 1950.

Three daughters were born to the Michelets. Jeanne Marie married Vernon Greer and had a daughter. Vernon, a son of a pioneer family, was killed in action in the Pacific during World War II. Jeanne later married Jim Langenegger, son of Ernest Langenegger. They have a son and a daughter. Jim served with the Air Force, rank of Captain, in the China-India Theater during World War II. He farms in the Hagerman area, and Jim and Jeanne are very active in the church, school, and community.

Lucille married Homer Mayberry. Four children were born to this union, two sons and two daughters. Lucille worked for many years as a nurse in Roswell hospitals and still lives there.

Margaret married R. Roy Choat who also served in the Air Force in England during World War II. His father was a banker in Hagerman. They have two sons. Roy is a farmer and rancher. He and Margaret are hard workers in many organizations in the Hagerman area.

Jim and Roy purchased the Michelet farms a few years ago.

THE J.A. JACOBSON FAMILY

By Volga Ward

Jacob Edward Jacobson and Mrs. Selma Louise Jacobson came to the Hagerman area in March, 1898, from Kansas. There were seven children: Walden, Volga, Lillian, Arthur, Florence, Gladys and Jacob (who lived only a few hours). The family was active in the Seventh-Day Adventist church.

Mr. Jacobson was an ex-miner and had gone to Alaska during the Gold Rush. He was an industrious, hard-working man, putting his family first in his life. He helped Jim Cowles drill one of Hagerman's first mineral wells. Then he started farming and developed good farms for himself and T.B. Platt. He passed away in 1914.

In the earlier years there was not always a doctor in Hagerman, and Mrs. Jacobson with a nurse, Ora Corbett, went out and delivered babies. Later the nurse left, and, because the people insisted, Mrs. Jacobson went to their homes and delivered the babies. Sometimes she stayed for days to help care for the mother and baby. She delivered and cared for twenty-one babies. Only twice was a doctor present. Mrs. Jacobson was a good, God-fearing, pioneer mother, helping people in many ways.

Walden lived in New Mexico from 1898 to 1945 when he moved to California. He helped his father on the farm most of his early years, and, when his father died, he had to give up his education and take over the farming operations. He was attending school in Texas and would have graduated that year. He married a teacher in 1921 and had three sons and a daughter. One son is a doctor, one a dentist and one a fireman. The daughter is a nurse and is married to a dentist. Walden is deceased.

Volga finished high school in Hagerman in 1909. It was only a ten grade school at that time. In 1911 she went to an academy in Texas and in 1913 finished a business course. She went to Washington, D.C., that fall and took her first position. Because of the loss of her father and sister, Lillian, a month apart she returned to Hagerman to be with the family. After a few weeks she found employment at home, working in the mornings for Kemp Lumber Yard from 8:00 to 12:00 for 50¢ and in the post office for Mr. Platt from 12:00 to 6:00 for 75¢. She was later asked to come to work as an assistant cashier in the bank for $40 a month. After learning all the phases of banking, she was left to run the bank alone, while the cashier, Pete Losey, took his week off to go hunting in the fall. Dad Losey usually sat either in the front or the back of the bank, giving her moral support, but he could not even open the safe.

In the fall of 1917 Volga left Hagerman and went to Union College, Lincoln, Nebraska, finishing a public speaking course. She returned home to earn more money so she could go on to college. Hagerman High School had just put in a business course the year before and asked her to teach that year. She finished college in 1922 and taught in Minnesota the next year. In 1925 she received her Master's degree from Nebraska University. Volga and her husband, Leslie Ward, M.D., live in Redlands, California. Their son, Ellsworth, operates a dental lab in Healdsburg, California. Their daughter is a coronary nurse and lives with her husband and two daughters in Redlands, California.

Lillian Jacobson grew up in Hagerman and attended the Hagerman school. She was killed in an accident in 1914, just one month after her father's death.

Arthur died at the age of six.

Florence grew up in Hagerman and finished high school there in 1921. She attended school in Texas, Nebraska and Washington. In 1925 she taught school (fourth grade) in Hagerman. She married G. Edwin Norwood, M.D. They had three daughters, but two of them are now deceased.

Gladys finished nine grades at Hagerman and attended Union College Academy in Lincoln, Nebraska. She finished a nurses course at Glendale, California. She married Arthur F. Kohler and had three sons. One of her sons is with the F.B.I. in Washington, D.C., one is in college and one died at an early age.

THE WILLIAM JAMES FAMILY STORY
By Mary E. Burck Tollett

William James and Jane Minerva Campbell married in 1878. They had three children, Mary Edna, William Campbell and Esther Jane. Mr. and Mrs. James, Willie and Esther arrived in Hagerman in November of 1909 and were joined by Edna in the spring of 1910.

WILLIAM JAMES (1846-1930) came from Nebraska to New Mexico for family health reasons after being advised by doctors to seek a warm, dry climate for his family. Soon after his first arrival in Hagerman by tourist train, he found and purchased ninety acres of irrigated land located at the junction of the Felix and Pecos Rivers. He named the farm "Red Bluff Farm" as the red bluff of the Pecos River formed a picturesque back drop for the land. Red Bluff Farm was owned by the James family until 1940.

Though his wife would have preferred a one-story home because of their crippled son, Mr. James loved good things and beautiful things and was at once attracted to the recently constructed two-story, eleven room house at 300 West Argyle Street. He purchased the house and many of the city lots in the Davisson Subdivision of Hagerman.

Mr. James returned to Nebraska to sell his property and move the family to Hagerman. Everything, including twelve Rhode Island Red hens and three stands of bees, was loaded into a railroad car for the trip. The family arrived in Hagerman via train but by mistake their car of possessions was set off in Kansas. They stayed at the boarding house until the car finally arrived. Strange as it may seem, the hens and bees were very much alive although the hens were temporarily blinded from being in the dark railroad car so long.

William James was a very successful farmer and was active in farm organizations and community affairs. He and Mrs. James were members of the Presbyterian church.

JANE MINERVA JAMES (1853-1936) was a frail woman and did not participate in many activities outside the home. She was an excellent needlewoman, cook and homemaker.

MARY EDNA JAMES (1878-1969) was a teacher in the Blue Hill, Nebraska, schools when her family migrated to Hagerman. She arrived in Hagerman in the spring of 1910 to help care for her mother who was very ill following pneumonia. She married Louis R. Burck in 1911, and they became the parents of the only grandchildren of the William James'.

WILLIAM CAMPBELL JAMES (1882-1926) the only son of the William James family was stricken with infantile paralysis when nine months of age and was severely crippled. Although he was not able to pursue a career, he was a source of much pleasure to his nieces and nephews during their childhoods. Willie was a member of the Presbyterian church and attended services regularly.

James Residence. This large, eleven room house was built by W.S. Davisson in 1906 and was bought by William James in 1909. It is located at 300 West Argyle. This house boasted a unique rainwater system . The entire house was guttered into a huge galvanized tank containing a charcoal filter. A carbide gas generator plant was used to furnish gas for lighting, cooking and heating. The large front porch with its columns was used for many family and neighborhood "get togethers" and, of course, by the younger generation for courting.

ESTHER JANE JAMES was born in Blue Hill, Nebraska, in 1890 and graduated from high school there. She became a certified piano teacher after attending the Webster Conservatory of Music in Artesia, New Mexico, and another conservatory in Lubbock, Texas. She taught piano to the children and adults of Hagerman for many years. She is a member of the United Methodist Church and was a charter member of the Epworth League, which was organized in the summer of 1910, and a charter member of the W.S.C.S. She was the church pianist in Hagerman for many years and worked wherever she was needed in the church, 4-H Clubs and Girl Scouts.

Esther remembers the good times of yesteryear such as hunting Pecos Valley Diamonds, meeting the trains at the depot and the home talent plays which were produced on the second floor of an old building on Argyle Street which housed a drugstore at that time. She recalls the train wreck of 1910, the hotel fire, the collapse of the Pecos River bridge, the dreaded grass fires and the chemical fire truck.

Although she never married, Esther is loved by many children. She did babysitting before retiring and is fondly called "Aunty" and "Miss Esther" by several generations. Her present residence is Sudan, Texas, where she has lived since 1953.

The deceased members of this pioneer family are interred in the family plot in the Hagerman Masonic Cemetery, and none of the descendants live in Hagerman at the present time.

WILL AND ALLA JENKINS
By Lois Jenkins Titus

Will and Alla Jenkins and their eight children settled on a farm two and one-half miles west and one-half mile north of Hagerman in October of 1929. They had bought the farm from Karner Blythe in 1924.

In 1941 they moved, house and all, to another farm one-quarter mile away which they purchased from Mr. Snipes, a Roswell businessman. An unusual thing happened to the sturdy old house. It had actually been moved to at least four locations. This "roving house" now sits on the Kern Jacobs farm west of town.

Only two of the members of the original family of ten now live in the Hagerman community, Ruth (Mrs. Mike Rhodes) and Vern. Others of the family are Paul and wife, Betty (Blount), who live on a farm west of Portales, New Mexico. Lois Jenkins Titus lives in Roswell, New Mexico. Naomi Jenkins Pierce lived in Artesia until her death in 1968. Lindon and wife, Joyce (King), live in Roswell, New Mexico. Wayne and his wife, Leola (Hermes), live in Lima, Peru. Josephine Jenkins Storey resides in Ridgecrest, California. Two young children, Maxine and Bernice, died at an early age.

Mrs. Alla Jenkins died in 1943. In 1960 Will Jenkins moved to Artesia, New Mexico, where he died in 1963.

Three of the Jenkins boys served in World War II, Vern in the army in Africa and Europe and Wayne and Lindon in the navy in the Pacific area.

W.H. KEETH FAMILY
By Dalton Keeth

William Henry Keeth of Kosciusko, Mississippi (1882-1966) was married to Elizabeth Testerman (1887-1963) in Avoca, Jones County, Texas, in 1903. They were the parents of seven children.

J.V. Keeth was married to Bertha Bailey of Hagerman. Their children are Dorothy Williams (Mrs. Homer) of Houston, Helen Harshey (Mrs. Richard) of Hagerman and John Henry of Roswell.

Clyde Keeth was married to Lula Green of Hagerman. Children from this marriage are Cynthia Howell and Josephine Howell of Los Angeles, California. He is now married to Leona Taylor and lives in Roswell.

C.H. Keeth (deceased) was married to Nina Morgan of Hagerman. They had one child, Karen Raye.

Miss Essie Keeth (deceased), a Laboratory Technician, passed away in 1956.

Jesse Keeth of Lovington was married to Joyce Steele of Whiteface, Texas. They had three boys, John (deceased), Shane and Bill.

Dalton Keeth was married to Pattie Wiman of Roscoe, Texas. Their children are Janet Sutter (Mrs. James), Lander, Wyoming; Jean Deal (Mrs. Norman), Greenville, S.C., and Jerry, at home in La Feria, Texas.

Lorene married Victor Nackard of Flagstaff, Arizona. They had four children, Freddie, Michelle, Philip and Vic. She is now Mrs. Lee Caffall of Artesia. Vic, her youngest child, lives in the home.

Our family, with earthly belongings, moved to the Pecos Valley in the fall of 1926 in a Model T Ford from a ranch near Tatum. My parents were among the many to lose their ranches in eastern New Mexico during the mid-twenties.

They had to sell the cows, forty were registered, for $16.00 per head and include the calves.

The Pecos Valley presented hopes for a new beginning, and so it was. What seemed to be a tragedy evolved into new assets in the way of churches and schools as well as financial gain. Papa rented land about six miles south of Hagerman. After three years he bought the Sunshine Oil Company, and the family moved to town. He was in business until he retired in 1957.

The Depression wasn't as hard on us as it was on most families. Having lost the ranch a few years earlier we were accustomed to getting by on the minimum. On the cotton farm, we were a "do it yourself" family except for cotton picking, and we did quite a bit of that.

The family was regular in attendance at the First Baptist Church where most of us made professions of faith in Christ as our Savior.

Occasionally my memory carries me back to those Sunday afternoon hack rides and the circumstances involved. A stray burro would at times roam through the country. Papa didn't feel we had enough grass for us to keep him. Jess would be commanded to take him off. Being an obedient son, he would ride him off for a couple of miles. He would just happen to have a hamstring and chain along which he attached to one of the donkey's front legs. The burro wouldn't go far.

On Sundays we often had other boys come home with us from church. We would hitch the burro to the hack and head for the hills on the east side of Pritchard Lake. On those fifteen foot peaks we unhitched the burro and shaves, tied the front axle to keep the wheels from being able to change directions and all but the burro driver got a breezy ride to the lake. When the burro was brought we went to the top for another thriller down the slope to and sometimes into the lake. This was climaxed with a good juicy watermelon snitched from the cotton patch.

THE KEY KLAN IN HAGERMAN
By Mildred Key Nash

There were ten Keys in our family circle when we moved to Hagerman that January day in 1928. I, Mildred, was the eldest of the eight children of Alex and Willie (Hawkins) Key and was then halfway through my sophomore year in high school. The others were Kova Nell, Richard, Marian, Doris, Maxine, Lex and Malcolm.

My dad had moved to the Pecos Valley in 1921, when, because of drought and World War I conditions, he had lost our homestead farm and ranch located between Weed and Mayhill, New Mexico, in the Sacramento mountains. He had borrowed money to buy cattle when they were high, and then, when the price dropped, he, like so many others, could not pay back the loan.

It was while he was farming a place north of Dexter that Hal Bogle, an extensive landowner neighbor, was impressed with Papa's industry, honesty and diversity, and made a deal with Papa to work for him. We had farmed for Bogle for several years around Dexter when he bought the Hagerman farm and offered it to Papa. It was on the fork of the Pecos and Felix Rivers, one mile east of the Pete and Jack Casabonne homes, on the curve of the railroad. We moved from the Twin Lakes, or Douglas Farm, one mile south of Dexter, on two hay wagons pulled by two spans of mules.

During the remainder of that year the "Key Kids" rode to school in a one horse drawn hack with a rumble seat. Two of us sometimes rode "Ole Copper," our saddle horse. The hack was fun for us and especially for our company. When the weather was warm we delighted in dragging our bare feet in the water as we forded the Felix River.

Later we acquired a 1926 Model T Ford, in which we rode to school for a year or so until busses started running. Then we walked a mile west to catch the bus on the Dexter-Hagerman highway.

Our nearest neighbors were Jim Cowles (bachelor) and the Charlie Coles (no relation), Charlie Michelets, Lations, Elton Lankfords, Mrs. West and the Menefees.

Papa always enjoyed the competition of exhibiting stock and crops at the Chaves County Fair and took pride in the ribbons he won. That annual fair, with its grand parades, carnival and fireworks was an occasion we looked forward to. I can see us yet — all ten of us piled in that Model T, "a'goin to the Fair!"

Because of his natural talent for regular carpenter work, as well as for design, Papa had a big part in the planning and construction of the complex cattle pens and loading chutes on the Bogle ranch headquarters located west of us. The ideas implemented were revolutionary in the cattle business.

We always had beautiful horses, as Papa loved them and was good with them. Several of us were avid horsemen and women and spent endless hours riding. In later years the boys admitted having ridden often over the Felix railroad bridge, running their mounts at breakneck speed through the salt cedars on the Pecos and climbing its steep cliffs, disregarding the horses' well-being completely.

We were always having company. Our guests loved the crowd of fun-loving kids, the horseback rides, the swimming in our private pools in the curve of the Felix River, hunting Indian artifacts, the merry-go-round that Papa built for us, the treehouse, digging caves in cliffs or hay and the big farm meals and freezer ice cream on summer Sundays and watermelon feeds.

The Key family was, through the years, very active in the Methodist Church. Mama, who had been a schoolteacher for six years before starting her family, served several years as teacher of the Junior Epworth League. In those days Hagerman, and all the Pecos Valley, had a great thing going with the church youth. Some of my fondest memories are of the wonderful programs and parties we had, of attending

Epworth League Assemblies in the mountains and elsewhere, which was a highlight for all who could go. Marian, Doris and Maxine, and sometimes the boys, took an active part in the church youth program also. Maxine was pianist for the Junior and then the Senior League. The girls sang duets, and we still get hilarious when we recall some of the comic skits they did on "fun nights at the church."

The girls also participated in 4-H, Girl Scouts and R.T.C., a social club, which afforded us many great parties during high school days. Mildred served as Girl Scout leader for two years after her 1930 graduation from high school. She was then working for Mrs. Blanche Hughes in the telephone office over the postoffice and bank.

The Key kids spent most of their growing up days at Hagerman, and, being always poor as far as material wealth was concerned, we had plenty of hardships. But we felt a sense of security, even during the depression years of the '30s, because of our stable, happy home, and the love of family and friends. The older we grew the more aware we became of the tremendously rich heritage we have in things which no amount of money could ever buy!

Everyone helped, not only with the routine chores, but with the mass production of fruit and vegetable canning. Mama canned for many years, using the water bath method, then began using a huge pressure cooker. The children helped each year with the hoeing and picking of the cotton. Although they had to miss school for several weeks each fall to pick cotton, my sisters graduated from high school with honors.

The most exciting time during the twelve years the Keys lived at Hagerman was the big Pecos and Felix River flood in May of 1936. Flood waters backed clear up to the railroad, one mile west of our house. Even though the house was built up three steps off the ground, the water was sixteen inches deep in the house. All the horses, cows and hogs had to be driven to higher ground, and the Key family took leave of their domain to spend three or four days and nights with the Elton Lankfords.

Mama, recalling the terror of that experience, said years afterward that the things which stuck in her mind, after knowing that her family was safe, was seeing her jars of canned stuff, fruits of hard labor, and a store house of food for the future, floating up out of the cellar and down with the current. Another pitiful sight was when her chickens flew from one floating thing to another, to finally have their perch washed from beneath them. A few that stayed on the pieces of barn, which lodged downstream, were saved. Had the flood waters risen six more inches, all the bedding and clothing which were stacked as high as possible would have been ruined. Lex, with the help of the Greer boys, removed two inches of red silt from everything in the house.

During the depression years Mama, determined to help her children obtain a higher education, enlisted family friends to save their Montgomery Ward scholarship coupons for her college-age girls. So our long time mailcarrier and good friend, Mr. Wimberly, and many others, were instrumental in Marian's, Doris' and Maxine's attending Eastern New Mexico Junior College (later E.N.M.U.) at Portales. Marian went on to graduate from Scarrit College for Christian Workers in Nashville, Tennessee. Several years later Maxine got her Masters from E.N.M.U. Doris married before finishing college and Lex later attended E.N.M.U. for one or two years before going into the service.

Both Lex and Malcolm served in the army during World War II. Lex went overseas, but Malcolm was stationed in the United States throughout the conflict.

I, Mildred, married Leon Nash in 1934 at Hagerman. We have two sons and one daughter. Our present address is Rt.1, Floyd, New Mexico.

Richard married Zelma Dorman in 1934 in Hagerman. They have two sons and one daughter. Their address is Rt.1, Morton, Texas.

Marian and Rev. Robert L. Main were married in 1942 in Nashville, Tennessee. They have three daughters, one son. Their address in 3829 Drummond, Houston, Texas.

Doris and Lloyd Jackson married at Hagerman in 1937. They have two daughters and one son. Address, 1315 S. Ave. G., Portales, New Mexico.

Maxine and Lowell Payton were married in Hagerman in 1938. They have one daughter and two sons. Address, Star Rt. B, Hobbs, New Mexico.

Lex married Hazle Harrison in Morton, Texas, in 1955. They have one daughter and a son. Address, Rt. 1 Box 120, Pasco, Washington.

Malcolm married Laverne Croft in 1944 in Rising Star, Texas. They have a daughter and a son. Address, 1208 S. Bassett, Eastland, Texas.

We lost our Papa in 1964, in Morton, Texas, at the age of eighty-one.

Mama died in 1970 in Morton at eighty-five.

Kova Nell, our precious afflicted sister, died in 1972 at Morton, Texas, aged fifty-seven.

We Keys get together once a year for a reunion and always do a lot of reminiscing about the "Good Ole Days" at Hagerman.

HISTORY OF JAMES H. KING FAMILY
By Ethel King Woods

James (Jim) King was born in Brown County, Texas, in 1885 and later moved with his family to Stonewell, Texas. At the age of twenty he met and married Bertha Kluting in 1905. They lived in a tent until their house was built. I, Ethel, was born in 1907. Two years later we moved to Emma, Texas, where Olga was born in 1909. From there we moved further west to Plains, Texas. Their third daughter, Beulah, was born in 1914.

Daddy had bought a car from a cowboy on the plains close to Lovington, New Mexico. One day he was driving to the ranch and was stopped by a Lovington sheriff. A man with the sheriff asked Daddy where he had gotten the car. He told them that he had bought it from a cowboy and gave them his name. The sheriff told Daddy the car and title had been stolen and the description he read fit the car. The man also told them that he had put a piece of iron with two red bolts at each end to hold the iron where the frame had been cracked. They looked and found the iron and bolts, so Daddy knew they were telling the truth. They took the car, the cowboy got the money, and it was a long time before Daddy could afford to buy another. I can remember how upset we all were.

We moved during World War I. There had been a drought, and, because of the war, many cattlemen had lost most of their possessions.

Daddy had a brother in Hagerman, so he went there in a covered wagon in 1919. Mother and we girls followed in a Model T car. Daddy bought the Ham's place, about 100 head of cattle and some horses. He rented a house in town.

Daddy and Mother joined the Christian Church. They and I joined the Eastern Star, and Olga and I were members of the Girl Scouts. Our leader was Mrs. Ditta Devenport. One of the important things she taught us was how to swim, and later, on a picnic, Olga and I helped save our mother from drowning.

The Ham place that Daddy bought was east of the Pecos River. He also leased land around there and bought the Bonigne ranch and land on the west side of the Pecos River. At one time he owned land up to the city limits of Hagerman.

During these years cowboys came from all around to help with the roundup's and branding. There was a lot of hard work and good times. The old home had such a beautiful yard that people came from all around to picnic and camp out.

I went to visit my Daddy's oldest brother in Southland, Texas, and I met P.R. (Son) Woods. We were married in 1923 in Levelland, Texas. Our only son, C.J., was born in 1925. In December we went to Hagerman and Son went to work for Daddy on the ranch. Son and I later filed on a section of land by the Ham's place and started buying and raising cattle.

When C.J. started to school we moved to the Bonigne ranch to be closer to the school. While living there Dad and Son planted a few acres of farmland. They took their farm products to the County Fair in Hagerman and were surprised but happy to win several ribbons. The cowboys with the green thumbs took quite a bit of teasing from the old time farmers. Daddy later traded the Ham place for the Walters ranch.

Olga married Stafford Brown in 1926 and had one son, Jimmy. After he was grown they divorced. She later married Ray O'Dell and moved to Truth or Consequences, New Mexico.

Beulah married Seaborn Price in 1929. They had two children, Charlotte Jo and Sammy, and lived most of their married life in Carlsbad.

The old home was torn down and a new one was built. Daddy and Mother lived there until the time of their deaths. Some of the outstanding things that happened there was the

Jim King

Jim King house.

marriage of their only granddaughter, Charlotte Jo, and in 1955, we girls gave a Fiftieth Wedding Anniversary open house party for them. Daddy was upset because people came from everywhere bringing gifts. He said if he had known they were going to bring gifts he would not have consented to the party. Later on, after looking at them and the cards, he thought it was very nice.

Mother passed away in 1964, and Daddy followed her in death in 1967. Olga died in 1970 and Beulah in 1972. They were all buried in the Hagerman Masonic Cemetery.

JAMES LUTHER KING

James Luther King (1868-1951) and his wife, Alice Coppleman King (1869-1939), and family came to Roswell the first time in 1915 by covered wagon from Bonham, Texas. After a few months they returned to Texas but in 1921 returned to Roswell. The father; son, Clarence and daughter, Willie, filed on a claim west of Hagerman near the Diamond A Ranch. The rest of the family attended school in Roswell.

In 1923 the family moved to Hagerman as the father was working for Continental Oil Company. They bought farms and started the blacksmith shop (later sold to Leonard George). The Kings and Streetys remained in the blacksmith business for many years.

Mr. and Mrs. King were parents of fourteen children but seven of them died in infancy. The remaining children who lived in Hagerman were as follows:

Nora King married Dr. Knight and lived in Ravenna, Texas, until his death. She returned to Hagerman in early 1940's and now lives in Roswell.

Eventhia married R.W.Streety (both deceased). They had two sons, Robert and Walter (both deceased), and two daughters, Jonnie Streety Stroud of Albuquerque and Ruth Merle Gunter of Roswell.

Luther James (Louie) moved from Hagerman in the late twenties and now lives in Medford, Oregon.

Clarence remained in the blacksmith shop until it was sold. He did custom combining for many years and still buys cattle. He has three daughters, Charlene Stewart of Alamogordo, Norma Jo Bohner of Lubbock, and Jean Idecher of Roswell. Following the death of his first wife

(Mattie Mae Barton), he married Bertie Merchant Bible, and they still live in Hagerman.

Willie married Conrad Christianson and lived in Hagerman off and on over the years. They are both deceased. They have three surviving daughters and one son.

Jeffie Ray married O.J. Atwood (deceased). She attended the Hagerman School. They moved from Hagerman in 1942 to Roswell where her husband was in small appliance repair for many years.

Rufus married Bess Meador. He graduated from Hagerman Schools. He and his wife have a store at Loco Hills, New Mexico. Their only son, Neal, lives in Hobbs, New Mexico.

— Information furnished by Jeffie King Atwood.

THE KIPER FAMILY

Phillip Edward and Lizzie Mae Cobbs Kiper came to Hagerman by train from a farm twelve miles north of Big Springs, Texas, in March 1912. At that time they had four children, H.A. Oscar, Eva Dee, Edna Dora and Charles Frederick. They came to Hagerman to work on the farm for S.W. Moore who owned several farms around Hagerman. The family first moved to a farm three miles northeast of Hagerman known as the Clark place. Mr. Kiper worked for $35 a month, six days a week from sunrise to sundown. The family moved from the Clark place to the Swan house, located one mile south of Hagerman, in 1913. They lived there until the winter of 1916 when they moved to the Frank Roland place located northeast of Hagerman. The family bought eighty acres of the Roland farm, forty acres of the Hall farm and 120 acres of the Lewis farm. Later Royce Lankford bought this from Mr. Kiper in 1946. Mr. and Mrs. Kiper retired in Hagerman and lived there until his death in 1968. Mrs. Kiper preceded him in death in 1954.

The three oldest children started school in 1912. They walked the three miles each way every day. Oscar was in the second grade and Eva and Edna were in the first grade. Miss Lucy Thomas was the girls' teacher.

Three more children were born to the Kiper family in Hagerman, Orville, born in 1914; Fielden, born in 1917 and Finis, born in 1921.

The family attended the Hagerman First Methodist Church.

In those days they had orchards producing apples, peaches, plums and pears. They also raised alfalfa hay which was the main crop. They raised a little feed and small grain. Alfalfa hay was selling for $6 a ton. Orchards were pulled in 1922 and 1923. Mr. Kiper was one of the first to raise a bale of cotton in 1921. He had to haul it to Carlsbad to be ginned. A little cotton was raised in 1922 and quite a bit in 1923.

H.A. Oscar married Neavada Carrie Rhodes in 1929 in Fayetteville, Arkansas. Neavada died in 1937. They had two children, Bessie Rue, born in 1931 and Caroline Janice, born in 1934. Caroline died in 1943. In 1938 Oscar married Ina Beatress Rhodes. They had three children, Elizabeth Neva, born in 1940; Doris Fayerene and Donna Wayelene, born in 1950. Oscar and his family moved to a farm three miles west of Hagerman where they are presently residing.

Eva Dee married Earl A. Camp in 1921. They had one son, Ray Lee, born in 1931. They lived in Carlsbad. Eva died in 1970. Earl and Ray Lee presently reside in Carlsbad.

Edna Dora married Arley Alvin Brock in 1923. They had two children, Alvin Edward, born in 1924 and Alvena Dell, born in 1933. They lived in Roswell. Arley died in 1968.

Charles Frederick married Ora Mae Stinnet in 1930. They had two children, Charles Edward, born in 1931 and Doris Lee, born in 1941. Charles Edward died in 1938. They lived in Dexter. Charles Frederick and Ora Mae divorced and Charles (Charlie) lives in Roswell and Ora Mae lives in the home in Dexter at the present time.

Orville married Delphine Lattion in 1932. They had four children, Orville Dennis, born in 1933; Rosie Jean, born in 1936; Eva Mae, born in 1937 and Betty Fay, born in 1942. Orville Dennis died, but the date is unknown. They live in Sheridan, Oregon, at the present time.

Fielden Alexander married Mildred Lorene Vance in 1935. They had three children, Willie Edward, born in 1936; James Hubert, born in 1937 and Mildred Annette, born in 1943. Willie Edward died in 1937. They lived in Roswell. Fielden died in 1949. Mildred Lorene married Leo Rogers Sellers in 1952.

Finis Edward married Zona Vee Mayberry in 1940. They had two children, Barbara Jean, born in 1941 and Danny Lynn, born in 1949. They lived in Roswell. Finis died in 1968.

THE B.F. KNOLLS
By Glynn Knoll

Benjamin Franklin Knoll with his wife, Lela Pearl, and their four youngest children, Coy, Irene, Sanford and Glynn, moved from Brownfield, Texas, to Hagerman in 1928. The move was made in the family automobile, a 1926 model Star, pulling a trailer made from a Model T chasis and a truck. After many years of dry land farming in Texas the fertile green irrigated farms in the valley had the appearance of a dream come true. R.N. Thomas, Daddy's nephew, was helpful in obtaining a lease on the McGregor farm, two and one half miles northwest of Hagerman, and this was our first home in the valley. After farming several years in the area Daddy bought and developed a 240 acre farm about five miles southwest of Hagerman, and lived there until his death in 1945. Daddy's crops were cotton, grain and alfalfa. He fed lambs bought from Jack Casabonne for several years. These lambs were driven from the Casabonne ranch near Hope and at shipping time the fat lambs were driven to the Mossman Spur for shipping. He bought the lambs for 3½ and 4¢ per pound in the early 1930's and later on in the 1930's for 6¢ per pound. These lambs were fattened on whole grain and alfalfa. He also fed yearling steers and they were fattened on rations ground on a hand fed mill. The farm is now owned by the J.W. Wiggins family and has been reverted back to grass.

Coy married Margaret Curry and lived in Hagerman until his death in 1946, when he was killed in a plane crash. Sanford married Ida Bea Lemon and they now live at Lovington. I, Glynn, married Juacile Barnett and we live at Hagerman. Mother, now ninety-five years of age, is in the Lakeview Rest Home in Carlsbad, New Mexico.

Footnote: By Juacile Knoll

Papa Knoll and Mother Knoll radiated goodness, kindness and love. They were honest, hard working people of German descent. Papa said to me many times, "Honey, we don't have in-lawitis where you are concerned; you are our daughter." Indeed I felt like a daughter enfolded in their love.

THE E.E. LANE FAMILY
By Alberta Lane

When I married Ed Lane in 1908 he was living on a 160 acre farm which he had bought from his mother after his four years in the Navy. The farm was in Missouri. I was the teacher in the one-room school which was adjacent to Ed's farm. We both were native Missourians. Our move to New Mexico came about through the friendship of Jim Williamson and Ed's brother-in-law, W.A. Brooks. The Brooks family owned a large acreage in Texas.

Mr. Williamson had lived near the Brooks family before moving to Hagerman, and it was he who influenced Mr. Brooks to come to the Pecos Valley to buy alfalfa hay. While in Hagerman Mr. Brooks was so pleased with what he saw that he bought a farm along the Felix River near the old bridge north and west of Hagerman. He then encouraged Ed and me to move to New Mexico to farm his land.

In November of 1911 Ed came to Hagerman on a freight train bringing all our belongings. I came on the Santa Fe train arriving January 1, 1912.

The house which was to be our home for about two years was small, only two rooms and not well built. There were many cracks left between the twelve inch boards used as siding. Shortly after my arrival another room and a big porch were added. The weather was dry and the wind blew dust. I think the wind was worse along the river. When the wind calmed down I would start my house cleaning, and I often measured a gallon of dust that I had swept up.

The water was very hard and not good for drinking. We had to haul water from a well near Greenfield. I could not get the clothes clean in the hard water, and I remember that someone suggested that we fill a barrel with water and add lye. After a time a scum would form which, when skimmed off, left the water useable for washing clothes.

We decided to build a cistern, but when the cistern was ready there was no rain. I asked the owner of the grocery store, A.N. Miller, when we could expect rain. He replied, "It doesn't rain here till June." Sure enough our first rain came on Decoration Day, and I had good rain water.

Our first child, Edwin, was born in October of 1912. Shortly after that we had more rain and the Felix River overflowed. We were awakened about four in the morning with water pouring into our little house. Before we could escape the water was waist high.

The first woman in Hagerman I met was Mrs. Lee Clark. She and her husband were managing a hotel. Earl Latimer, Sr., was the barber.

I was delighted when I found the Presbyterian Church as it was exactly like the one I had left in Peculiar, Missouri. The minister, Mr. Simpson, died soon after we came, and the Rev. H.J. Cumpsten and his family arrived in May of 1912. I particularly enjoyed the friendship of the ladies in the Ladies Aid Society. Along with others, I met Edith McKinstry and Edna Carter at my first meeting.

Front row, l. to r: E.E. Lane, Lila, Beatrice, Blanche, Mrs. Lane.
Back row: Edwin, Evelyn.

We bought a farm on the same road farther north from the bridge and moved there in 1914. We continued to farm Mr. Brooks' land. I was delighted to get into a bigger house (two stories), and we did much to improve it. At-that time the house was surrounded with apple and peach orchards. Many people had orchards; however, we often had late frosts, and the fruit would be killed when the trees were in blossom.

Ed bought other land including ranch land east of the Pecos. I did a lot of cooking not only for the farm help but for the ranch hands, particularly at roundup times for branding and dipping.

Ed was a lover of horses, and we often got our horses through relatives in Kentucky. We also had many Shetland ponies. The three older children rode the two and one-half miles to school in a buggy drawn by a Shetland for several years. Then they abandoned the buggy and rode horse back until the bus service started. They tied up their horses at the hitching post at the Presbyterian Church, fed them at noon with hay stored in the church barn and watered them at the public horse trough across from the depot near the artesian well.

Our closest neighbor was Howard Russell who lived alone for many years. He was seclusive in many ways, but he was a fine scholarly man and a good friend. He seemed so lonely that I invited him to eat with us often and always at holiday time. He loved the children, and they loved him and his stories. He sometimes wrote stories about the children, their pets and playthings, or a Christmas morning in our household. These stories were published in various newspapers but mostly in the *Kansas City Star*.

In the mid-twenties Mr. Russell surprised us all by marrying Lucy Rowley, a lady from Arkansas. She was a dear friend, too, and returned to Arkansas after Mr. Russell's death.

We had five children in all. After Edwin there were four girls, Evelyn, Beatrice, Lila and Blanche. They all finished high school in Hagerman but attended colleges out of state. Edwin lived on a farm near Hagerman with his family for several years before moving to Colorado in 1948.

Ed died in 1959. We had celebrated our fiftieth anniversary the year before. I continued living on the farm until 1970 when I moved to Albuquerque to be near my daughters, Evelyn, Beatrice and Lila.

In spite of the wind and dust and the hard water, I love Hagerman and my many friends and memories there. We had such good times together; Hagerman is really my home. The family, as of June, 1975, is as follows:

Edwin married Frances Mountcastle, and they have three children, Ed Lane III, Philip and Janet. Ed and Frances live in Ignacio, Colorado.

Evelyn married J. Douglass Williams, and they have three children, Lane, Jim and Helene. They live in Albuquerque.

Beatrice married Frederick Leckman and lives in Albuquerque. They had two children, Patricia and Stephen. Stephen died in May, 1973.

Blanche married Albert Tompkins and lives in San Bernardino, California. They have two sons, Hal and Bill.

LEONARD M. LANG FAMILY
By Nell L. Casabonne

Leonard M. Lang was born in 1878 and raised in Brenham, Texas, a son of German immigrant parents and one of thirteen children. There he met Lula Barnett, the daughter of a farmer and a Primitive Baptist preacher, and they were married in 1900 at Wood, Territory of Oklahoma. They moved to Clifton, Texas, where he worked for the railroad. After Mother developed asthma and lost two infants, it was decided in 1905 to move to New Mexico. His oldest brother and wife, Otto and Anna Lang, had moved to Hagerman several years before, so they came to be with them. When he arrived Dad went to work in his brother's saloon as a bartender. Our Mother worked as a nurse caring for tuberculosis and asthma patients who came to New Mexico's high, dry climate for these diseases and who mostly lived in tents. They built a home in east Hagerman and Dad served as sheriff for one year and deputy for several under Judge Bailey. In October of 1908 a son, George R., was born to them. In 1909 Dad went to work at the Wool and Hide Co., a position he held for several years. Later he was employed by Roy Lochhead as foreman at the Hagerman Alfalfa Mill. In December, 1913, a daughter, Evelyn (now Mrs. Homer Collom) was born.

In 1916 they made a decision to homestead land and settled on a claim three miles on top of the Caprock due east of Hagerman. As times were hard and homesteading did not provide a very good living, Dad worked for neighboring ranchers, hauling freight, building windmill towers, barns and some ranch homes. He also took train loads of livestock to the Kansas City market for neighboring ranchers, caring for them along the way and seeing that they arrived in good condition. While he was away, his own herd of Herefords and the ranch were looked after by George, Evelyn and Mother. Two more children arrived during this time; Nell (now Mrs. Johnny Casabonne) born in 1919 and Richard D. in 1921.

As we lived so far from town when the two oldest children reached school age, a private teacher, Miss Margaret Lane, was hired who lived in our home and taught them for several years. As more children moved into the area a small school was established which was also taught by Miss Lane. When George reached High School age he moved to Hagerman and boarded with the T.B. Platt family.

In the drouth years of 1922 and 1923 the livestock had to be moved off of the range, so the family made a move back to Hagerman and leased part of the Harry Cowan farm south of town where we lived for a year or so. After selling the ranch to the Taylors of Maljamar, Dad bought a farm three miles east of Hagerman in 1925. All of the children attended and graduated from the Hagerman school. In August, 1937, our mother died, followed by George, who was killed in an automobile accident in 1939 at Belen. In 1945 Dad retired, selling the farm and buying a home in Hagerman, where he lived until he passed away in 1962 at the age of eighty-four.

THE OTTO LANG FAMILY
By Herb Lang

Otto and Anna Lang came to Hagerman from Clifton, Texas, in 1903. They had three children, Accua E., Freda L. and Herbert F.

Mr. Lang's occupation was barroom owner. He was one of the original petitioners to create the First National Bank and owned stock in the bank. He built the brick building which served many years as a general merchandise store and several years as Post Office. He built his home which later served the Zimmerman family until their children finished school. He also started the Hagerman band and purchased many of the instruments from his own pocket. The band continued after the Lang family left Hagerman and up until the time the United States entered the First World War. The Hagerman band gave a concert almost every Saturday night during the summer and fall.

Mrs. Lang and children later returned to Hagerman. Accua was killed in the first World War. Mrs. Lang died in Hagerman. Freda (Mrs. Alma L. Nail) and her husband still reside here.

Herbert was married to Bessie Anderson and moved away from here for several years but came back to Hagerman where he now resides with his wife. They are the parents of three daughters, Gretchen (Mrs. Ross Smith), Judy (Mrs. Clarence Harshey), Susan (Mrs. Ray McCullough) and a son.

Otto Lang Saloon, O.G. Lang behind bar.

ERNEST LANGENEGGER

Ernest Langenegger is a strong and sturdy man for his years. His good memory and stories of the past give a person the feeling of returning to Hagerman in the early 1900's. Sometimes when there is a question about the early days, the common solution is, "Ask Ernest Langenegger."

Ernest's father John Albert Langenegger was originally from Switzerland but came to Hagerman from Elbing, Kansas. The family spoke German and Ernest still remembers the language well enough to speak it. John Albert, a son, Albert (Shorty), and Ernest first came to Hagerman for Mr. Langenegger's health. They built a house one mile east of the Washington Ranch and when it was finished Ernest's mother, Anna Boss Langenegger, another son, John, and a daughter, Bertha, came to Hagerman to live.

Most of the family left Hagerman shortly afterwards but Ernest remained. Later John returned and the two young men caught and broke wild horses, often hiding in the bushes until the horses came to water, then they roped the horses in such a way as to keep them under control. They also worked as cowhands for the Diamond A Ranch and others. In the winter when there were no jobs they shot cottontails. The largest kill consisted of 625 rabbits in one day. The rabbits were then gutted, packed in sacks and shipped to Denver, Colorado, for 75¢ a dozen.

Ernest lived at the boarding house on the Washington Ranch when he first came to Hagerman. The ranch was located about two miles south of Hagerman across the railroad tracks. The buildings were made of adobe and were quite an attraction in the early days. Bill Washington was the owner and one of the earliest settlers in the Hagerman area. The ranch was the setting for many parties, dances and celebrations in its time. According to Ernest, Mr.

Washington came to the area in 1872. The house had eighteen bedrooms, a kitchen and dining room. Billy the Kid stopped there occasionally. The Washington premises also boasted "one of the largest barns ever seen," with forty-two horse stalls. A race track was also located there for a short time. Anyone who wanted to race brought his best horse on a Sunday, prepared to win. Side bets were placed among onlookers and racers. Later Sam Gootch took over the ranch. Trouble and fights began to happen at the races and Ernest remembers helping tear down the track in 1907.

Some of the homesteaders and the nesters were greatly hated by the first landowners and many disputes, fights and "dirty dealings" took place. Capt. Mossman who claimed a large amount of land was one of the men hated by the homesteaders and nesters. Sheriff Johnny Peck came to arrest Ernest for shooting at Mossman one day. At the time Ernest was helping Mr. Ehret stack hay. Ernest just laughed and said, "Johnny, I'm honored you think I shot at the old son of a b----." But when Mr. Ehret discovered the shooting had occurred at the same time Ernest had been stacking hay for him, the sheriff left. Someone had indeed tried to shoot Mossman and, according to Ernest, had shot out the back window in his car as he passed by.

Sometimes the nesters wrapped gunny sacks around their horses feet to leave no tracks while they spied on the big outfits fencing off a water hole. Shortly afterwards the fence was burned down, but authorities found no horse tracks in the area. They often sat on a hill with guns ready should the threats of "running the nesters out" become a reality.

There were many graves on the prairies in those days. Reportedly, if an alien came to the country to work and was owed too much money by his boss, he was shot and buried.

When Pancho Villa took over Juarez, Mexico, the fighting was an exciting adventure to the early settlers and many traveled to El Paso to sit on Mt. Franklin and watch the battle through field glasses.

Ernest and Hazel Moon were married in 1910 and to this union were born Ernestine, Ross, Bill, Ida, Jim and Jack. Hazel passed away in 1925.

In 1924 Zula Nations Knight came to Hagerman. She had come to Tolar, New Mexico, between Melrose and Fort

Sumner in 1902 in a covered wagon with her parents. While homesteading on this place both parents died within ten days of each other. They left six children, four very small ones and one married one. The younger children went to live with the older ones. Zula went to live with a married sister and remained there until she married Clyde Knight in 1916 and moved to Roswell, New Mexico. In 1927, Zula lost her son, Lem, during the polio epidemic of that year.

Ernest and Zula Knight were married in 1929 and now live in the town of Hagerman but lived on a farm southwest of Hagerman for many years.

Ernest started farming in 1910 southeast of town for Mr. Curtis. He sowed 100 acres of hay and for those days that was a lot of hay. He later farmed for Mr. O'Dell around 1924 and then moved to the Fife farm where he had to pull out the orchards to prepare to farm cotton.

Ernest's sons all live in the Hagerman area, farming and ranching. All have contributed greatly to the community by serving on boards of every kind. His two daughters live in other states, Ernestine in Texas and Ida in Oregon.

Ernest says you can say those were the good old days if you want to but the good part was that people were more honest then and if you had a friend who was really your friend he stood by you thick or thin.

THE JOHN LANGENEGGER FAMILY
By Their Children

Mother recalls she met Dad when he came by her grandfather's ranch with a pack of greyhounds while he was coyote hunting. At the Nail ranch they had a pet loafer wolf that they had to keep chained to keep it from hamstringing the cattle. When lunging after the greyhounds, the wolf broke the chain and was fighting the hounds. Mother and her sisters were trying to hold the wolf's chain to keep him from killing the hounds. They finally wrapped the chain around a post and Dad fast departed with his hounds. Later he was employed by her grandfather as a cowboy, and this led to their courtship and later marriage. John Langenegger and Annie Bell Hamilton were married in Roswell in 1918.

Mrs. Langenegger was born in Anson, Texas, in 1898 and came to New Mexico with her parents, Mr. and Mrs. James L. Hamilton, and her grandparents, Mr. and Mrs. T.J. Nail, in 1901. They came in two covered wagons and drove a herd of cattle with them. They spent the first winter in the Capitan mountains. In 1902 they moved to the Pecos Valley where her father and grandfather homesteaded northwest of Lake Arthur. In 1911 they moved northeast of Hagerman where her grandfather had a ranching operation. She lived there until she was married.

John Langenegger was born in Elbing, Kansas. His parents had originally come from Switzerland. He came to New Mexico in 1906 with his parents and remained until 1912, when they returned to Kansas. He came back in a few years and was employed on the Bill Washington Ranch as a cowboy. He recalls that they trailed cattle from the Mexican border to Black River and that it took three months. He was paid $1 per day. He was then employed on the Circle Diamond Ranch, breaking horses and doing general ranch work. At the time of their marriage he was employed by Fred O'Dell on his farm. On June 8, 1918, he was inducted into the service and sent to Camp Mabry at Austin, Texas. Later he was sent to camp in Florida and he sailed from Newport News, Virginia, on an European boat on September 1. The boat had been used to haul animals and the men called it a "cow boat." After twenty-one days at sea they docked at Brest, France.

Their first child, Wanna B., was born in 1919 while he was overseas. He returned to his home in 1919 and was employed at the Hagerman Alfalfa Mill. In 1920 a son, John Walter, Jr., better known as J.W., was born. In 1923 another daughter, Bessie Mae, completed the family.

In January, 1924 Dad leased the Oscar Green farm and the family moved there. In 1927 Dad bought the forty acre Henry Hannah farm. We continued to live on the Green farm until we moved to the Hannah farm which became known as our home place in February, 1929. Former Hagerman High School principal, R.N. Thomas, had lived on the Hannah farm until this time. In 1931 Dad bought from J.T. (Tolly) West twenty acres directly south from the Hannah place. In 1933 the Mitchell place across the road to the east was purchased. We remember the morning the home on that place burned. Our family was at the breakfast table when we discovered they had a fire. The burning shingles were blowing over our house and the fire department wet the roof of our house to protect it. The down payment for the Mitchell place was made with the bonus money the government paid the World War I veterans who served overseas. At that time most of this forty acres was in apple orchard with a few peach and pear trees scattered about. Dad, with the help of Buck Boyce and teams of mules and horses, pulled most of the orchard. A few trees were saved for fruit trees but on February 8, 1933, a hard freeze came and all these trees were killed. We had a wood heater and lots of wood which Dad had from the trees he had pulled. Bessie Mae's after school job was to haul the wood in with a little red wagon to fill the wood box. The hard freeze came the night after the day Dad had butchered two hogs for Mr.

J.W. Wiggins in the wind and heat. At about 10:30 that night Dad went out to see if the tarps he had covered them with were still on, and discovered they had already frozen as hard as rock. From this they knew they were in for a cold night, and Mother stayed up all night stoking the heater. In 1936 100 acres were purchased from Rich Carter, former Hagerman farmer who was then living in Carlsbad. In 1938 the last of the acreage was purchased. This was the Green farm on which he had first started his farming operation in 1924.

By this time Wanna B. had finished high school and in 1939 she and Stenson, better known as "Cork" Andrus, were married. They are the parents of three boys, Billy Ray, Jerry Lee and Louis Dibrell. In 1941 Bessie Mae married Vencil Barnett. Their children are Kaye Moore, Carolyn Anderson and Johnny Barnett. In 1946 J.W. married Anna Bell Tulk and they had one son, Johnny Millard (Rusty) Langenegger. J.W. passed away in 1962.

It was a happy and memorable occasion when Mother's and Dad's golden wedding anniversary was honored by their daughters with a reception in the home of Vencil and Bessie Mae on January 28, 1968.

Mr. and Mrs. John Langenegger, wedding picture.

The following is taken from the *New Mexico Magazine,* — 1935 issue

Written by Wilfred McCormick

Few here in Hagerman will ever forget one eventful evening, years ago. The director of a traveling Wild West Show bellowed an offer of twenty-five dollars to the man who would ride their "Figure Two" horse the length of the arena.

John Langenegger crawled through the ropes.

"I reckon I can use some of that money," he drawled lazily. "Where's your nag?"

The showman seemed to eye him scornfully. John's gingham shirt was open at the collar, unadorned by any fancy bandanna. His pants were the faded bib overalls of a typical farmer. To complete the outward impression of being a novice at the game, John was wearing shoes instead of boots!

The director, thinking this rube volunteer would be even easier than the average for their famous outlaw, gave haughty assent to the ride. He suggested a side bet. It was promptly called. Other money passed to stake holders.

John climbed into the saddle.

What happened is history-in Hagerman!

"Figure Two" proved that he could buck, all right. But he was trying to unseat one of the greatest horsemen in New Mexico, and his cause was hopeless. The unknown "sucker" was an easy winner, efficiently demonstrating to some three or four hundred delighted patrons that he could have ridden the horse the rest of the night.

"An' why shouldn't I?" scoffed John afterwards. "That's the way I make my bread an' butter-forkin broomtails, just like that, for forty a month. This was just a little overtime!"

THE ELTON LANKFORD FAMILY

By Florene Menefee

Elton Lankford, a widower, brought his five children to Hagerman in 1924. Moving to Hagerman at the same time was his twin brother and his wife, Elmer and Bess Lankford.

In the early summer of 1924 the Lankford brothers bought a farm north-west of Hagerman. This farm was unimproved. Mrs. Elton Lankford passed away in 1924, but, having already made plans to move, the brothers rented a farm north of Hagerman owned by Guy Robinson and embarked upon a new life in what we thought was a desert.

The family came from Sulphur Springs, Texas, to Roswell in a 1921 and a 1924 Model T Fords. This required three days traveling time.

The day we left Texas, the fifth day of November, was the day Ma Ferguson was elected Governor of Texas. On the tenth day we set up batching facilities in a house on the farm. Late in the evening on the fifteenth day the household goods and livestock arrived by freight train and the car was docked at Russell Spur which was located at the Casabonne Curve.

Elton Lankford accompanied the freight car which took ten days to arrive. At the time of the move there was a quarantine on cattle for anthrax in New Mexico and the car was held up in Clovis. By the time the car reached Roswell the horses legs were swelling and the seven head were unloaded from the car and driven to Hagerman. The cows remained in the car and were unloaded at Russell Spur.

The children, Ray, Royce, Florene, Everett and Delpha, were enrolled in the Hagerman school from which they all graduated. Four of them went on to college. One, Ray, completed his college work. We commuted to school on foot, horseback, buggy, Model T Ford, Model A Ford and later by school bus driven by Earl Stine.

On our first day in school we inquired as to where the Baptist Church was and on Sunday morning found our way to the church where we received a warm welcome from such families as the Levi Barnetts, Adam Zimmermans, E.A. Whites, G.B. Newsoms, W.E. Dodsons and many more.

In the fall of 1926 our father bought a farm three miles north of Hagerman from E.P. Malone of Cottonwood. He made this his home until 1947 when he retired from farming. He built a house in town, has rent property and an interest in cattle feeding. Our father has fifteen grandchildren and twenty-four great-grandchildren.

There are many people to whom we could pay tribute for making Hagerman a wonderful place to live. We learned from them that this place was not a desert but truly the Land of Enchantment.

THE FRANK LATTION FAMILY
By Micheline Lattion Claunch

Frank Lattion with his parents and seven brothers and sisters sailed from Switzerland to America in about 1894. After sailing on the great Atlantic for many days and then traveling by train for many more days they settled at Hagerman and did farming and later moved to Dayton, New Mexico. Agriculture was their dream. The Lattions became prosperous and very happy in their newly adopted country with all of its freedoms.

Frank and his brother, Tom, had seen many acres of grass, stirrup high, that was unused because of the lack of water. This inspired them to start drilling water wells for the farm on the plains and in the Caprock area. When it was necessary they would make the two day trip from the Caprock area to Dayton for their supplies, visit the relatives and attend church. The Lattions were all of the Catholic faith. Their Bibles were written in French.

Frank and Tom took the time, on these occasions, to visit with their new friends and thereby to learn the language of their new country. Some of these friends were John and Felix Cauhape, the Runyan brothers and Don Crockett — all from the Dayton, Penasco and Hope area.

The two young men worked many months at drilling before my father found his dream ranch location, just below the Caprock, thirty-five miles east of Hagerman. Dad drilled the well for his ranch and put up a big Samson windmill with the bottom of the tower walled in. He even had a door and a window in the well house and greatly admired his very own first water well. Then my father, with the help of

Tom, built his first house, a neat small one-room rock house. Tom then returned to the family at Dayton to farm, being a farmer at heart.

Dad built a fine herd of Hereford cattle, worked hard and spent many lonely evenings dreaming of his school mates in the "old country". So in 1913, once again, he and his mother crossed the Atlantic to Switzerland for a visit. This time he found his true love, Rosalie Doralie. They married and returned to America on the new steamer *Queen Mary*.

Father left his bride, Rosalie, at his sister's, Mary Michelet, in Hagerman while he returned to the ranch. He didn't have the heart or the courage to take his Rosalie to the one-room house, so he worked long hours and built a pretty three-room house for her.

Mother, being a girl from the city and having heard stories of wild cowboys in America, was frightened when Dad was away from home and would always pull the window shades down. But she soon lost her fright and learned to love the young cowboys, Clyde and Bill Zimmerman, who stopped by occasionally.

When the oldest children reached school age our schooling became a great problem, as there was not enough children in our area for a school. My parents had to make a decision, whether to move to town or remain on the ranch, north of Cedar Point, and figure out another way for us to get our education. So Dad got two burros for my brother, Raymond, and me to ride to the Clabe Kile ranch, four or five miles away. We stayed with the Kiles through the week and rode back home for the weekend. Cordie Kile was our very first schoolteacher.

Clyde Browning and Dad spent much time in getting a school bus route established to the two-room school house at Mescalero, thirty-five miles away. What a happy day it was when Dad came home with a new truck, built into a school bus! He was the bus driver because the Lattion ranch was at the end of the bus line. David Marly, an eighteen year old boy, was our schoolteacher then. One day we all decided to play "hookey," got our "Karo syrup" lunch buckets and ran as fast as we could to the Caprock. Mr. Marly soon joined us, bringing his lunch along and we all had a lovely day picnicking, climbing the hills and wading in the spring water (or perhaps it was just a water hole). Present were children of the Clyde Brownings, Allen Doyles, Lyman and Jack Graham, the Williams, Waldrops, Yorks, Roberts, Tulks, Sunny James and the Lattions.

On cold days our teacher, Mr. Marly, would cook a big pot of soup for our dinners. Each child furnished his share of the ingredients. So you see we had hot lunches fifty years ago. Then in about 1931 we started going to school at Hagerman where we all finished our high school education. Dad was the bus driver, as once again we were on the end of the bus line.

By this time Dad had sold our ranch to Adam Zimmerman and we had moved to a ranch down in the sand country, south of the original home place.

Dad had taken mother and us children to Dayton to visit the relatives when one night when we were staying at our Uncle Phil and Aunt Christine Ramuz house Adam Zimmerman came to tell us that our Dad had fallen off the windmill tower. He was badly injured but still alive.

Our Dad thought that Adam Zimmerman would be there to help him put up a new windmill wheel but got impatient waiting for Adam so he decided to start the work alone that morning. He climbed to the top of the tower and began dismantling the old wheel, a section at a time. Then he would lower each section to the ground with a long rope. All went well until the rope tangled around his foot and jerked him to the ground. He lay unconscious for several hours. He had on heavy shoes that laced, and, after he became conscious, he found a wire close by and managed to catch it through the shoe laces. This helped to hold the broken leg a little more securely. He worked his way on his back, using his elbows, to the house which was about 100 feet away. Both wrists were broken and the bone was protruding through the flesh of his leg just below the hip. He reached the house by sundown and somehow got into the house and on the bed by dark. But he had to fight a hog off during this torturing ordeal. The hog smelled the blood from the severe head injury which almost took the sight of one eye. He managed once, with the help of a broom for a crutch, to get to the kitchen where he found a gallon of frozen milk. This all happened in February and Dad had opened the doors and windows that morning, before climbing the tower, to air the house. It was very cold and Dad's feet and ears were frost bitten. Finally after eight days and nights Adam Zimmerman and a friend drove up to the gate. The first thing they saw was Dad's favorite horse tied to the wagon almost dead from starvation. They rushed inside, and, at the sight of Dad, Adam almost fainted. Dad assured them that he would be O.K. if they would get Rosalie and Dr. Stroup. He recovered after many months in bed.

Gladys and Raymond were both bitten by rattlesnakes. Dad was gone from home when Gladys was bitten, so after much difficulty, twelve hours later we got her to town and the doctor. Mother had given her first aid the best that she could, but the child almost died. When Raymond was bitten he was brought to the Michelets' and with the help of Dr. Brown survived.

Our mother had learned to speak English by studying the Montgomery Ward catalog. So in the 1920's after the P.T.A. was organized at our little school on the Caprock she was often invited to speak. Her favorite topics were America and her native land of Switzerland. Her English was perhaps not perfect, but to me beautiful, as she unfolded her feelings about the new land of America that she loved.

Our parents shared a great love for each other and their children, and our lives went on happily. In 1929 our mother's dream of visiting her relatives with her husband and children was about to become a reality. We had written for our passports to Switzerland, planning to start on our journey in May, 1930. The Montgomery Ward catalog was in constant use and many hours spent in planning the trip. The family was also making plans for a new brother or sister who was to arrive in December of 1929.

Our dreams came to a sudden end when our mother died on January 5, 1930, leaving a two weeks old daughter, Geraldine Noel, who died in June, 1930.

Our father married again and in 1954 died in Levelland, Texas.

Eda was the first of the Lattion children to marry when she married Fred Philan (deceased). They had three daughters. Eda is now married to Allison Shambrook. They have one child.

Micheline married Vernon Walker (deceased). They had three children. Micheline is now married to W.H. Claunch.

Francis married Charlie Walker (deceased) and had two daughters. Francis is now married to George Partridge.

Anna Mary married Curly Derrick and has two sons.

Raymond (deceased) was married to Lois Pinkenton.

Gladys married Dwain Jones and has two children.

Rose Blanche married Barrett Ingram. They have four children.

HARVEY W. LITTLE
By Clara Little Tankersley

In 1905 Harvey W. Little, a young man of twenty-one years, left Kansas and came to New Mexico, partially because of his health, for he had suffered with asthma most of his life, and partially because of the incentive to "Go West, young man." He worked for a year on the Hagerman Ranch southeast of Roswell and there learned something of the ways of cowboys. But life as a single man was not for him. On October 23, 1906, he married his schoolgirl sweetheart, Cornelia M. Weekes, in Eskridge, Kansas, and together they came back to New Mexico by train. They spent a short while in Roswell, where his sister, Laura Rutledge, was living, then later moved on to Hagerman and settled on their homestead six miles west of Hagerman, a short distance south of the Felix River.

Their first home on their homestead was a floored tent until they could complete excavation for a dugout, which also served as living quarters. They later built a small house, about 12' x 12'. This little house and dugout served as their living quarters during their homestead days. During these days their family grew to include two sons, Ronald and Ernest. Harvey tried farming on their land but this was not successful because of the lack of water, and so finally had to give it up after about three years. This land is about one-quarter mile east of the Artesia Highway and is just as barren today as it was seventy years ago.

Sometime during their homestead days Harvey's father and mother, Jason P. and Mary A. Little, came to New Mexico and also lived in the area of the homestead, but on the other side of the road. Another family, the Waters, also lived in that area for a while. While living in Hagerman, Jason P. Little, now past seventy, built a home at the west edge of town. This home was later referred to as the Pete Losey home. The building is still in good repair and occupied. Soon after completing the home, the parents moved back to Missouri where Jason Little died in 1911. This was a day to remember in the Little family. This was Harvey's birthday, also the birthdate of their first daughter,

Clara. Mrs. Harvey Little continued to make her home in Missouri and died in 1922.

Harvey Little and his family lived on various farm lands in the area — the Cline place, Charley Young place and the Vicker place, where their second daughter, Frances, was born in 1914. In November, 1915, Ernest died.

From the very beginning of their new life in New Mexico Harvey and Nealy were very active in the Hagerman Baptist Church and reared their family under the influence of this little church, and, in their adult life, the children have been faithful members of a Baptist Church wherever they have lived.

Around 1917 or 1918 the family moved to town and Harvey worked for the township as maintenance man and operator of the town water pump, which was located two and one-half miles west of Hagerman. He continued in this work until 1922. In 1921 another son, Joe, was born. Shortly after this the family moved back to the farm where Harvey farmed for two seasons. In December, 1924, the family moved to Roswell, where he was engaged in plumbing.

Cornelia Weekes Little passed away in Roswell in 1962 and Harvey W. Little passed away in 1963.

Ronald H. Little married Dollie Monk in 1926 and there were five children. They were divorced and he later married Mabel Danforth in 1939. He is retired from the Union Pacific Railroad and lives in Kansas City, Kansas.

Clara V. Little married Earl G. Tankersley April 18, 1930. They have one daughter, Viola Patterson. Clara is employed at Sears, Roebuck and Co., Roswell, as secretary and personnel assistant. Her husband, Earl, is Municipal Judge, Roswell.

Frances L. Little married Luther C. Tankersley, April 23, 1932, and they have three children, Bruce Tankersley, Janice Spencer and Joan Enfield. Frances is a piano-organ teacher with her own studio. Luther is retired from American National Insurance Company, Roswell.

Joe W. Little was married to Edith Faulk and they have three sons, James, Jerry and Ernest. Joe was a radio announcer in Carlsbad and was drowned while making a broadcast of a flood in the Lake McMillan area in 1966.

THE LOSEYS

Grandfather Losey, George Willard Losey, was a successful farmer and business man just outside of Omaha, Nebraska. Like so many people in that area, he became disgruntled with the winter weather and started hunting a warmer climate in which to go into business. Sometime in the mid-winter of 1910 he caught the Santa Fe train and came into the Pecos Valley. He liked Carlsbad but couldn't find what he wanted in the way of a business there. After spending several days looking, he started back out on the Santa Fe. George Losey has a postcard in his possession dated February 11, 1911, saying that Mr. Losey was in a little town in New Mexico called Hagerman, and he had found the business he wanted, the town he wanted to move to and the place he wanted to live. He said he was closing the deal on the First National Bank of Hagerman.

His wife and family were still in Nebraska. There were several sons and one daughter, Mayre. He wrote them to sell what they had in Nebraska and come down to Hagerman where they were going to live. This they did. Grandmother Losey, her youngest son, Willard Andrew (Pete), and daughter, Mayre (Auntie Babe to many of her friends), arrived in Hagerman sometime in the spring of 1911. Grandfather Losey purchased a big two-story white house in the 500 block of West Argyle. He lived here until his death in the early thirties. Grandmother Losey died in 1918.

In 1915 Pete married Eva Hillian. She had come to New Mexico in 1910 from Des Moines, Iowa, where she had been teaching school. She was born and raised in Winterset, Iowa. Eva taught in the Hagerman schools several years, before and after her marriage.

Their first home was a big white house west of the intersection of Argyle and the highway. This home had been built by a Mr. Little, and the grounds were spacious. The

Loseys added beautiful flowers, trees, and fish ponds. It became one of the showplace homes of the town.

Pete and Mayre worked with their father in the bank, which was prospering as most banks did in those days. Following Grandfather Losey's death, Pete took over and Mayre continued to work in the bank. Later she married Vail Stewart but remained active in the business until her death.

Pete and Eva Losey had two children. George Mark was born in 1925. He attended Hagerman schools until his senior year, when he transferred to the New Mexico Military Institute at Roswell, New Mexico. He stayed there for two years of college, then attended Washington Lee University. He married Ruth Cannaday of Roanoke, Washington, in 1947. They have a son, and a daughter, and now live in Marshall, Texas.

Jean, the Losey's daughter, was born in 1932. She attended Hagerman schools and Colorado Women's College for two years. She was married to John Wortman in 1951 and was killed in an automobile accident in 1952.

The Losey's second home was located at the east end of Argyle. This lovely brick home and the farms were sold by Mrs. Losey following her husband's death. She moved to Carlsbad in 1952 and remained there until her death in 1959.

Pete Losey played a big role in the development of Hagerman. He was best known for his business ability, but he supported many worthy causes, organizations and the church. He loved hunting and fishing.

In regard to his banking ability, the story has been told by many people, other than family, that when the crash hit in 1929 Pete Losey's First National Bank of Hagerman was one of three banks in the United States which kept it's doors open and remained solvent.

— Information supplied by George and Ruth Losey

THE LUSK FAMILY
By Helen Curry from information supplied by Mrs. J.E. Lusk

Oliver G. Lusk and his wife, Sina, moved to New Mexico from Texas in January of 1917. They were the parents of six children, J.E., W.C., Arthur, Wilburn, Roma and Lillian. Mr. Lusk was a farmer and settled on a claim twenty-two miles east of Hagerman.

In 1920 the family moved to Hagerman. They remembered that there were hitching racks all over town and the only place to buy gas was in front of A.N. Miller's store.

In the winter of 1917 when Elvin, J.E., was fifteen years old he drove a freight wagon from Hagerman to Carl Sam's ranch near Lovington. He worked four horses to the wagon. He would leave the ranch before daylight so he could get to town and load the wagon. He spent the night in the wagon yard. Early in the morning he would start back to the ranch. If everything went all right he would get unloaded by 10 p.m.

On one of his trips he got caught in a snow storm between Hagerman and the ranch. He had no water for the horses but he did give them grain. Everything was covered by several inches of snow so he could not cook breakfast. He had some frozen bread for that meal.

In 1920 Elvin married Bess Myers and they lived most of their married life in Hagerman. Elvin drove a school bus for many years and the children all loved him. Every Christmas he had candy for each child.

Elvin also served as town marshall for a good many years. If any one was ever in need Elvin was right there to help. He was loved and respected by all. He and his wife were faithful members of the Church of Christ. Elvin passed away in March of 1972.

None of the other Lusk family members remained in Hagerman for a long period of time.

THE McCORMICK FAMILIES
By Wilfred McCormick

The first dentist was brought to Hagerman in January of 1907 by William McCormick, a moderately well-to-do farmer from the north central part of Illinois.

William McCormick along with other prosperous mid-western farmers came to the valley after seeing "Magic Lantern" pictures of the region. They were all furnished free railroad transportation out to the new land to see for themselves that the promoters hadn't been lying. Mr. McCormick was one of those who liked what he had seen, so he resigned as chairman of the board of county commisioners; he sold his farm, and disposed of some of his livestock and most of the usual farm-and-home equipment.

Those were the days of large and closely-knit families. Only two of William McCormick's children, both of whom were practicing doctors, remained in Illinois. The rest all came in a three-day train trip to settle, hopefully, on a 160-acre tract of gramma grass land some five miles west of Hagerman about half a mile north of the dry-bedded Felix River.

Dr. Ivor B. McCormick, a recent graduate in dentistry from the University of Illinois, with his young wife and two children of his own were among those who came.

His father, William, was descended from a famed line of distinguished McCormicks — Cyrus, who invented the reaper, etc. The mother, Elizabeth, was a Van Doren, descendent from Dutch nobility.

With a substantial nest egg remaining after his purchase of this new land, William McCormick built an elaborate home on the property. The house was mid-western style, square, two stories in height, and had a large basement within the foundation. Also he built huge, Illinois-type barns for some prize horses and cattle that he had brought with him. He even built a tall "smokehouse" for curing meat, perhaps among the first to be seen in this area. The wagons and buggies were brand-new; one of his buggies had rubber tires and considerable brass trimmings, which with ornamental harness on a high stepping sorrel made quite a show in those early New Mexico days.

Meanwhile, of course, work had started on the artesian well that was to bring the real elixir of life to the farm. And as drilling continued, deeper and deeper, already William McCormick and his sons were busy setting out orchards, planting alfalfa and corn — corn certainly, because he had come from hog country and a farm just wasn't considered a farm without a considerable showing of pigs.

But somehow, something went wrong. Those artesian veins, fed from the snows and rains of the White Mountains to the west, proved to be tricky. Both to the north and to the south of Mr. McCormick settlers had hit those veins. But Mr. McCormick's well flowed for only a few hours that first evening. Water was visible in the pipe, however, just a little below the surface so he took the advice of "experts" and installed a pump. This was powered by a Charter 12-horsepower gasoline engine. It would be quite primitive by today's standards, but sufficient then to pull water out of the ground for perhaps a week. In the meantime, a large dirt reservoir had been built and duly "puddled," and ditches were in readiness for the crops.

Then the water failed again. It was decided that he should lower the centrifugal pump into a pit some thirty feet beneath the surface and the surrounding water table. That should give him all that he needed. So he started on the pit.

One morning before the pit was finished, the McCormicks awoke to see that a tent had been erected inside the fence on the northwest corner of their land. A covered wagon was nearby, a team grazing in hobbles. Aside from being within the McCormick's fenced pasture, this was not particularly unusual — covered wagons, two or three of them a day, used to labor along the dusty road that went past the house.

When the camper was still on the premises the following day, William, Jr., youngest of the McCormick boys, rode over to see if somebody needed help.

What he found was practically unbelievable.

This land was his, the nester claimed. It had been free government land, so he had filed legal papers entitling him to homestead it. In vain the McCormicks attempted to argue that they had paid out good cash money for a title to the 160 acres and it was rightfully theirs.

A trip to the county seat at Roswell was made. And the records showed that the nester was right — William McCormick's deed to the land was fraudulent; now he would have to remove all of his improvements within a stated time.

Either that — or he could buy the nester out!

That's what Mr. McCormick had to do and the price was exorbitant. Not only did he pay a huge "ransom" to get the other man to move off of his property, but he then had to file homestead rights himself and agree to comply with the laws of the day over a period of several years before the property would become legally his.

The wallop took all of Mr. McCormick's remaining nest egg. Flat broke now, he could only keep trying to get water that might still enable him to make a living from the crops that he had planted. The lowered pump was not a success, though it did furnish him enough water to raise one year's crop and to get the orchards started. For that year the 160 acres became a genuine show place.

Then the well went dry again. Faced with no future now, most of the sons and daughters with their families left for other regions, not to return.

Dr. Ivor McCormick and a sister, Alice, remained with the old folks; another sister, Grace, had married and lived on a farm of her own. William McCormick's income had now shrunk to his pension as a Civil War veteran, plus the few dollars he could pick up selling milk, butter, eggs and vegetables from the garden; this small plot was irrigated from a shallow windmill-type well that supplied their drinking water.

Through most of this, Dr. McCormick, the young dentist, had been the principal worker and foreman. Now something had to be done — and fast. So he went to Santa Fe to take the state examination preparatory to setting up a practice in one room of the big house.

But soon tragic news was forthcoming. He had flunked the examination. He dared not treat or even receive any patients until this legal requirement would permit him a license. A recent graduate of one of the world's foremost dental and medical schools, it was difficult for Dr. McCormick to figure how he could have failed — the examination had seemed quite easy at the time.

However, since exams would not be held for another year, and something had to be done in the meantime, he succeeded in renting a forty-acre field of alfalfa along the railroad tracks of old Russell Spur, just north of the Felix River. He and his loyal wife, Nellie Jordan McCormick, built a crude shack about fifteen feet square and moved in with their two children. They had a small castoff stove in one corner, which they could feed with Mesquite-root wood to cook over; and they had to carry water across the tracks from the neighboring Michelet place — the Jacques Michelet family had a flowing artesian well there, but it was heavily saturated with sulphur. By letting the water stand overnight, however, it lost much of the offensive smell and taste and could be used for the table.

With a cow from the original McCormick herd, a few chickens, and a team of horses, the young dentist went to work long hours hoeing ditches, hiring out with his team to neighbors, and putting his kids in the Greenfield country school, several miles to the north and west.

But adversity wasn't through dogging him yet. He lost his first crop of hay just after he had mowed it — a heavy rain that night made it completely worthless. Furthermore, the shingled roof of his shack leaked like a sieve; not enough pitch to the roof.

Perserverance paid off, however, and he did well enough that year to rent the neighboring Adair place. He moved the shack about a quarter of a mile to the west and attached it to an already existing two-room house. Now he would have an additional twenty acres to farm along with the Doran place.

Meanwhile, examination time rolled around again in Santa Fe. Hopefully, confidentially, he made the trip, and again he found the questions easy for an applicant so recently out of university.

But again word came that he had failed!

That was a bitter wallop, because in the meantime a number of Hagerman and Dexter people had admired his courage and had pledged him their "work" just as soon as he could legally set up practice.

Determined this time to pass that dental examination, he bought a huge book of questions and answers; it was supposed to cover the field of dentistry completely. For two long hours each night, and for one hour each morning just after daybreak, he would have his young son read him the questions — unpronounceable words, but phonetically near enough to give him a clue as to what the question meant — and he would recite the answers. He had gone completely through that book by the following spring; certainly now he should be ready.

But the results were once more the same. Sorry, but he had again failed to meet the minimum requirements!

The real big change occured one morning when a delegation from Hagerman led by Frank Anderson, who owned the livery stable, came calling on the dentist-turned-farmer. Anderson's message was crisply blunt. Hagerman needed a dentist. If Dr. McCormick couldn't qualify, then they were going to search elsewhere. First, however, he proposed they do some investigating into the reasons for the dentist's three successive failures.

The committee was not long in securing an answer from a member of the Board of Dental Examiners. "Dr. McCormick," he explained, "had never turned in an articulator."

An "articulator" is a molded set of teeth, both uppers and lowers, fitted into bees-wax gums over a mechanical frame which shows the "bite" when hinged together.

The committee passed this information along to Dr. McCormick, who was promptly aghast. Nuts — somebody was lying! Not only had he taken pride in constructing an articulator, but he had at least four witnesses who could testify to having seen him build it and had then been actually present to see him turn it in to the proper person.

When confronted with this evidence, and threatened with exposure, the examiner — a dentist with an established practice within twenty-five miles of Hagerman — lamely admitted having somehow misplaced the articulator. Probably he had done something of the same sort on two previous occasions; nobody will ever know.

At any rate, Dr. McCormick was hastily issued a license. He went on to complete his farm contract for that year, then moved his little family into Hagerman. Their first home was the so-called "Bowen place," belonging to the canal company. This was a deep but narrow frame building facing the railroad tracks. Dr. McCormick, with only a few primitive tools, such as an old foot-pedal engine and what they used to call a "Morris Chair" set up his office in the northwest room of this building.

During that first year he commuted on the train to Dexter on Tuesdays of each week, servicing Hagerman on the other six days — and nights. Those were the times when nobody was ever turned away with the toothache or ordered to take an aspirin and report to the office next day. Across the years, in countless hundreds of nights, Dr. McCormick was rousted out of bed to help some sufferer, while some member of his family shivered in the cold to hold a kerosene lamp for light into the patients' mouths.

Two big changes occured the following year. For one, Dr. McCormick bought an old barber chair to replace the Morris model; and for another, he was able to buy a home on South Winchester street for $1500 from "old man Beal." Eventually he later scraped enough together to purchase one of the real new-fangled chairs with its fountain cuspidor and with adjustable features that would make his patients more comfortable and at the same time afford him better working angles.

Dr. McCormick, in addition to maintaining an old-style office patronized chiefly by people who didn't have any money, did other jobs. For a time he had a small herd of Holstein cows and they sold milk and butter, getting up before daylight in "fly time" and milking after dark to avoid the same pests that kept the cows restless. He was also, in turn, the town Marshal, the Chief of the Fire Department, bookkeeper for the Hagerman gin. Then for some twenty years he hit on something that he enjoyed — and mastered: He was the combined Police Magistrate and Justice of the Peace. But there was little money in the latter, because he settled more than half the cases out of court, for which there was no fee. Nevertheless, his reputation as a jurist eventually became so widespread that he was frequently called to Roswell to sit for the magistrates there in important cases.

With the war years, people suddenly had a little money in their pockets to pay his fees, which had never gone up. They were one dollar for an extraction, forty dollars for a complete set of uppers and lowers!

At any rate, for the first time in his life Dr. McCormick began to take in money.

Then in 1945 the first of three strokes took away the use of his right hand. To a dentist, this was complete disaster.

Dr. McCormick survived until 1952, courageously cheerful though awaiting the end. He was buried in the Hagerman cemetery with Masonic rites, having long been a Mason. For that matter he had always been a devoted "joiner," member also of the Eastern Star, Odd Fellows, Rebeccas, Encampment, Knights of Pythias, and Woodmen of the World.

"Greatness" is such a variable term. Therefore, measured as one who brought relief from pain to thousands of suffering people, one who spent a lifetime making friends and no known enemies — surely Dr. McCormick was indeed a great man in the making of Hagerman that it is today.

THE "DOC" McCORMICK KIDS

I am pleased by a request to supplement the "McCormick Story" by a followup story on the generation of McCormick kids, whom Nellie and Ivor left behind.

Let's start with the youngest — Rowena went all the way through the Hagerman schools and subsequently attended Eastern New Mexico University which was then a fledgling college. After that, in the depression years, Rowena became a beauty operator for a while before her marriage to Red Meeker. To them were born two attractive girls. After Red Meeker's passing, some time later, Rowena married Frank Sanford. This couple had one son. Rowena — now widowed — is employed part-time by the Atomic Energy Commission as an Information Specialist.

Agnes also went through the chairs of the Hagerman school system. She learned the beauty operator's trade, worked in Hagerman for several years, then operated her own shop one summer in Ruidoso. At the outbreak of World War II, Agnes took special training and became a Dental Hygienist at the Prisoner of War Camp south of Roswell. She was employed there for the duration and then married one of the soldiers, Sergeant O.F. Clark, and they had two sons. Agnes died in 1964 and is buried in the family plot at Hagerman in the Masonic area.

Oldest of the three McCormick girls was Elsa, who had come to New Mexico as a baby from Illinois. Immediately upon graduating from Hagerman High School, Elsa enrolled in Barnes Business College at Denver. Later while in the Normal University at Las Vegas, New Mexico, she met S. Omar Barker, already gaining fame as a western author and poet. Mr. Barker was then on the teaching staff of the University. Elsa left the Normal for a couple of years to teach in Hagerman, then married Omar Barker for the start of a new era in her life.

Elsa became a prominent western author in her own right, first in short stories, then as a featured novelist.

Elsa and Omar built their first home in Sapello Canyon and after living there for many years, they have moved to Las Vegas, New Mexico.

My wife, Helene, is a western writer herself.

There are two Wilfred McCormick youngsters, a daughter and a son. Their mother was Eleanor Paddock of Hagerman, who lived long enough to get them beautifully launched, and then was laid to rest in Albuquerque, New Mexico.

For the first time in my life, I am now subdued and mellow enough to yield to a pinch hitter! So here is what the English Department of Eastern New Mexico University once had to say of Nelle and Ivor's boy:

Wilfred McCormick is one of the most successful and versatile authors of our time. He is believed to have more hard-cover novels in the libraries and schools than any other author, living or dead.

McCormick's first book was published in 1948, and all of his many books (over 50) are still in print.

He lives in Albuquerque, where he has long been active in community affairs.

ABOUT THE McKINSTRYS
By Elizabeth McKinstry Stoskopf

How I wish the history of Hagerman had been instigated a few years ago when my mother was still alive. Writing things like this were "her cup of tea." Or when the McKinstry men were alive, for they loved to talk and spin tales of the past. Their Irish heritage always showed through.

The McKinstrys were instrumental in the shaping of the little town of Hagerman. They must have made quite an impact upon their arrival, if for no other reason than they were so large physically. The men were six feet and over, and the women were tall and stately, too. I've often thought how the McKinstry men were born forty years too soon. They could have had a family basketball team with five tall men of six feet and over and two substitutes.

Remember as I tell what I know that for me it is rather like looking through the wrong end of binoculars, and it is only from my point of view. It is so far, far away and in the almost forgotten recesses of my brain.

Originally the James McKinstry family came from Armagh, Ireland, in about 1888. James McKinstry and his wife, Sarah Boyd, must have had the true pioneer spirit. To break family ties in Ireland and bring a family of youngsters to this country took an adventuresome type of individual with a lot of faith in the future. More than once I asked my dad, "Why did Grandfather McKinstry come to this country in the first place?"

Dad quoted his father and answered in words to this effect, "In Ireland there was no future. Land was scarce, so for a family mainly of boys the United States looked more promising."

To this country with the parents came Thomas, the only child of the age that had to become naturalized, Elizabeth,

William, John, Jim, Sam, Harrison, Adeline, and Fred. Edith was born in this country. All the younger children became citizens when Father and Mother McKinstry became naturalized citizens.

The family settled south of Chicago, Illinois, around Gilman, Onarga, and Danforth, and they lived there or in that vicinity for fifteen to eighteen years. The family were all farmers at the start and as the children were growing. However, William became associated with the Illinois Central Railroad, and as I grew I always thought of Uncle William as being my rich uncle. Fred went to school and became a lawyer, married and settled around the Kansas City, Missouri, area. Jim, Sam and my dad batched in Illinois after Father and Mother McKinstry went to New Mexico. I heard my dad tell of shucking corn when it was so cold he was sure his fingers or ears would be frost bitten.

The next move of most of the McKinstrys was to New Mexico. I'm not sure what transpired, but I have some old, old papers — a warranty deed between my dad and J.J. Hagerman and wife, Anna, on February 28, 1905. (Interesting along this line is that it was in the Territory of New Mexico and under the laws of Colorado.) At this time the printing was done in Roswell, and Hagerman must not have had a bank either, because there are receipts or coupons with the First National Bank of Roswell on them. If we think interest is high now, in 1975, I found interest rates in 1905 at 6%, in 1910 at 10%, and in one place a note stated if not paid in full at maturity, it shall draw 12% per annum, and that any failure to pay any installment of interest, the holder could collect principal and interest at once. Scrooges lived in that day, too! Also interesting was the fact that with the purchase of every piece of land were the water rights issued by the Felix Irrigation Company — this was in 1905, but by 1910, it is called the Northern Canal of the Hagerman Irrigation Company. Also I see by the papers I have, that in 1910 there was the First National Bank of Hagerman. I was more or less amazed that land sold for $200 an acre in 1910.

Grandfather and Grandmother McKinstry bought land northwest of Hagerman in 1905 and built their home on this land. Adeline and Edith moved here with their parents.

The McKinstry family. Seated, l. to r.: Harrison, Mother (Sarah) McKinstry, Edith, Father (James) McKinstry, and Tom. Standing, second row: Fred, Jim, Sam, and John. Standing, third row: Adeline, William and Elizabeth.

As for my dad, he married Ethel Mae Wilson. Mother graduated in 1909 from Hagerman High School. Olive Harshey, Ed Wranosky, Volga Jacobson, Edna Parks and Tola Lemons were in her class. D.A. Paddock, father of Miss Grace Paddock, was the teacher of the class. Mother received the honor of being the first graduate to see her daughter, Elizabeth McKinstry, receive a diploma from her Alma Mater. Mother and Dad were married in 1915. I remember Mother saying that she didn't know whether she fell in love with the tall, slender, Irishman, or with his good looking team and fancy harness.

The McKinstrys must have helped shape Hagerman in many ways. They no doubt were prominent farmers, but also helped build organizations. I found a paper which said that H.L. McKinstry was a member of the Hagerman Alfalfa Growers' Association in the Territory of New Mexico on February 1, 1910. The McKinstrys, while not paragons of religion, belonged and helped in the churches there, especially the Presbyterian.

My dad went to college in Valparaiso, Indiana, in 1911 and 1912, but he came back and went to farming again. Daddy must have had one half interest or owned land close to the McKinstry homeplace. Anyway, when Dad was about to get married, there are papers in which he bought land again, and then when Grandmother McKinstry died in 1917, he must have bought out the heirs, because there are papers for all of this.

Two of the McKinstry men migrated again. My dad and mother moved to Kansas in 1946 to be closer to my family. Sam and Loveta moved to Muleshoe, Texas, because their kids were there. To me it is sad that no McKinstry with the name as such lives in Hagerman. Willis, my husband, and I have two daughters.

A memory that stays with me especially was the summer that polio struck after a July 4 celebration at Lake Van — this must have been somewhere from 1927 to 1930. The Lane family was hard hit with several members having it. Lemuel Knight from my class at school died. My friend, Dorothy Sweatt, had it, and never did fully get over its effects. The youth of the Pecos Valley were asked to stay at home the rest of the summer, but some of us would go horseback riding to pass the time, and we thought this wasn't breaking the rule of congregating and spreading germs.

I also remember my uncle, J.E. Wimberly, running the *Messenger* and setting type and running the linotype. Later Uncle Ed delivered mail. In those days it wasn't against the law to do a lot of things, and Uncle Ed lent a helping hand to many a poor soul in trouble. In later years Mother was managing editor for the *Messenger*, and she and I both wrote the gossip column, A Line from E.M.

For me living in the Pecos Valley and near Hagerman was a wonderful place for a childhood. My parents and I had wonderful neighbors, my Uncle Tom and Aunt Millie, the Blythes, the Van Sweatts, the Utterbacks, the Andrews, the Heitmans, the Harsheys, the Lanes, the Menouds, the Richardsons, the Sam McKinstrys — just to name a few. I never knew as I grew up that Hagerman didn't have just the best of everything. I thought it had everything needed for happiness. And doesn't it still?

THE TOM McKINSTRY FAMILY
By Ede McKinstry Harshey

Tom McKinstry and Camille (Millie) Wright were married in Gilman, Illinois, where Papa was engaged in farming. Their children were Ruth, Ede, James and Edmund.

Our family together with mother's parents, Jonathon and Marie Wright, moved to Hagerman in February 1909. Papa had come ahead on a freight train together with the farm equipment, horses and a cow, as well as all of our household goods. The rest of our family arrived sometime later, also by train. I can remember us staying with Grandfather and Grandmother McKinstry in their home in Hagerman until we moved to the McKinstry farm home northwest of Hagerman.

A few years later Papa bought the McCoy place and we moved into the two story house with pillars on the front porch reaching from the ground floor to the roof.

Our family were members of the Methodist Church and Mother joined the Seventh Day Adventist Church in later years.

All the children attended Hagerman schools but Ruth died in 1915 from diphtheria.

I was married to Lloyd Harshey in a home wedding with the Reverend C.C. Hill of Roswell officiating. James married Fay Senn of Dexter and they had one son. James was later married to the former Bess Jones. Edmund married Auda Barnes of Dexter, and she passed away in 1933. Later he married Lula Denham and they have one son.

Grandfather and Grandmother Wright proved up on a claim west of the John Emerson ranch and shortly after this time, in 1922, Grandfather died and Grandmother lived with us. About this time we bought the J.E. Blythe place and sold our place to the George E. Wade family.

In addition to his farming interest, Papa was also an auctioneer and received the honorary of Col. Tom McKinstry. He was well known and held many, many sales throughout the Pecos Valley. His varied interests included owning stallions, jacks and bulls for breeding stock.

Grandmother Wright passed away in 1927.

In 1940 the farm was sold to M.D. and Marie Menoud and Papa and Mother moved into Hagerman on Morgan Street where Papa died in 1940 and Mother in 1959.

THE JIM AND SAM McKINSTRY FAMILIES AND THE AUSTIN SWANN FAMILY

By Jean McKinstry Allison and Peggy McKinstry Smith

Austin Swann and daughters, Eva, Minnie, and Loveta, stepped off of the train at the depot, making their first appearance in Hagerman in 1908. They came from the Jacobia Community in Hunt County close to Greenville, Texas. They spent the first night there at the Hagerman Hotel, and Loveta remembers that they even had a porter to handle their luggage which really impressed her. As it developed, the porter was a very good singer, and Loveta later accompanied him on the piano as he sang.

Austin had bought a farm south of town, but the people who were living in the house had illness and were unable to move out. So they, Austin and daughters, remained at the hotel for about a week. These people who were living in their house were Seventh Day Adventists, and they invited the Swann family to church the first Saturday they were there. The girls went and met many of the early Adventist members, the Walden Jacobson family, the Greens, the Charlie Coles, etc.

In 1910 John Swann, a brother of Austin, and family moved from Greenville, Texas, to Hagerman and moved to the Austin Swann home south of town. Austin and daughters rented and moved to a house in Hagerman on West Argyle. During this time Mr. Swann did bookkeeping for a business (unknown but probably a real estate firm) owned by a Mr. Vickers where the Tollie West family business was later located.

Loveta Swann graduated from Hagerman High School in 1910, the second graduating class. She had thought she would graduate with the first graduating class the year before, but a grade had been added, and she had to go an extra year and failed to graduate with friends Ethel Mae Wilson (McKinstry), Ada Lee Crozier, Edna Parks and others.

The John Swann family moved back to Greenville in 1911, and Tessie, John's daughter, stayed with the Austin Swanns in order to graduate the following year, 1912, from Hagerman High School.

During this time the McKinstry boys, Sam and Jim, sons of James McKinstry also of Hagerman, began to court the Swann girls. Jim and Sam had two horses at their disposal which they traded back and forth when they went to visit the Swann girls: Old Jeff who was reliable, and if you had him, you could tie his reins to the buggy and give your full attention to your girlfriend while he headed for home. Then the next time would be your time to take Jo, a fancy, high-strung horse. However, one night Jim tried tying Jo's reins to the buggy and courted disaster. A boy in a white shirt on a bicycle darted out unexpectedly and Jo, being very nervous, jumped causing the buggy to turn over. Naturally Minnie, Jim's girlfriend, was quite upset about this, and her family had a hard time getting the true story because she knew Papa would not look favorably upon her spooning.

On November 7, 1912, Minnie Swann married Jim McKinstry and Loveta Swann married Sam McKinstry in a double wedding ceremony in their home. Their sister, Eva, made all of their trousseau clothes. Before the wedding, Mrs. F.A. Adair, wife of the Superintendent of Hagerman Schools, hosted a bridal shower for Minnie and Loveta, one of the first wedding showers in Hagerman. Also Jim and Sam's mother, affectionately called Mother McKinstry, gave her future daughters-in-law an afternoon party to introduce them to her friends, among them: Mrs. T.B. Platt, Mrs. F.D. Mitchell, Mrs. Hinkle (the banker's wife), Mrs. Harter (a farmer's wife), and others. Jim and Sam's sister, Mrs. Edith McKinstry West, gave a formal dinner party for the young couples.

After their wedding, the young couples lived at the McKinstry home in town several months until Minnie and Jim moved to the Tollie West farm home. Sam and Loveta remained in town, but the couples later switched homes and Jim and Minnie moved back to town. Later Jim and Sam bought another place close to Hagerman, on the highway where Jim and Minnie lived for years and where Peggy, their daughter, was raised. In about 1920 or 1921 Sam and Loveta purchased the old Dr. Stallard home in Greenfield and had it moved to their Hagerman farm, about four miles northwest of Hagerman, where their three daughters, Sammy, Jean, and Mildred, were raised. The house which had been on this farm was bought by Sadie and Ernie Bowen and was moved to Hagerman. Their son, Junior, was born in this home. This house is still located in Hagerman on the Southeast corner of Argyle and York streets.

Austin and Eva Swann moved back to Greenville in 1914, but they only stayed a little over a year and came back to Hagerman in 1916. About this time Austin bought the house in Hagerman on N.W. York and Sterling. It was here in 1920 that Sammy Nan, daughter of Sam and Loveta, was born. Nearly three years later in 1922 Veta Jean was also born in this home. Sammy remembers well in 1926 when Jim and Minnie brought twelve day old Peggy, their newly adopted daughter, to introduce her to the family. Then one year later in 1927 Sam and Loveta had another daughter, Mildred Adeline, born in St. Mary's Hospital in Roswell.

In 1922 Eva Swann married Elza Powell, but sadly Elza lived a very short time after they were married. Later Eva married Ben Jack West.

The Swann girls had been Baptists before marrying, but after marriage Minnie and Loveta worked with their husbands in the First Presbyterian Church. Loveta was the church organist from this time until they left Hagerman in 1952, nearly forty years. Eva went to the Methodist Church with Ben Jack and was a tireless worker. Peggy, Sammy, Jean, and Mildred all joined the Presbyterian Church as young girls.

Jim told of helping to break the land out of saltgrass where the First Presbyterian Church was built in 1906. He became an Elder in this church and Sam was active in community organizations. He was a board member of the Hagerman Irrigation Co. from 1910 until he moved from Hagerman. Sam was also a member of the Hagerman School Board for twenty some odd years, serving as president for most of that time.

An interesting "family" story comes from Sam's being on the school board: Loveta was afraid to stay at their country home with the children when Sam was attending the meetings. Therefore the family always went with him and waited in the car. On one particularly windy night a loose board was blowing against the building and Mildred, being quite young, asked, "Is that the board Daddy belongs to?"

Jim and Sam, operating as McKinstry Brothers, had one of the first registered Hereford cattle herds in the Pecos Valley in addition to their farming interests.

Minnie was an expert seamstress and enjoyed making elaborate dresses for her nieces, her daughter, her granddaughters, and even her great-granddaughters.

The McKinstry girls all attended Hagerman Schools and Sammy, Jean, and Mildred are all graduates of Hagerman High School. Sammy and Jean recall that one of the favorite activities of the school classes was horseback picnics to local "sites." These outings could be either during the day or at night, but the night jaunts were the favorites, and there was much "pairing off" on these.

Mildred married Kenneth Osborn of Dexter in 1948 in the First Presbyterian Church of Hagerman.

Peggy married Edward Smith in the Presbyterian Manse in Ruidoso, New Mexico in 1952. She had two daughters by a previous marriage. Edward also had a son from a former marraige. Peggy and Edward raised all three of the children in Hagerman.

Austin Swann died at Hagerman in his daughter Eva's home in 1930, and he was buried in the Jacobia Cemetery close to Greenville, Texas.

Minnie and Jim McKinstry continued to live in Hagerman. In 1962 they celebrated their golden wedding anniversary. Jim died in 1963 and Minnie in 1964, and both are buried in the Hagerman Cemetery.

Sam and Loveta McKinstry moved from Hagerman to Muleshoe, Texas, in 1952 to be closer to their daughters, Sammy and Jean Allison. Sam died there in 1955. Loveta still teaches piano in Muleshoe and is an active Guild Piano Teacher as well as a Nationally Certified Teacher of Piano.

Peggy Smith still lives in Hagerman and manages the bookkeeping and tax service business started by her late husband, Edward. She also has farming interests that include the original McKinstry Brothers acreage as well as some of the land that Tom and Harrison McKinstry once owned.

Sammy and Oscar Allison live in Muleshoe, Texas, and have four children.

Jean and Harold Allison also live in Muleshoe, and have five children.

Mildred and Kenneth Osborn live in Lovington, New Mexico, and have four children.

THE JOHN L. MANN FAMILY
By Nadine Hanson

The young cowboy, John L. Mann, worked on several cattle drives, driving cattle from Texas to Kansas on the Goodnight Loving trail and the John Chisum trail. He was born in 1863 and moved with his wife, Flora, and two children, John and Nadine, to Hagerman in 1928 from Pecos, Texas. They came to Hagerman to open a grocery store and operated it until they retired. This store was located in the L & K Cafe building on the north side of Argyle St. Their first home was across the street, east from the old Methodist Church, on Argyle St.

Flora Mann was born in 1872 and died in 1956 in Hagerman. As a young girl she helped her father who was a doctor in Pecos, Texas. John L. Mann died in 1948.

John L. Mann and Flora Mann had eight children of which I am the only surviving one. I, Nadine, married Allen Hanson, and we live in Roswell.

THE RICHARD MANSFIELD FAMILY
By Bill Mansfield

My father, Richard Mansfield, and my mother, Laura, and I moved from Roswell to Hagerman in the summer of 1914. My sisters, Bess, Amy and Nell, did not make their permanent residence there as Bess taught school in a rural community east of Dexter and lived with a ranch family. Amy and Nell were employed in Roswell when the move to Hagerman was made so they retained their jobs. They are now living in California.

Prior to moving to Hagerman, my father had an engineering contracting business in Roswell and did considerable work installing machinery in the new alfalfa mill in Hagerman and later in another being built in Dexter. These mills were becoming very popular in the alfalfa growing areas of the western United States. Roy Lochhead was the owner or operator of these mills and he offered my father the position of superintendent. He accepted in 1914.

I entered high school in Hagerman and graduated with the class of 1918. There were eight boys and one girl in that class. The other boys were Karner and Frank Blythe, Harrington Wimberly, Lester Walters, Aubrey Evans, Ray West and Dick Lathrop. Beryl West was the only girl. O.R. Gable was school superintendent and Miss Perdita Morgan, later Mrs. T.D. Devenport, was class sponsor.

Growing up in Hagerman was a rare privilege. The best people in the country lived there. We were more like a family then just residents of a community.

I shall always remember one hot summer afternoon in 1915. Three other boys and I walked to the Felix River to swim in a favorite spot near the flume. First we raided farmer Jacobson's watermelon patch and left our clothes on the bank while we swam. Bathing suits were not generally in use by boys at that early date. After an hour or so we returned for our clothes to find they had completely disappeared. Thinking some nearby farm boys had played a trick on us, we searched every bush for half a mile up and down the river but found no clothes. By this time it was getting dark and rather cool, and we had visions of four nude boys dodging around the side roads to be as inconspicious as possible on the way home. At this point farmer Jacobson drove up in his buckboard, gave us a good tongue lashing and announced we could have our clothes as soon as we paid him for the melons we had taken. None of us had any money but we did some very desperate bargaining with him and he finally said we could pay him later. We gladly did, but this is not the end of the story.

The next Halloween night we decided to get even with him. He drove his horse and buggy to town and tied it to the hitching rack at Miller's store. We unhitched the buggy and pulled it to the schoolhouse yard. We completely dismantled every piece of it and hauled the pieces to the top of the schoolhouse. It was there for three days while they figured out a way to get it down. We never told anyone about who was involved in such a scurvy trick on the old gentleman. We probably would have been expelled from school, had we been found out.

In 1923 Florrie Blythe and I were married and moved to El Paso, Texas. My father and mother moved to Detroit, Michigan, about 1930 and after that spent their retirement years in Long Beach, California.

E.J. MASON FAMILY

Ezra J. Mason, his wife, Alice Benton Mason, and children, Cassius, Wingetta and Melvina, arrived in Hagerman in 1904 from Gratton, Michigan. Mr. Mason was experienced in fruit evaporation and all its accessories. For twenty-six years he had managed one of the largest fruit drying establishments in Michigan. Mason's dried fruit was known all over the United States and Canada. He bought and improved 120 acres in the vicinity of Russell Heights, Hagerman.

While in the Hagerman community he was an important figure in the development of the town. As a citizen and neighbor he was highly esteemed. He was a Presbyterian and a Republican. He passed away in 1918, and Mrs. Mason died in 1952.

The two daughters both died at a young age. Winnie was married to Henry Johnson and Mellie married Charles Tallman.

Cassius Mason bought and homesteaded land about four miles northwest of town, and he and his father improved the land and built a home on it.

In 1912 Cassius married Mary Boyce. They bought a furniture store from Henry Johnson and established the Mason Funeral Home.

For twelve years Cassius was postmaster. He was appointed an aide-de-camp on the Governor's staff, with the rank of Colonel, by Governor John Miles. He was a member of the Town Council, fire chief and Mayor for several terms. He became a member of the Masonic Lodge in 1906 and served as Master of the Lodge and Worthy Patron of the Order of Eastern Star. The first Silver Beaver award in the council was given to him for his work in scouting. He served as President of the New Mexico Funeral Directors Association and the New Mexico Board of Embalmers.

Mary and Cassius were the parents of two sons, Steve and Garner, and a daughter, Betty. Another daughter, their first child, died in infancy.

Cassius Mason passed away in 1955 and Mary still resides in Hagerman.

The E.J. Mason house, northwest of Hagerman.

The E.J. Mason rose hedge, 1912. Mr. and Mrs. Mason in background.

THE MENEFEES
Information from H.R. Menefee

John P. Menefee and Mendozia Robinett Menefee came to Hagerman in 1928 from Lamesa, Texas. Mr. Menefee was a farmer and rancher and the family joined and actively participated in the Methodist Church. They were the parents of ten children, two daughters and eight sons, all of whom attended the Hagerman school, except Valera. Valera graduated from the Lamesa, Texas, High School. After several years the family moved to Hope and then to Artesia. Mr. Menefee passed away January, 1971, at the age of eighty-six. Mrs. Menefee still resides alone in the family home in Artesia and will be ninety years old in 1975.

Their daughter Valera became the wife of Frank Curry. He went into the ministry and served Methodist Churches in New Mexico and Texas, and, in 1963, he came to Hagerman as pastor of the local church. From here they were sent to Clark Memorial Church in Artesia, New Mexico, which he served until retirement. They still reside there. Marvin and Lawrence Menefee both became Methodist ministers. Marvin's wife was formerly Mayre McIntosh of Hagerman. They lived in Midland, Texas, when Marvin passed away in October, 1972.

Lawrence married Ann Cox of Abilene, Texas, and he has held pastorates in Texas and New Mexico. At the present time they are serving a church in Espanola, New Mexico.

Alton Married Lena Bonomo of Roy, New Mexico, and resided in Silver City, New Mexico, at the time of his death in 1964. Gladys married W.J. (Bill) Burck, son of Mr. and Mrs. L.R. Burck of Hagerman, and they live in Langehorn, Pennsylvania. Glen married Joan Norris of Maxwell, New

Mexico, and farmed with his family west of Lake Arthur, New Mexico, until his death in 1973. Clayton married Maxine Parks of Paris, Texas, and lives in Albuquerque, New Mexico.

Donald married Betty Brown of Artesia, New Mexico, and farms in the Artesia area. Lynn married Helen Myers of Raton, New Mexico, and is living in Alamogordo, New Mexico.

Howard is the only one of the children to remain in Hagerman. He and Florene Lankford, also of Hagerman, were married in 1933 and have been engaged in farming ever since. They are the parents of two sons and two daughters.

Wesley Menefee married Beth Ballard and farms in the Cottonwood area. Truman married Maribeth Jolly of Albuquerque, New Mexico, and lives in Dallas, Texas. He is Chief Computer Analyst for Republic National Bank in Dallas.

Sharla Rae became a teacher and is living an interesting life as a teacher with the Department of Defense. Presently she is teaching in Wiesbaden, Germany, and was married August 2, 1975, to Major Donald Hamilton of the United States Air Force. His home is in Columbus, Ohio.

Linda Kay is the wife of Barry Jones who was raised in Electra, Texas, where they presently reside and he has a supermarket.

Pop always said the way to find where the Menefees lived was to go down the road to the house that looked like school was out for recess and that was the place. For a while after we moved to the farm north of Hagerman, which was close to the railroad track, one little brother was so scared the train was going to run over him that if he could not get to the house when the train passed, he would grab a post, a tree, or the spokes of the water wagon wheel and hold on for dear life. I won't call any initials but his name was Donald.

THE E.D. MENOUD FAMILY

By Marie Menoud and Jack Menoud

Eugene D. Menoud swapped his native Freiburg, Switzerland, for Eddy County in 1891, the result of recruitment efforts by Roswell's Charles H. deBremmond, a French immigrant. Mr. deBremmond sailed to Europe seeking hearty, able-bodied men to settle in New Mexico. Menoud was one of the "adventurers" who returned with him.

In 1893 Menoud found employment, and his future bride, in Carlsbad's Crawford Hotel. He was a bellboy; she, a chambermaid.

Idella Florence Fair, born in Kokomo, Indiana, moved with her family to Kansas when she was a small child. In 1893 she moved to Carlsbad with Mr. and Mrs. J.A. Crawford, builders of the Crawford Hotel. She and Mr. Menoud were married in 1896.

The Menouds raised two sons and three daughters. Before settling in Hagerman in 1921, the family lived in Roswell from 1906 to 1920. They moved to Greenfield in 1920 and stayed for a year before going on to Hagerman. Eugene Menoud died in 1943, followed by his wife in 1947.

The Menoud's eldest son, Maurice Denzel (Bud), married Marie Kristine Olsen, who came from Kansas with her foster parents, Mr. and Mrs. E.N. Hedges in 1908. Bud and Marie had two children, Florence and Eugene. Florence (Mrs. Alfred Yingling), is wife of an oilfield driller and mother of two children. She lives in Roswell. Eugene married Berna Dean Sperling Evans. They had five children. Eugene died in 1972. Berna lives in Carlsbad.

Mary Louise, the eldest Menoud daughter, married J.W. Harris and moved with him to Oregon in 1924. Several years after the death of her husband, Mary Louise married H.E. Bailey and still lives in Springfield, Oregon.

Alfred D. (Jack), the Menoud's younger son, married Byrda Dorman who came to Hagerman from Texas in 1931. Jack and Byrda had two children, Gloria and Donald. Donald died as an infant. Gloria (Mrs. Lupe Martinez), the wife of a bank employee, is an instructor at Eastern New Mexico University — Roswell. She has two children. They live in Roswell.

Alice married Thomas Woody and raised three children. Betty (Mrs. Bob Futrell), the wife of a civil service employee, is a housewife and mother. She has two daughters. She lives with her family in Warner Robins, Georgia. Mr. Woody makes his home with the Futrells. The Woody's two sons, Dennis and Clifford, live in Pecos, Texas, where they own and operate the Case Equipment Company. Dennis had three children. Clifford has one son. Alice died in 1958 in Dexter.

Grace, the Menoud's youngest daughter, married James G. McNamara. They had three children, JoAnne, Jimmy and Mary Bell. The two younger children died as infants. JoAnne (Mrs. H.E. Prince), the wife of a building contractor, is a housewife and mother. They have two children. James died in 1965. Grace lives in Roswell.

The Menoud family bought the Chedester farm one and one-half miles south of Hagerman where they moved when they first came to the small community. They later bought two other farms in the area which were sold before Mr. Menoud passed away. Mr. and Mrs. Menoud bought a home in town and were living there at the time of their deaths. Bud and Marie bought the Tom McKinstry farm northwest of Hagerman where Marie still lives. They were one of the first Farm & Home Administration borrowers in Chaves County. Jack and Byrda bought a farm east of Hagerman where they have lived since 1943.

Farmers and stock farmers since coming to Hagerman, the Menouds have raised cotton, alfalfa, small grain and other crops and grasses. They baled hay for the public for several years also. The Menouds helped to build the first cotton gin in Hagerman and hauled cotton and seed from the gin for many years.

Jack attended barber school and worked part-time in Roswell and for the Latimer Brothers in Hagerman and Dexter. He also bought cotton for several years.

Louise attended beauty school and worked in Roswell before her marriage.

Mr. Menoud was a Catholic and Mrs. Menoud was a Methodist. The Menoud children are members of various denominations. Bud and Marie were active members of the Presbyterian Church throughout their married life; Marie is still a devoted member. Bud, at the time of his death, was an Elder in the church. Their children were also members of the Hagerman church. Louise has been a devoted member of the First Christian Church in Springfield, Oregon, for forty-two years. Before her first husband died, they were honored for having twenty-five years perfect attendance in church. Jack and Byrda have been active in the United Methodist Church throughout the years. They each have served in many capacities in their church, Sunday school, United Methodist Women, Methodist Men and Methodist Youth Fellowship. Their daughter, Gloria, and her family attend the First United Methodist Church in Roswell. Alice was a member of the Dexter Presbyterian Church and her children are active members in their home communities. Grace, a member of Trinity United Methodist Church in Roswell, enjoys women's work and attending Sunday school. Her daughter's family are members of the Tabernacle Baptist Church.

Although the Menoud family were hard workers, they found time to enjoy life. There are many stories they could tell about the days of yore, their first Ford car, their riding horses, home parties and country dances. The children are justly proud of their family heritage. The father was an immigrant from Switzerland who spoke only French when he arrived in the United States. He soon learned to speak Spanish and went to night school to learn English. The mother was a descendant of Charles Curtis Carroll, who helped frame the Constitution of the United States and signed the Declaration of Independence.

Mrs. M.D. (Marie) Menoud and Mr. and Mrs. A.D. Menoud (Jack and Byrda) are still enjoying the activities of the community, which they and the family have helped to build, and are proud of the part the family has had in making it a wonderful place to live.

Jack and Bryda have worked with the Boy and Girl Scouts, 4-H Club and the Rainbow for Girls. Jack is a Past Master of Felix Lodge #29, Past Patron of Harmony Chapter #17, Order of the Eastern Star. Byrda is a Past Matron of Harmony Chapter and is the present Treasurer. She is Mother Advisor of the Order of Rainbow for Girls. Jack is a charter member of the Hagerman Lions Club and is serving his twenty-second year as Chairman of the Hagerman Cemetery Association.

THE A.N. MILLER FAMILY IN HAGERMAN, NEW MEXICO

By Harold R. Miller

My Grandfather, A.N. Miller, was born in Shelby County, Indiana, in 1842. He enlisted in the 33rd Indiana Volunteers of the Union Army in the Civil War in 1861 and was captured in the battle of the Cumberland Mountains and served six months in Libby Prison. He was discharged in early 1865, and in 1866 he moved to Kansas where he took up a homestead. From Kansas he moved to the Indian Territory where he operated an Indian Trading Post. About 1875 he moved to Arkansas, and in 1878 he moved to Leadville, Colorado, during the great silver mining days. In 1882 he moved to Los Angeles and from there to San Diego. In 1891 he moved to Llano, Texas, where he remained about one year and then moved to Iowa. In 1894 being attracted by an advertisement of cheap irrigated land in the Pecos Valley of New Mexico, he moved to Hagerman, coming by way of Dallas, Pecos, Texas, in what was called an emigrant car. This trip was made entirely by rail.

He brought with him his family consisting of his second wife; a son, Edward C. by a former wife; my father, Robert N. Miller, who was born in Arkansas in 1877; my father's brother, Bert M. Miller, and my father's sister, Pearl Miller.

Grandfather purchased a farm of about forty acres just east of Hagerman which was purchased after Grandfather's death by W.A. Losey. This was a rather large house and cost grandfather six hundred dollars. My father, Robert N. attended school in Hagerman under Miss Blackstone.

Sometime in 1896 Grandfather established the A.N. Miller & Co. general store which remained in business in Hagerman until the end of 1926.

In 1896 my mother, then Harriet E. Hicken, came to Hagerman to visit her sister, Mrs. George E. Berry. The Berrys had purchased a farm about a mile southeast of the town site. She met my father and they were married in Hagerman in early December of 1896. To this union were born four children, Harold R. in 1897; Victor A. in 1898; Edna in 1901 and Marjorie A. in 1904. Our mother passed away in 1909 and is buried in the Hagerman Cemetery. Grandfather Miller passed away in 1926 and was buried in the Hagerman Cemetery.

About 1895 the wife of A.N. Miller, the son, Bert M., and the daughter, Pearl, moved to the state of Washington. Grandmother Miller and Uncle Bert never returned. Pearl made several visits to Hagerman through the years. My father, Robert N. Miller, spent thirty years with the A.N. Miller & Co. Store. He was active in the Baptist Church, the Woodmen of the World, the Odd Fellows, the Masonic Lodge and the Eastern Star and was, shortly before his death in 1930, Worthy Grand Patron of the order of the Eastern Star for the state of New Mexico. In 1928 father was married to Ethel Smith who survived him. He served as Justice of the Peace for Hagerman for a number of years and also served as a member of the Board of Education for the Hagerman Public Schools for a number of terms.

The children of Robert N. and Harriet E. Miller all attended and were graduated from the Hagerman Public Schools. Harold, Victor and Edna attended the University of New Mexico, and Marjorie attended Albuquerque Business College specializing in typing, dictation, and bookkeeping. Harold and Victor each served in World War I. In 1919 Victor left Hagerman and never returned and presently is retired and living in Glendale, California. Edna left Hagerman in 1920 and never returned. She presently resides in Albuquerque, New Mexico. Marjorie left Hagerman about 1922 and made her home most of the time until her death in 1964 in Albuquerque where she was office manager for the Rio Grande Conservancy District.

Harold worked with the A.N. Miller & Co. general mercantile until the end of 1926. In 1920 he was married to

Anne Catherine Attebery of Greenville, Texas. Harold was quite active in Hagerman during his adult years, being twice Master of Felix Lodge No. 29 of the order of Ancient Free and Accepted Masons, was mayor and a member of the City Council for a number of terms and served part of two terms as a member of the Hagerman Public School Board. In 1931 he, his wife and two sons moved to Carlsbad, New Mexico, where with the exception of his service in World War II he has lived since.

When the Miller family moved to Hagerman there were no telephones, no electric lights, no automobiles, no radio, no television, no coal, and we obtained our water for drinking, cooking and washing from a tank car brought to Hagerman from what was then Eddy (now Carlsbad). Our fuel was mesquite roots for which we paid three dollars a cord. Newspapers and magazines were brought in by rail. Our communication with the outside world was by letter or Western Union telegraph service. The railroad at that time came into Hagerman from the south and did not extend north of Roswell. It was affectionately referred to as the Pea Vine Railway.

There was a minimum of entertainment in those early days. Every one went to Sunday School and Church. The boys swam in the irrigation ditches and the Felix River in the summertime. There were baseball and basketball games, top spinning, marbles, and "shinny-on-your-own-side," played somewhat like La Crosse with improvised clubs and a tin can. Yet they were happy days. Everyone knew every one. People helped each other. A man's word was his bond.

SAGA OF JACQUES L. MICHELET

By Louise Brown Sleeper

Many years ago, in the early eighties, an enterprising Englishman became interested in the Pecos Valley in New Mexico as a farming area. The Felix River was beautiful at that time, flowing several feet deep and plentiful with perch and catfish. The promoters for the Pecos Valley began distributing literature to other countries and a young man from Switzerland became interested because the seasons of his own country were so cold and short.

Jacques L. Michelet was born in 1859 in Canton de Valais, Switzerland. He sailed on the ship, *The Savoy*, from Le Havre, France, to New York City where he worked sometimes as a cook and a porter in hotels to be able to continue his travels. He brought little cash from the old country because of frightening tales of Indians, and he was unable to speak the English language. From New York City he traveled to New Orleans and Lake Charles, Louisiana, through Texas and on to St. Louis, Missouri, working his way from place to place. After traveling a few years he decided to go back to Switzerland to attend to his business interests.

In his youth Mr. Michelet had worked in a bakery and learned the business so well that he built his own bakery shop. He was well educated, had performed his military duties, so his thoughts and dreams turned to the "New World," the "Land of Opportunity."

He leased his bakery, cleared other business and again he landed in New York City. His desire was to go directly to the Pecos Valley of New Mexico after reading about the advantages of the long growing season and the beautiful sunsets. The best route to go, he was told, was to sail to Galveston, Texas, take a train to Pecos, Texas, and on to Eddy (later called Carlsbad), New Mexico. From Eddy he rode the stage coach north to the Felix River.

At that time the stage route was ten miles west of Hagerman. Mr. Michelet walked from there following the Felix River. When he saw that the Felix joined the Pecos River about two and a half miles northeast of Hagerman he decided to homestead his farm on the north side of the Felix River. The soil was sandy loam, so different from his native Alps. From his education in surveying, he visioned the possibility of building a dirt dam about two miles west with a ditch along side of the river to his farm.

In the meantime a Swiss Colony had settled in Eddy and Mr. Michelet pursuaded Marie Lattion to come from Switzerland to Eddy. She and her brother Gene lived in Eddy for a year. Marie worked as a maid for a family until she and Jacques married in 1893. Many times Mr. Michelet walked to Eddy to see Marie and back to his farm, a distance of 60 miles each way. There were no fences and he would often encounter wild cattle. At one time a large group came charging at him and he had to wave his hat and yell blood-curdling screams to frighten them away.

Marie stayed in Eddy until Mr. Michelet built an adobe house on their land. It was one fourth mile from the Felix River and handy to haul water until a cistern was built. He planted poplar and fruit trees around the yard. The trees grew to such beauty and shade that the area was greatly admired. Many families in the vicinity enjoyed Fourth of July picnics there. The large orchards were very productive because the climate was so perfect.

During the slack times of his hard labor on the farm, Mr. Michelet hired out to help in the development of the Pecos Valley. The farm was slowly being improved but he needed to buy necessary implements and stock. He helped in planting large orchards and surveying much of the country. There were lakes, bogs and swamps from Roswell to Eddy and many rains during the growing season. He walked to Roswell and Eddy when necessary to attend to business matters.

As soon as he was able to buy horses and implements, the farm was put into cultivation. The dirt dam project was started and the ditch surveyed. A scraper and a team of horses were used and it was difficult and hard work. The scraper was about three or four feet wide with wooden handles on each side. As the horses pulled the scraper had to be worked manually. The horses assisted by pulling with a jerk to turn the scraper over and dump the load where necessary. This was slow, tiring and required patience with the team. The two miles of ditch had to be plowed and the dirt removed by the scraper. When the project was finished, the water from the river flowed freely to the farm, watering the orchards and other trees.

The sandy loam was plowed with a small plow, sometimes with only one horse, but, when the salt grass land was plowed, two horses were used. The plow had two handles. This was to hold on to and keep the plow on the edge of the furrow. The lines from the bridle bits were put over the shoulder and under the opposite arm in order to keep one horse in the furrow, using the shoulder to help guide the team. Mr. Michelet had to hold to the plow and walk in the furrow. It took many days to plow the acres to be planted. After plowing, the land had to be disked and leveled. The leveling was done with heavy timbers, nailed together to form a rectangle.

Sugar beets were planted but were not a success because the distance to the processing plant was too great. Sugar cane was grown and hauled to Lake Arthur, eight miles south of Hagerman, but only enough for home use was made into syrup.

The acres of green alfalfa were Mr. Michelet's pride. He planted all his land by hand. He would tie a twenty-five pound sack of seed around his waist, walk back and forth across a field, take a handful at a time and throw it far out, swinging his arm around and let a portion through his fingers. The alfalfa grew three feet high and one quarter inch in diameter. He bought a mower and, using two horses, managed to cut it. The mower was small for such rank hay, and it took time and repairs. After cutting the hay had to be worked into shocks. This was done with a rake. The teeth were curved and four inches apart and when let down, gathered the hay. A lever was stepped on to dump the hay in windrows, then arranged into shocks. One day while Mr.

Mr. and Mrs. Jacques L. Michelet.

Mower.

Buckrake and bailer.

Michelet was raking, a bumble bee's nest was disturbed and the swarming bees stung the horses. The team ran away and Mr. Michelet was thrown under the rake in front of the teeth. He was rolled over and over until the rake was pulled over a ditch and he was dumped. He had two broken ribs and was unable to work for a long time. Someone told him to blow into a bottle to strengthen and mend his ribs but he refused because of the pain. It took many days to bale the hay. The baler had to be set flat on the ground and the wheels removed. Between the front wheels was a large, very heavy iron called the dead man. The weight of the iron was to hold the baler to the ground. The wheels were removed to lower the plunger and the team could step over it each time they circled. The plunger pushed the hay back to where the blocks and bales were divided. The baler had to be moved often. Once when the baler was ready to be moved, one of the horses refused to pull. Mr. Michelet slapped the balky one with a line and the horse laid down. Soon she got up, pulled just enough to move the wheel on

Mr. Michelet's toe and the loudest Swiss yodeling of all times was heard.

A buckrake was used to push hay to the baler from the field. It was about twelve or fourteen feet wide with long teeth in front made of two by four lumber. Two horses were hitched on each side. The teeth lifted the shocks and when loaded moved the hay to the baler. It was quite a skill to hold the horses even while pulling the loaded implement between the rows of trees without breaking a tooth on the buckrake. Repairs took time, and time was precious when only eight or ten tons of hay could be baled in one day. It took all day to make a trip to Roswell for farm repairs and implements. Sometimes it was necessary to spend the night along the road. When the hay was baled it was loaded on a home-made sled, built from timbers, pulled to the corrals and stacked to feed or sell. Later wagons were available.

Firewood was hauled from across the Pecos River. It was an all day job to ford the river and dig the mesquite roots. On one of the return trips for firewood one of the horses balked in the middle of the stream. There was much excitement because the horse nearly drowned. Mrs. Michelet held the horse's head up while Mr. Michelet unloaded the mesquite on the bank of the river. The horse got up and the wagon was pulled out.

Mrs. Michelet's parents and family came to the Pecos Valley, too, and lived a few years, working on the farm. They later bought property southeast of Artesia.

Mr. Michelet got his naturalization papers in 1903 and cast his first vote for Theodore (Teddy) Roosevelt. Being thoroughly satisfied with the accomplishments of his hard labor, he went back to Switzerland to dispose of his bakery and other interests. Returning to Hagerman he purchased more property and built a new eight-room house one and one half miles northwest of the old place, on elevated ground out of danger of floods from the two rivers. He had an artesian well drilled to irrigate this part of the farm.

Mrs. Michelet's parents and family settled near by and helped with the farms and children while Mr. Michelet was away. By that time the family had grown. There were six children, Rose, Blanche, James, Charles and skipping four years they hit a double and had twins, Louis and Louise.

The children were vaccinated for smallpox by their father. One of the children was vaccinated first. The doctor sent a small needle vial filled with the fluid and instructions to make a small scratch on the arm of one of the children rub the vaccine into it. After this became infected a needle was sterilized by holding it over a coal oil lamp. Then a tiny scratch was made on the arms of the other children. The needle was then used to pick up some of the infection and it was rubbed into the scratch. It was successful with no ill effects.

The children all graduated from the 12th grade in the Hagerman school. The mare, "Old Black," that pulled the surrey with the fringe around the top, every day of every year, deserved a diploma, too.

In 1913 Dad purchased an Overland car for the family. It had brass decorations with large wheels and wooden spokes. There was a tank on the running board. When it was filled with carbide and water it furnished gas for the lights. This was very repulsive and it was not long before a new model car was purchased.

Mr. Michelet passed away in 1942 and Mrs. Michelet in 1943. They were the oldest settlers in the Hagerman district of Chaves County.

Were these the "Good Old Days?"

The children of the oldest settlers of Hagerman were, Rose, Blanche, James, Charles, Louis and Louise. Rose and Blanche started to school together. Their parents spoke French so they knew very little English and had a very difficult time. Their first teacher, Mrs. Harry Cowan who was very understanding and sympathetic, assisted them, and they progressed rapidly. Both graduated from the twelfth grade together. Blanche was valedictorian of her class. They both taught school for a few years then married the Casabonne brothers. Pete and Blanche had two sons and two daughters. Rose and Jack had one son.

James and Charles also started to school together and graduated together. James liked his pleasures and Charles was very studious. Charles was valedictorian of his class. He was a member of the school board for fourteen years and a Trustee and Elder of the Presbyterian Church for many years. He married Roberta Williamson. Their son, Bobby, married Betty Johnson and they have two sons and a daughter. James was an excellent mechanic. He married Jeannette Jacobson and had three girls.

Louis and Louise also graduated together. Louis delighted in telling everyone his twin sister would never have graduated had it not been for him. He was valedictorian of our class and was a dispatcher for the Santa Fe Railway for many years. He married Billie Donnell and they had one daughter, Mary. Louise married Vedder Brown and they had two sons and a daughter.

F.D. MITCHELL FAMILY
By Erv Mitchell

The F.D. Mitchell family came to Hagerman in 1906. They lived a quarter of a mile due east of the schoolhouse. Most of the acreage was in orchards, and the house, surrounded by flowers and trees, was a show place.

Mr. and Mrs. Mitchell contributed much to Hagerman. They were civic minded people who worked for the betterment of the community. Mrs. Mitchell was very active in the Presbyterian Church, often playing the organ, which she helped obtain as a gift from a church in Chicago.

She was instrumental in starting the Thursday Club and the Woman's Club, which prompted her grandson, Erv Mitchell of Roswell, to write: "In the early days of Hagerman, the women of the Woman's Club wished to build a meeting place, so they set forth to print a cook book to earn funds for it's building. The nature of the project was disclosed to prominent women of the country and solicitations were made for their best and favorite recipes. Response was good, the book was published, the proceeds from the sale of this book did in fact build them a woman's club.*

"My grandmother, Mrs. Franklin D. Mitchell, was one of the prime movers of this project, I believe, and she was quite a literary personage in her own right, having had numerous pieces of poetry published in the leading magazines of the day. My grandmother was also a voracious reader. She became very involved in her reading.

"One afternoon she asked grandpa to harness Pet as she needed to go to town. This was done and she departed. She failed to return. We harnessed up the buckboard and went towards town, where we found her and the buggy. Both reins on the ground, her nose in a book, oblivious, Pet grazing happily on the salt grass in the middle of the field in front of Tolly West's home.

"My Grandpop, F.D. Mitchell, was never much of a smoker, but he did enjoy his pipe for the evening and one day found he was completely out of tobacco. The prospect of getting to town for tobacco at that late time in the evening overwhelmed him. He seized the basket of pipes, proceeded to the front door of the farmhouse, opened the screen door and threw the basket of pipes over the fence. He never smoked again."

The Mitchell house burned to the ground in February of 1929. Mr. and Mrs. Mitchell moved to a small house in town before moving to California in 1930 with their daughter, Helen. Mr. Mitchell died in 1937 at the age of eighty-four and ten years later Mrs. Mitchell died. She too was in her eighties.

* Instead of building a club house, the Woman's Club bought the old Cowan house and remodeled it into a club house and library.

THE MONTAÑO FAMILY AND THE TONY TRUJILLO FAMILY

Abel Montaño and his wife, Mollie Stewart Montaño, both now deceased, moved to Hagerman in October, 1924, from Lincoln County. At the time employment, particularly agricultural employment, seemed to be more gainful than most ranching endeavors in Lincoln County. So, it was in search of employment that brought the Montaño family to Hagerman.

A noteworthy item is that during the period of approximately 1920-1940, several families from southeastern Lincoln County (San Patricio, Hondo, Lincoln and Arabela) moved to the Pecos Valley and settled primarily in the Hagerman-Dexter area. It was as if there was a great migration during those years of people seeking alternative employment possibilities.

Five children were born to the Montaños: Louis, Vivian and Flora (twins), Salomon and Abel Jr. Of the five children four reside in Hagerman. Louis is married to Margarita Quintero; Vivian is married to Tony Trujillo; Flora, who resides in La Luz, New Mexico, is married to Daniel Sedillos. Salomon and Abel Jr. reside in Hagerman.

In 1930 Louis, Vivian and Flora attended the one-room country school at what was known as the Felix Ranch. The ranch was managed at the time by Mr. Van Sweatt. The teacher was Miss Meador.

Vivian and Tony Trujillo were married in 1943 and in 1944 Tony opened Tony's Grocery and Service Station.

Four children and thirty-one years later Mr. and Mrs. Trujillo are two of the long-time merchants in Hagerman.

The Trujillo children are Jake, Benny, Margie and Tony Jr. All of them graduated from Hagerman High School and Eastern New Mexico University at Portales.

Jake is teaching at E.N.M.U.-Roswell Campus and is married and lives in Roswell. Benny is married, lives in Clovis and is head of the Upward Bound Program at E.N.M.U. in Portales.

Margie is in Albuquerque attending the University of New Mexico working toward her Ph D. in psychology. Tony Jr. is married, has one child and lives in Albuquerque. He is a R.N. working at the Veteran's Hospital.

The family is active in the Catholic Church and at present Tony Sr. is president of the Hagerman Board of Education.

J.P. MORGAN FAMILY
By Perla Morgan Clark

Being tired of northern winters, James Patrick (Jim) Morgan and his wife, the former Elizabeth Grace (Lizzie) Wright, decided to move their family and farming interests to the Pecos Valley of southern New Mexico.

They sold their farm near Wakefield, Nebraska, and Jim, Lizzie and young son, Jesse, went by train to Hagerman, New Mexico, arriving in April, 1914. Their daughters remained in Nebraska as Perditia was teaching school near Hoskins, and Perla was teaching in the Lone Star School near Coleridge. Alta Marie stayed with Perditia in order to finish the school year. They joined their parents in May. Jesse entered the second grade and Alta entered Hagerman High School in September, but the older daughters returned to their schools in Nebraska for another school year.

Jim and Lizzie rented the Ed Lane farmhouse, then a house in Hagerman until they purchased their home on Argyle Street and the Rosehedge farm north of Hagerman. Jim was a member of the Town Board. He and his wife were very interested in community development and helped in church and school activities and all other worthwhile projects.

Perditia (Ditta) and Perla began teaching in the Hagerman Public School in 1915. At that time, one teacher taught all subjects (including special classes) to two grades in one room. One grade or class would have their study period, while the other worked at the blackboard, read aloud, answered questions orally or discussed current subjects.

Alta graduated from high school in 1918 and taught in the Berrendo School near Roswell and later in the school at

Hagerman. She and her sisters attended the New Mexico Normal University at Las Vegas during summer sessions.

Great sadness came to them in the spring of 1919 when Elizabeth (Lizzie) Wright Morgan became ill and passed away. Jim continued to live in his home and keep up his farm work with Jesse in school and his daughters teaching school, until their marriages (Perditia in the Clovis school and Perla and Alta at Hagerman).

Aaron F. Clark and Perla were married in 1920; Robert W. Cumpsten and Alta were married in 1922; and T.D. Devenport and Perditia were also married in 1922.

In 1924, Jim and Flossy E. Wixom, daughter of Mr. and Mrs. B.H. Wixom of Greenfield, were married in Roswell and made their home on the farm near Hagerman. Their marriage was cut short by her sudden death in 1926. During the sad, lonely time that followed, the son and daughters spent as much time as possible with their father. Jim Morgan passed away in 1936 in Wayne, Nebraska, while staying with a sister.

James Patrick Morgan.

Jesse graduated from Hagerman High School in 1925 and entered New Mexico A. and M. at Las Cruces. He and Martha (Peg) Evans were married in 1929. Jesse graduated from New Mexico A. and M. in 1929 with a B.S. in Mechanical Engineering and received a commission as second lieutenant in the United States Army Reserve.

After graduation, he worked for a time in California, then in the testing laboratory of the New Mexico State Highway Department as a laboratory engineer. Jesse was called to active duty in the army in 1941 and served in tactical schools and armored divisions. He retired in 1946 with the rank of Lieutenant Colonel. Jesse began teaching at New Mexico A. and M. in 1946 as Assistant Professor of Mechanical Engineering. He then served as Assistant Dean of Engineering (1959-1967) with additional duties as Cooperative Education Program Coordinator.

Jesse and Peg are parents of three girls and a boy. Since his retirement from NMSU, they have moved to Laguna Hills, California.

The Morgan girls, l. to r: Alta, Perla, Perditia.

THE T.J. NAIL FAMILY

Thomas Joseph Nail, born in Bosque County, Texas, in 1854, and Mildred Annie Short, born in La Grange, Texas, in 1860, were married in Texas in 1878. They were the parents of five children, William, Mollie Ellen, Tommy LeRoy, Clint Ross and Alma Leonza.

The family moved from Texas to New Mexico in 1902. They came in a covered wagon, bringing a good herd of cattle, some horses, chickens, pigs and all their household possessions. Mr. Nail bought a ranch in the Capitan area. He was forced to leave because the forest reserve grazing rights would not feed all of his cattle. At his next stop the Cottonwood water supply turned out to be alkali, and the family was forced to move on. Mr. Nail found some land southwest of Hagerman on which he could file and walked to Roswell to make his claim. The land lay a mile west of the Calvin Graham home. The family lived in a tent until Mr. Nail could get an adobe house built.

Alma remembers his childhood fear of storms because the strong winds sometimes blew the tent down and scattered their belongings. The family dug a well, about forty feet deep, and later a windmill was put on it. Mr. Nail sometimes drove a wagon with sideboards to South Springs where he could buy a full load of apples for two dollars. These would be preserved by drying. Prairie grass grew as high as a horse's stomach and the range was open. The grass was also cut and stacked for winter feed.

About 1911 farmers began to take up the land so cattle grazing soon began to disappear. The Nails bought a ranch east of the Pecos River and built another house. During World War II, two sons, Clint and Alma, volunteered, and because Mr. Nail was not able to run the ranch alone he and his wife moved to Hagerman. The couple spent the remainder of their days in Hagerman.

Alma is the only living member of his family. After the war he and his wife Frieda lived on farms and ranches in the Hagerman area. While he was gone to war, Frieda worked in the Noah West-Carl Hanson Apple Shed. Alma and Frieda, now retired, live on a farm west of Hagerman, once owned by the Jenkins family.

Each of the Nail children received most of their education in the Lake Arthur School. Their parents were strong Christians of the Baptist belief. The oldest child, William died in infancy, Mollie married Jim Hamilton. They were the parents of three daughters, Annie Belle, Loula Mae and Bessie Lee. Tommy was married to Annie Pitts. They were the parents of seven children: Alma, Sadie, Mildred, Tom Jr., Birdie, Annie and Elizabeth. Clint was married to Margaret Ellen Clark. They had two sons, Joe and Jack. Clint was engaged in ranching business with his father most of his life.

THE GEORGE BERRY NEWSOM FAMILY
By Carroll Newsom

The G.B. Newsom family came to Hagerman in 1906.

George Berry and Eva, the parents, with seven children came from Alvarado, Johnson County, Texas, by train, bringing with them their personal belongings and some farm machinery and fencing for the eighty acre farm located between the G.L. Truitt and Sam McKinstry farms, on the Felix River three miles northwest of town.

At that time the land was unimproved, and, with the help of Mr. Truitt and perhaps some other neighbors, they built the house and barn. Mr. Truitt and family had come two years earlier from the same part of Texas.

The Newsom children were: Worthy, Vivian (deceased), Clyde (deceased), Myrtle (deceased), Donal Lee (deceased), Paul and Ruth (deceased). Four more children were born after moving to Hagerman. They were Carroll, Juanita, Raymond and Irene.

Worthy married Delia May and Clyde married Alice May, sisters, who lived, at that time, in the Cottonwood community.

Myrtle and Juanita found secretarial work in El Paso, Texas, and married there. Myrtle married Joe Ashford and Juanita married Frank Pino. Donal Lee married Alma Dodson of Hagerman and Ruth married Ernest Dodson of Hagerman. Paul married Elna Smith of Hagerman and Vivian married Fred McGee also of Hagerman. Irene married Hugh Pittman of Cloudcroft and Raymond married Bobbie Paris in Galveston, Texas. I, Carroll, married Alma Jane West, a Dexter girl.

Life for these early settlers was not all easy. Transportation, of course, was on horseback or in horse drawn equipment. When I was a very small boy, it was a real treat for me to get to ride into Hagerman on a wagon with Dad when he went for supplies. He always gave me two or three pennies to buy stick candy.

We children all attended school in Hagerman, going by horse and buggy. Not until the younger ones started to school was there a car for transportation.

To supplement the income from the farm, we baled hay for Sam McKinstry and his brother, Jim. This work always started as soon as school was out in the spring and lasted until school started again in the fall. Our father also did most of the road work in the Hagerman area. This included dragging the roads with four horses to each drag and also building the bridges that went under the roads.

The Felix River at that time had water running freely. It was deep enough that we could swim in it almost anyplace, and some holes were deep enough that we could dive into them from the top of the river bank. In those days it was quite a treat after a hard day of baling hay to take a refreshing swim in the Felix River.

The children all had chores to do and they worked hard and studied hard and played hard when there was time left over.

We never had much in the way of toys or candy or fruit, except at Christmas time. Nothing ever smelled quite as good nor tasted so wonderful as the oranges and apples and assorted nuts and hard candy that we found in our Christmas stockings.

George Berry Newsom died in 1939 and was preceded in death by Mrs. Eva Newsom in 1934. Both are buried in the Hagerman cemetery.

I will close with a paragraph by Andrew Carnegie that seems most appropriate for my parents: "Give me the life of a boy whose Mother is nurse, seamstress, washerwoman, cook, teacher, angel and saint all in one, and whose Father is guide, exampler, and a friend. No servants to come between. These are the boys who are born to the best fortune."

REMEMBRANCES OF THE FRED O'DELL FAMILY
By Herb Lang

Having spent many hours, days, weeks and even parts of years in and around the O'Dell family I have many memories, most of which are very happy memories. Indeed I had more fun than most youngsters in that period of time. I will add here that Volney Bowen also shared in our joys and sorrows of the time with the O'Dells, especially Roy.

The first thing I know of Fred O'Dell and Myra Barnes was that they met and married in Gordon, Nebraska. Mr. O'Dell told me that when he married the only thing he had was a buggy and the fastest team of horses in the country.

I do not know if they went directly to Clarendon, Texas, perhaps they did, but Fred quickly prospered and became successful. It seems for some reason that he was dissatisfied with the policy of the bank in Clarendon, so he started one of his own. He also owned the town hotel, cafe and surely considerable land because he knew considerable about farming and owned lots of horses. I never knew why the family left Clarendon.

Mr. O'Dell got the lease on the school section at the southwest corner of Hagerman, known as the "Winters Place" in 1916. Roy and several men drove a large herd of horses across country, perhaps 100 head. These men and Roy were fishing after their arrival here, and this is the first time that I ever saw Roy. They inquired of us native boys what kind of fish inhabited the river, as they would not bite the hook but continuously took hold of the cork and pulled it under. Of course the place was loaded with gar fish.

It wasn't long after this that all of this hunting and fishing began, most of the details I will skip, except to say that in my opinion Roy O'Dell killed more quail than any man who ever lived. One amusing thing, at least in retrospect, when Bess and I were first married we came to New Mexico for a vacation. Roy and his first wife, Elizabeth, Bess and I went quail hunting. We killed too many birds and after stashing away as many as possible in the car, Roy had the bright idea of putting the birds in the bosom of the girls waists. No game warden would think of finding them there. Everything turned out O.K. except that the poor quail were lousy. There was considerable itching but it was not very hard to be rid of the things.

Also the times when the nimrods came in with a flock of quail, put a large tub on the back porch of the big house, for the feathers and entrails. Then Mother O'Dell baked biscuits and fried quail. Its surprising how much of such fare three young fellows can put away, and how good it is. I know, for I have been there.

Then when we got old enough and bold enough to take the girls out, we must have been quite a bother. O'Dells had a player piano and no matter how late it was we ended up at Roy's house and played that blooming piano. Never once did Mrs. O'Dell fail to get up out of her bed and serve us hot chocolate and cookies or perhaps sandwiches. She always said that she was glad to have us, for then she knew where we were, and that we were safe and out of mischief. Yes, we had a good time.

When O'Dells came to New Mexico there were three banks on four corners in Roswell. Fred told me this; the first of the banks that he went into he asked for a loan of twenty thousand dollars and was summarily refused. He walked across the street to another bank and told the man he wanted to borrow the amount mentioned above. The man reached for a note and said, "What is your collateral?" He told the man he did not want to borrow any money but wanted to deposit forty thousand dollars, but didn't want to put it in a bank that didn't have any money. The man from the first bank followed him around all afternoon trying to get him to put half the amount in his bank, but of course only got laughed at for his trouble.

Mr. O'Dell told me that he had his money in banks in seven cities; if one went broke it would not hurt him much.

He told me the names of the cities, these I remember: Chicago, Omaha, Denver and San Francisco.

Guy was the older of their two boys. He went to France in the first World War as a member of old Battery A, headquarters in Roswell. This was a most congenial family. I never heard Mr. or Mrs. O'Dell say one cross word to the other.

There are a jillion things that I could say about these people, and still there are many that have faded behind the veil of years, after all it has been more than fifty.

Now, although it is against my better judgment, I will tell what I know and have been told about Fred O'Dells last two days on earth.

At this time I was in Illinois, but, of course, my folks sent me the daily papers regarding this sad occurrence and also of the trial.

Milt Robinson like Levi Barnett, it seemed to me as a boy and still to this day, were poured in seperate molds and then the molds broken. Whoever may read this will have to take my word for it, Milt Robinson was a MAN. There is no one left to substantiate this but me.

Milt and his family lived in the tenant house some 200 yards south of the big house and he was farming a part of the section. Some controversy arose between them. Each one milked a cow in a lot behind the big house. That evening when the milking was done Mr. O'Dell told Milt not to be in that lot the next morning. I understand that Milt said he would be there. During the hours of darkness Milt stood a loaded 30-06 rifle inside the door of the shed adjoining the lot. The next morning Milt got to the lot first and when Mr. O'Dell came out to milk Milt shot him down and then shot him again after he was down. O'Dell had nowhere near reached the gate to the milk lot. I have seen the stake where the body lay but have forgotten the distance but it may have been as much as fifty feet.

There is a story that Fred O'Dell shot first with Roy's pistol. Man and boy, I knew Roy as well as anyone could know a person except a blood relation and I know that he thought as little of a pistol as I. Of course I was in Illinois and couldn't possibly say that he did not own a pistol. My

The Fred O'Dell home.

mother and sister were getting breakfast in the house where Roberta Michelet now lives and they only heard two shots that morning.

I do not remember the time of year in 1924 that this happened, but I was on the train coming to Hagerman soon afterward and met Guy O'Dell. Guy told me that he and Roy were sleeping in the same bed when their father was killed but his story as told to me and the story told to me later by Roy were as different as day and night. Be that as it may, no two people can witness to anything the same.

While I was at home in Hagerman at that time, Milt was in the county jail in Roswell. My uncle, Leonard Lang, and I went to the jail to visit him for a few minutes. I would be leaving for Illinois in another day or two, and as I bid him good-bye a tear trickled down each cheek, and I've never forgotten his chuckle and parting words. "Kid, don't worry about me, you've heard of people staying in a place like this till it rotted down, but I am coming out of here, and I'm coming quick."

Jim King and Milt had been friends and partners in the cow business in Texas many years. The next time I came home the first thing I did after greeting the members of my family was to go see Jim. My first question after our customery greeting was, "How did Milt come clear?" He told me he never missed one word of that trial and he could not tell me the answer. He said it was cold blooded murder.

My sister, Freda Nail, met and talked with Milt briefly in Clovis. He had been to the fat stock show at Fort Worth to mingle with the thousands of people that attended that show in those days. He said, to Freda, that it did not help, Fred O'Dell walked side by side with him wherever he went. He told her that Fred O'Dell went to bed with him at night and got up with him in the morning.

Mrs. O'Dell never really got over her great loss. The last years of her life were spent in a wheel chair.

Guy and his mother went to Hot Springs, New Mexico (now Truth or Consequences) soon after Mr. O'Dell's death. Roy with the help of Bernice Barnett farmed the section for several years. For some reason Guy and Mrs. O'Dell did not approve of Roy's wife Elizabeth and it seems this had something to do with their overruling Roy and trading this farm for Radium Springs, near Las Cruces. This was probably the greatest mistake any O'Dell ever made. Radium Springs proved to be practically worthless.

The four members of the O'Dell family and Olga King O'Dell, Roy's second wife, are out there a mile west of Hagerman sleeping, and here I am with my memories most of which are still green in spite of being seen through the mist of years.

THE NED AYMER PALMER FAMILY
By Neva Palmer

Ned Aymer Palmer married Isabel Reid in Kansas. Three children were born to them, Gladys Elizabeth, Mary Vivienne and Edward Reid.

The Palmers decided to move to a warmer climate so they came to New Mexico. After seeing the Pecos Valley Mr. Palmer bought some farm land near Hagerman. The family went back to Kansas to make ready to move here.

Mr. Palmer and a friend came back to build a house on his property and the family came in 1905. Another daughter, Neva, was born in 1908.

Gladys taught school in Tularosa for a couple of years, then obtained a position in the Hagerman High School as teacher and principal for five years. She then went to Roswell where she taught until retirement in 1965. One of her students while she was in Hagerman was Wilfred McCormick, who became a well known author. He dedicated one of his many books to Gladys Palmer. All together Miss Palmer taught for fifty-two years in New Mexico. She passed away in 1970.

Vivienne taught in Roswell until 1925, then married a rancher, Pete Louissena. They are both deceased. Their daughter Mary and her husband, W.W. Roach, now manage the ranches. They have one son.

Edward went to Arizona and there he married Violet Birdno. They lived in Tucson, where he worked for the Railway Express Company for forty years. They are the parents of a son, Edward, Jr.

Neva taught at the LFD school four miles from Roswell for six years. She then accepted a position with the Roswell City Schools which she held until her retirement in 1973. She still resides in Roswell.

After Mr. Palmers death in 1918, Mrs. Palmer moved to Roswell and opened a hat and dress store, The Bon Ton. She died in 1952.

THE FRANK PARKS FAMILY

By Audre King and Dianne Andress

James Franklin (Frank) Parks and his wife, Viola Buck Popnoe Parks, arrived in the Pecos Valley by covered wagon about 1904. With them were their two daughters, Johnie and Frankie, and also Mrs. Parks' children, Inez, Pearl, Tox, Buck and Ira Popnoe. They told of their trip from Lubbock, Texas, driving their cattle and riding through buffalo grass as high as the wagon wheels.

The Hagerman canal was being dug and St. Mary's hospital was under construction at that time.

Our grandparents, the Parks, settled on a claim near Lake Arthur.

The Popnoe boys and our grandfather worked on the canal and drilled wells throughout the area. The Parks family soon moved to Hagerman so that Johnie and Frankie could attend the Seventh Day Adventist Church School.

Our grandfather was a deeply religious man and can be remembered sitting under the apple tree studying his Bible. He was a vegetarian, a hard diet to follow in those days. The Parks and Popnoe kids laughingly used to tell of their mother hurrying to prepare a chicken when grandfather left to drill a well. This was a welcome feast after eating so many eggs and so much peanut butter.

Our grandmother was a busy lady, caring for her family of seven children. She also took care, for awhile, of the two small motherless girls of William Crockett Parks III, who was our grandfathers brother. W.C. Parks III had brought his daughters and come to the boom area after his wife's death in Colorado. He, too, worked on the canal and the drilling rigs. He later married Mary Cook who was a seamstress. They migrated to the Hondo Valley.

Our mother, Johnie Parks Latimer, told us that her parents were afraid of the gypsy people who came through Hagerman from time to time, so they always warned their children to get in the house when the gypsies were seen coming.

Our grandparents' home is now owned by Earl Latimer and can be found on West Morgan Street. It has been remodeled with three of the original adobe rooms included in the present structure.

Ira and Tox Popnoe migrated to Montana and Buck to California. Pearl married Harlan Pritchard and Inez married Cliff Glass. They settled in Dallas and San Antonio respectively.

Frankie Parks married Bill Wyatt of Roswell. She now lives in Uvalde, Texas.

Johnie married Earl Latimer in 1915 and they had four children. Audre is married to Roy King. They have two children. Dr. Earl Latimer, Jr. is married to the former Patricia Ruth Miller. They have three children and live in Roswell. Glenn was married to Millie Taylor (deceased). They had a daughter and Glenn lives in Roswell. Dianne is married to Ottie Andress. They have four children and live at Jemez Springs, New Mexico.

Mrs. Viola Parks was still a Hagerman resident at the time of her death in 1947. She was preceded in death by Frank Parks in 1921, when he was killed. Both Mr. and Mrs. Parks are buried in the Hagerman cemetery as well as our mother, Mrs. Johnie Parks Latimer, who died in 1969.

A SAD DAY FOR THE PARKS FAMILY
By Herb Lang

In the summer of 1920 Frank Parks took a cow out to the Stine place, located one and one-fourth miles northeast of town and now known as the Walter Elliott place. Jerome and Walter Delavan lived just across the road. Jerome was mentally ill and had been treated at Las Vegas previously. He had six men on his list to kill whom he said had "railroaded" him.

It seems that Jerome Delavan called Mr. Parks over to his house to talk to him as Mr. Parks was starting back to town. Mrs. Stine noticed that Mr. Parks came around to the north side of the Delavan house and sat down and leaned against the wall of the house, and then went over in a prostrate position. Mrs. Stine thought that possibly Mr. Parks was sick, so she called someone in town for help. When help arrived Mr. Parks was dead and his body was taken to the Cassie Mason funeral home. Cassie noticed a small blue hole which seemed to be a hole just about where the heart is located.

Guy Robinson, the deputy sheriff, was sent out to question Delavan. About the only information that Guy got was the evidence of a round hole in the screen door that Delavan pointed out. Guy got the message immediately and turned to return to his car, but just as he was about to enter it Delavan shot him in the back with a 22 rifle, injurying him.

This whole thing was a bit unbelievable to me, to say the least. All and sundry were out there with their high powered rifles shooting holes in that house, trying to smoke the man out. There were no windows on the north side of the house and people could talk through the wall without any risk, but to no avail, all he wanted was the six men who had "railroaded" him.

By this time it was dark and several cars were sent to the south side of the house to shine their headlights into the house. I believe that it was Johnny Peck, the sheriff, who shot Delavan in the wrist with a high intensity cartridge causing Delavan to lower the position of the gun that he was cradling in his hands. Then Jody Zumwalt, deputy sheriff, shot Delavan with a load of buckshot being afraid that Delavan might shoot.

Dr. Brown pronounced Delavan dead.

As for Mr. Parks, it just should not have happened, he was a kind and gentle man. He saw me kill a sparrow once with my ---- I am not supposed to use that word anymore, I think they call the things sling shots now-a-days. Mr. Parks upbraided me but good, reminding me that God noted the fall of every sparrow. We lived neighbors to the Parks family at one time, and although Mrs. Parks hair was white as snow, she was still very pretty. Mr Parks was the first man that I had ever heard call his wife by endearing names — sweetheart and honey. This is common now-a-days but not so when I was a boy.

FOOTNOTE:

John Max Andress, great grandson of Frank Parks, recalls his grandmother Latimer telling him that the family thought, at the time of the killing, the reason Jerome Delavan shot his grandfather was because both Mr. Parks and the sheriff wore the same type of hat. There was no known reason for Delavan to dislike our great-grandfather but he did dislike the sheriff.

J.W. PARKS FAMILY
Information from Edna Parks Carter

John W. and Sarah Parks brought their family, Tessie, Edna, George and Vergil, to Hagerman in 1906. They came from South Haven, Kansas, via train.

Mrs. Carter tells that her uncle had come three months previously and built the barn on the property which was located at the north end of Cambridge Street.

When the family arrived they stayed at the Clark Hotel until they made ready the barn to live in, until the house was built. The house was planned by Mr. and Mrs. Parks and was started soon after their arrival. It was finished in the fall and they had a celebration inviting all their friends and neighbors to inspect the house and have ice cream and cake. The beautiful house still stands north of the high school.

Mr. Parks farmed the acreage putting in alfalfa and fruit trees. As so often was the case, the fruit crops did not always turn out. After a few years the Parks moved to their homestead south of town.

The family was very active in the Presbyterian Church. Mr. Parks helped with the building of the Presbyterian Church. He also served as elder.

The Parks children attended the Hagerman schools.

They were a musical family. The girls played the piano and sang, and the boys were members of the town band and the church orchestra.

Tessie married Roy Walworth and Edna married Rich Carter. Both men were Hagerman residents at the time but moved away after a few years. Tessie now lives in Arizona and Edna has lived in Carlsbad for many years. Both are widows.

George and Vergil both served in World War I. Both of them are married and live in California.

Mr. and Mrs. Parks eventually moved back to Kansas. The family was greatly missed.

THE WARREN N. PERRY FAMILY
By Henry and Obera Perry

The year 1905 found Warren N. Perry dissatisfied near Belleville, Kansas, so he and two other men, Mr. Wranosky and Mr. King, decided to go west and buy rich irrigated land.

Warren and wife, Nanna Sorum Perry, had two children, Henry George and Elsie Marie.

Their possessions were loaded in an immigrant car on the Santa Fe Railroad and the families came by passenger train. Warren purchased a ten-acre apple orchard at the west and south edge of Hagerman. There was a nice house on the place where Nanna used her lovely homemaking talents.

One summer the Wranoskys, Kings and Perrys decided to go to Capitan in the mountains to the west. Covered wagons were made ready and loaded with supplies. The three families traveled and camped together for several days. It was an enjoyable vacation.

In 1906 a daughter, Rosalie, was born to Warren and Nanna. Nanna's sister came to Hagerman and opened a millinery shop. Their brother, George, also came for a visit.

Warren filed on a 160 acre tract of land ten or twelve miles west of Hagerman, proved up on it, then sold it.

In 1908 or 1909 tragedy struck the Perrys when Nanna passed away leaving Warren and three little ones. The children were taken to Kansas where the two girls lived with the Sorum grandparents and Henry lived with the Perry grandparents. Warren returned to New Mexico, sad and lonely. He started drilling water wells and kept busy from east of the Pecos on into Dexter and Hagerman vicinity.

In 1917 Warren married Grace Van Doren, a widow living west of Hagerman. He then went back to Kansas and brought the children home. Rosalie did not stay long, she cried so much to go back to Grandma's house that she was sent back to Kansas. Henry and Elsie stayed. Grace became very ill and died soon afterwards.

Henry quit school (where he was a popular ballplayer) to help his father with ranch and farm work. In 1924 he met Obera Thomasson and in 1926 they were married. They lived on the 640 acres of land Henry had filed on in 1922.

Elsie was married and had one daughter. She is now deceased. Rosalie married and has an adopted son and lives in Nebraska.

Henry and Obera are the parents of ten children: Mildred (Mrs. E.B. Finch) lives in Dexter; Henry Jr., Nanna Mozelle, Irma Jean (deceased), Wanda Faye, Thomas Warren, Myrna Sue, Betty Ann, Peggy Lou and Mary Elizabeth all live in California.

Warren Perry married Zoie Smith in 1927, and was living in Albuquerque at the time of his death.

Henry and Obera lived on their claim seven and a half miles southwest of Hagerman for nineteen years. In October, 1936, the family had gone to Lake Arthur to church and upon returning found their house and all their belongings burned. J.W. Coffee, a good friend, gathered donations for us and we purchased a 12 x 14 tent, stretched it up and lived all winter with our five children. Henry had to sell cattle to build a house.

Dr. E.J. Hubbard of Dexter was our family physician, delivering nine of our children at our ranch house — never failing to come when we needed him.

Henry and Obera sold the homestead in July, 1944, and in September were headed for the San Joaquin Valley of California. They bought a home in the small town of Waterford where they still reside, now enjoying grandchildren and great-grandchildren. They also enjoy Senior Citizen's Club.

WILLIAM F. PHILLIPS FAMILY

William Franklin and Martha Hannah Phillips, with their three children, William Franklin, Jr., Owen Wilbur and Mary C., moved to Hagerman in the spring of 1914. They lived on a farm about a mile and a half southwest of Hagerman and engaged in farming, fruit farming and stock raising. They were affiliated with the Methodist Church and Masonic fellowships.

William Franklin, Jr. (Frank) married Lucy Ervin Pettigrew; Owen Wilbur married Bonnie Belle Bradley; and Mary C. married Ira V. Cook.

William Franklin (Bill) Phillips died in 1926, Martha Hannah (Mattie) in 1954 and Owen Wilbur in January, 1975.

The family appreciated the people, climate, advantages and joys of living in the beautiful Pecos Valley.

THE PILLEY FAMILIES
By Fred and Vera Pilley

James Thomas Pilley, his wife, Sallie, and six sons left Beaufort County, North Carolina, and came to Buffalo, Texas, seeking relief for two of their sons, Herman and Abner, who were suffering from asthma.

The family came to Hagerman in a covered wagon, still trying to improve the boys' health, in February of 1915. The climate here at Hagerman seemed to agree with the asthmatics, so my mother, Sallie, Herman, Abner and I all filed on homesteads at "deep tank" about twenty miles east of Hagerman. My father continued to farm the Texas property and came to Hagerman to be with us as often as he could.

In the fall of 1915, when school started, I moved my own little family into Hagerman. I rode the twenty miles to the homestead at night and back to town to work almost every day in order to comply and prove up on the homestead and to take care of my family. In December of 1916 Nannie and our infant daughter passed away, so my mother moved in with me, from her homestead, to help me raise my children.

In 1920 a relinquishment to all four of the homesteads was sold to Cap Mossman. I was engaged in farming for fifty-four years until I retired in 1974 when we sold the farm located three miles southeast of town to Wayne Pilley and we moved to 201 Perth Street in Hagerman.

I married Vera King Chapman in 1938 and we have one son, Fred Eugene, Jr., who married Joan Troublefield and now lives in Roswell.

My father, James Thomas, died in 1942 and was preceded in death by my mother, Sallie, in 1934.

I was a charter member of the Church of the Nazarene, organized in 1923. I have served on the board since 1925 and have been Sunday School superintendent, teacher and treasurer for many years.

I was also instrumental in getting the roads graded southeast of Hagerman so the school bus and the mail service might serve that part of the rural area.

Gladys married Henry Basden, and she is now deceased.

Leonard married Dalphne Brown, and they live in Hagerman.

My brother, James Luther, and his wife, Sallie, had six children. Claude married Hazel Kelso; J.B. married Violet Wheeler; Avenal married Grady Dalton; Johnnie, Alma and George all married, but I don't know to whom.

My brother, Edward Thomas, and his wife, Ella, had five children. Mary Ellen married Bill Olive, Sallie married Feno Bramblett, Francis married Thurman Stephens, Herman (Jack) married Clyde Bogart and William A. married Lucille Beeman and they live in Dexter.

My brother, Ivey Herman, married Bertha Greer and they had one son, Jim, who married Patricia Potter of England.

Claudius died as a very young boy and Abner never married.

My five brothers, sons of James Thomas and Sallie Pilley, are all deceased.

E.M. REED FAMILY
By Thomas J. Reed

Elias M. Reed and his wife, Alice, moved with their children to Hagerman in 1912, where they resided on the Washington Ranch.

Mr. Reed was a farmer, stockman and minister. The sons were Quincy D., Eugene O., and Thomas J. Daughters were Hettie, Aldia, Margaret and Maude.

Quincy was a widower with a small son. After leaving Hagerman he remarried and made his home in Galesburg, Kansas. Eugene lives in Elgin, Illinois. Thomas married a local girl, Mabel Wranosky, and they, too, live in Galesburg. Hettie passed away in 1931 in Auburn, Nebraska, where she lived with her husband. Aldia and husband made their home in Lawrence, Kansas. Margaret married after leaving here and she also lived in Lawrence until her death in 1967. Maude died at Hagerman in 1915 of diphtheria.

Tom and Mabel keep in touch with Hagerman friends, having visited a few times and occasionally writing to the editor of the *Hagerman Star*. The family left here in 1918.

Although we have been away from New Mexico these many years, we have very many happy memories of our years there. Our children and grandchildren are scattered all over the world. We have traveled extensively over the United States, from east to west, north to south and into old Mexico. I made a trip into Trieste, Italy, in 1945.

After carrying the mail on a rural route for about forty years I have slowed down considerably.

THE RHODES FAMILY

William Joseph and Mary Matilda Rhodes moved to Hagerman by train in 1924 from Manila, Arkansas. The Rhodes family were farmers from the beginning. They sold the black gumbo land they owned in Mississippi County, Arkansas, and headed for New Mexico in 1923. The Rhodes family farmed one year in Carlsbad, New Mexico. All farming in those days was done with horses and walking plows.

The family first moved to a farm three-fourths of a mile northeast of Hagerman. They lived there until 1928 when they moved to Lake Arthur on the Rogers' farm. They later moved to a farm south of Hagerman. Later they bought a farm near Buffalo Valley and then moved to town. Mrs. Rhodes retired in Hagerman until her death in 1954. Mr. Rhodes died in 1971.

There were ten children in the family when they moved to Hagerman: Zebia Blanch, Opal Maude, Elinck Earl (Jack), Ina Beatress, Neavada Carrie, Woodrow Wilson, Mike Leaman, Ruby Irene, Bernice Marie and Lee Roy. Maryland Julian (John) and Willard Ray were born in Hagerman.

Woodrow, Lee Roy, John and Ray served in World War II. Woodrow was killed in the service in 1945. Ray was injured in the war.

Zebia Blanch married Charlie Curtright. They had seven children. Zebia died in 1971. They lived in West Memphis, Arkansas.

Opal Maude married Sherman Wrinkle. They had five children: Barbara Dean, Glenda, Donald Wayne, Phyllis, and Wilburt. Barbara is in Athens, Greece, with the U.S. Army. Glenda is in Ulysses, Kansas. Donald Wayne is in Lancaster, California, where he is a school principal. Phyllis is in Phoenix, Arizona. Wilburt is teaching in Simi, California. Opal and Sherman live in Lovington, New Mexico.

Elinck Earl married and had four children. They lived in Joplin, Missouri. Elinck (Jack) died in 1969.

Ina Beatress married H.A. Oscar Kiper. They had three children: Elizabeth Neva, Doris Fayerene and Donna Wayelene. Elizabeth is in Walnut, California, teaching school. Fayerene is in the state hospital at Ft. Stanton, New Mexico. Wayelene lives in Hagerman, farming the Kiper farm.

Neavada Carrie married H.A. Oscar Kiper. They had two children: Bessie Rue and Caroline Janice. Neavada died in 1937. Caroline died in 1943. Bessie Rue lives in Rancho Cordova, California.

Mike Leaman married Ruth Jenkins. They had four children: Frank, Clifford, Kathleen and Jane. Frank, Clifford, and Kathleen live in Hagerman where they are farming. Jane lives in Roswell, New Mexico, where she works at Levi Strauss. Mike and Ruth live in Hagerman.

Ruby Irene married Arther Littlejohn. They had three children: Donny Jim, Patricia and Mickey. Donny Jim died in 1950. Patricia lives in Abilene, Texas, and Mickey is attending Eastern New Mexico University at Portales. Ruby and Arther live in Roswell.

Bernice Marie married Willis Schierholt. They had three children: Lavoy, Gerald, and Glen. Lavoy lives in Carlsbad working in the mines. Gerald lives in Reno, Nevada, and Glen lives in Green River, Wyoming, working in the mines. Bernice died in 1965. Willis lives in Green River, Wyoming.

Lee Roy married Wanda Haley. They had two children: Gary and Darrell. Gary and Darrell live in Las Cruces, New Mexico, where they are attending New Mexico State University. Lee Roy and Wanda live in Hagerman.

Maryland Julian (John) married Bertha Mae Lawing. They had one daughter, Paula. She lives in Hagerman, farming. John and Bertha live in Hagerman.

Ray married Peggy Bailey. They had two children: Ray is in the hospital in Fort Lyons, Colorado.

THE W.E. RIDGLEY FAMILY
Information from Mae Graham

William E. Ridgely and his wife, Myrtle Hoyt Ridgley, came to Hagerman in the spring of 1911 from Logan, Kansas.

Mr. Ridgley had been a farmer in Kansas and after coming to New Mexico he worked on the railroad and did farm work.

There were ten children in the family but only two remained in Hagerman and raised their families here. Mae was married to Elmer Graham before the family moved to Hagerman and came two years later. Carl Ridgley married Lela Robinson and did farm work. The others were Agnes, Dave, Frank, Glen, Albert, Gene, Jennie and Mattie.

GUY ROBINSON FAMILY

Guy and Mattie Florence Robinson came from Logan, Kansas, a small town in Phillips County in northwest Kansas, and arrived at Lake Arthur on New Year's Day. Mr. Robinson purchased a farm on the Pecos River just north of the mouth of the Rio Felix and moved there in 1912.

The family came through by rail in an immigrant car bringing household goods, personal belongings, one milk cow, four horses and two mules. The family consisted of five children, Arthur, Cecil, Lela, Paul and Dwight. Thelma was born later at the farm.

Besides farming, Mr. Robinson served as deputy sheriff for approximately eighteen years and during this time was shot by Walter Delavan's brother who was mentally unbalanced. Mr. Robinson carried the bullet the rest of his life. Frank Parks was killed at the same time. Mr. Robinson also served on the school board.

Arthur married Essie May Thompson, a step-daughter to Buck Boyce, and had two boys and two girls. Arthur passed away in 1969 at Denver, Colorado. One of his sons, Lester, served in World War II. Lela, now deceased, married Carl Ridgley, also from Logan, and they had thirteen children, four girls and nine boys. Cecil, now retired by the Santa Fe, had two children, Floyd and Judith Ann. Paul married Bertha Scoggin (deceased) and had five children. Leman Dale died at age four; Kenneth was killed in 1974 in a small plane crash while flying over the ranch; Delbert has six children and farms at Lake Arthur; Pauline, married to Lennie Harper, lives in Albuquerque and they have three boys; and Betty, married to George Greenwood, operates a ranch in Santa Fe County.

Dwight was one of the basketball boys on the team when Hagerman took State Championship and went to Chicago. He married Shorty Rowell's daughter and has one girl. Dwight died of black diphtheria in 1921.

THE ARTHUR B. RUSSELL FAMILY
By Eva Russell Crook

Arthur B. Russell was born in Oregon, Missouri in 1853. Dora Dene Brown was born in Iowa in 1854. They were married in Missouri and were the parents of eight children. Mr. Russell owned a good river bottom farm in Missouri but became tired of the mud and disagreeable weather of his home state and decided to look elsewhere for farm land. In January of 1895 he came to New Mexico. He homesteaded on a quarter section of land about four miles southwest of Hagerman and sent for his family. He began building a house which was partially finished when his family arrived and dug a well for water by using pick, shovel and dynamite.

Mr. Russell did not return to Missouri to help his family move. Mrs. Russell, being the capable woman that she was, loaded her five children, two milk cows, four horses, one sow, some chickens and their household possessions on an immigrant train and came by way of Pecos, Texas, to Hagerman. They arrived in April of 1895 and were greeted by a strong wind and sandstorm. This gave Mrs. Russell a bad impression of her new home.

One of Mrs. Russell's first projects was to set up a barrel in the back yard to soften water for washing and other cleaning jobs. This was done by adding borax or lye to the water. Her chickens also got a weekly dose of this water. There were never any sick chickens after this. The milk, butter, cream and cheese were kept sweet by suspending them part way down in the dug well. Later, when a windmill replaced the dug well, a window cooler was used to preserve their food.

Mr. Russell went into the business of raising sheep. There were no fences between his home and the Capitan Mountains so the open range was large. Neither were there any salt cedars. He and his sons, with the hired help, herded the sheep and were sometimes gone for weeks at a time. When shearing time came the sheep were driven to a lake just south of the present town of Lake Arthur. Here camp was set up. A chuck wagon was run by the cook, Gumbo, and the family and hired help remained here until the job was finished. Friends and passersby often dropped in for one of Gumbo's good meals and to help if needed. It is of interest to note that the town of Lake Arthur is named after this lake and Mr. Russell.

Mr. Russell also had a public dipping vat. There was no charge for using the vat but the user furnished his own dip. Corn and alfalfa were raised on the farm and the tall prairie grass was cut and stacked in the feed lot to be used for winter feed as needed. In the winter of 1906 this hay saved the lives of the Russell's livestock. It snowed sixteen days out of eighteen. Fences, roads and everything were covered with snow. The men were out with the sheep so Mrs. Russell cut the wires around the feed lot and let the livestock in to eat the hay.

Some of the early day neighbors of the Russells were the Calvin Grahams, T.J. Nails, the Riccabrands, Fifes, Bogarts and the J.W. Wiggins. There was also a family by the name of Hitchcock who homsteaded across from the current Gomez Club. Mrs. Hitchcock and two of the children died and were buried in the pasture near the home. Later, when Mr. Hitchcock decided to leave his homestead, Mr. Russell told him he would tend the graves if they were fenced.

When a new family moved into the community the Russells were one of the first to show their hospitality by inviting the new comers to eat and stay the night. Butchering time was a community affair. All the neighboring men would come to help and bring their families. Each evening everyone returned to their homes, taking a good supply of meat with them. This was repaid at their next butchering. The women gathered to make lard and soap. Turkeys were also dressed in this manner.

The oldest child of the Russells was Roxie Edna. She attended Hagerman school and was married to Jim Clark. They had one daughter, Margaret Ellen.

Ethel Buelah was the second child. She also attended school in Hagerman. She married George Bryan whose family ran the Bryan Hotel in Hagerman. They had three children: Ruby Faye, Lela Mabel and John Arthur. Ethel kept boarders and George ran a butcher shop.

Maude the third child was a victim of Bright's Disease. She returned to Missouri to live with her grandmother and passed away when a teenager.

Edgar Harrison was the first son. He attended school in Hagerman. At the age of thirteen he suffered an attack of appendicitis. When the doctor arrived, an operation was performed on the kitchen table but it was too late to save Edgar's life. After his funeral the family was invited to the Riccabrands for supper and to spend part of the evening. When they later returned home someone had stolen all their chickens.

Alvin Ross was four years old when the family moved to New Mexico. He attended school in Hagerman. He married Fern Harvey whose parents ran a bakery in Lake Arthur. They had one daughter, Pauline.

Harvey Shelborn (Sheb) was the first child born in New Mexico. He lived most of his life on the homeplace. He was married to Leona Davis.

Eva Thelma was also born on the homeplace. She attended school in Lake Arthur and Hagerman. She married John Bishop Crook and they lived most of their married life on a farm south of Lake Arthur. They had one son, Thomas Arthur.

Paul was the youngest child. He attended school in Lake Arthur and Hagerman. He lived most of his life on the homeplace until his marriage to Shirley Thornbern when they moved to Artesia.

Eva, in reminiscing, remembers many of the ups and downs of the early days in New Mexico. She remembers the big snow of 1906. Hunting rabbits was a common pastime and also furnished meat for the table. In those days children walked to school if they lived close enough. Some rode horses or mules or drove buggies. At the noon hour the animals had to be watered at the town watering tank several blocks from the school. Many races resulted from these trips when the teachers were not watching.

The family worshipped in the Community Church which held its first meetings in the depot. Both Russell Papa and Russell Mama, as they were affectionately called by their many friends, were active and interested in all progressive activities of the community. They lived the remainder of their lives on the homestead and are remembered as beloved pioneers of the Hagerman community.

AN EXPERIENCE AT HAGERMAN
By Howard Russell

Early in the fall of 1903 a distinguished judge, a prominent real estate dealer and the writer sat in a western law firm discussing the possibilities of American youth making headway under adverse circumstances.

The real estate man made the assertion that were he set down in the most unpromising part of the country and if he had $100.00 to start he could make a fortune in a few years. The judge agreed but thought New Mexico the most God-forsaken part of the country. I doubted the statement but having no claims to bind me I agreed to make the experiment and although not a young man, I started the next morning with $1000.00 in my pocket to seek my fortune and landed in this part (Hagerman) of the great American desert.

After looking around a little I bought forty acres of irrigated land from Mr. J.J. Hagerman. I paid him $800.00 cash and gave my note for $400.00 to pay the balance.

On Christmas day 1905 I had finished staking off and fencing my property and commenced to build my little house. It was the most cheerless Christmas I ever spent.

I finally got my home built, a team bought, a barn put up and secured a few chickens. With the balance of my money I paid for some hay and feed for my horses and then began the tug of war.

The ground was so hard that I could not plow a furrow until I irrigated the land. I knew nothing about irrigating and my frantic efforts to control water would now appear amusing were it not heart-rendering.

In due course of time I succeeded in getting my entire forty acres broken and in crop of some kind, with an orchard of 500 trees started but I did not have a cent left and a second time in my life I felt the pinch of hunger, for my own cooking was not very tempting.

I began to realize that milk was a necessity and so I bought a cow and calf for $6.00 which proved a splendid bargain. The cow was so poor that she could not stand on her feet. I nursed her for weeks and finally pulled her through. She proved to be one of the best cows I ever saw and raised me three calves. I worked out and secured the six dollars for which I bought her. I purchased four pigs on credit and secured a fifth for a dollar. I now bought an old crippled horse for a couple of loads of hay, but I was obliged to sell my best horse to get funds to go back to my old home to bury my child.

This left me in pretty bad shape but I had a colt growing and managed to pull through. I had some of the best kind of people for neighbors and they were always ready to help me out.

The following are the result of my efforts:

A splendid little farm all set in alfalfa and orchard for which I am offered $6,000.00, three horses and a two year old gelding, four cows and two calves, 300 grape vines, 42 pigs, 6 pure bred poland chinas, a fine lot of chickens and twenty-five hundred fruit trees. I harvested 73 tons of alfalfa hay last year and will have 100 tons this year.

In short I came here with a little over $1000.00 and I could now sell out and go away with $6000.00. I came broken in health; I am now enjoying the luxury of a strong and vigorous constitution and have found time for doing a little good in this world besides.

I write back to my old friend, the judge, that I know his faith in the possibilities of American opportunities is well founded and that in another three years I will walk into his office with $12,000.00 in my pocket.

I have abundant faith in the Pecos Valley. Let me assure you that there is growing up around you a community whose productivity will far surpass your most dazzling anticipations and wealth will flow into this favored region by the millions.

The above story was found in *The Messenger*, April 19, 1907. Interesting news articles written by Howard Russell often appeared in the Hagerman papers of 1906 and 1907. Many people remember Mr. Russell driving his horses and buggy to town, singing as he went along. It has been told that he very often failed to remember his parked buggy in Hagerman and walked home. His small house still stands on his old farm located north and west of the Felix bridge. The area around his farm was known as Russell Heights. He later married a school teacher and Mrs. Russell was very active in the Presbyterian Church.

MR & MRS. JAMES A. SANDERS
MR. & MRS. J. LESTER OGLE

By Veva Ogle Knoblock

These facts are remembered through the recollections of an eleven year old child as I was that age when we left Hagerman in 1928.

James Sanders and his wife, Lucretia, came to Hagerman in the early 1900's, probably around 1910, from Ringwood, Oklahoma. How or why they made the move, I do not know. I have been told that they first operated a hotel across the street from the Baptist Church. Later they homesteaded south east of Hagerman.

In 1912 Lester Ogle came from Ringwood, and he and Elva Sanders were married. After their marriage, they moved to Cunningham, Kansas, where their two children, James and Veva, were born. In 1920 the Ogle family moved back to Hagerman by Model T Ford to be near my grandparents. Dad and Mother homesteaded 160 acres south of town about two and a half miles. Dad worked at the alfalfa mill for several years. In 1923 we moved into town. Dad became the janitor at the schoolhouse and we lived across the street south of the school. About this time my grandparents moved to a farm across the road from Mr. and Mrs. Wiggins.

Dad was a practical joker. I remember hearing tales of his sprinkling "itching powder" in the athletes' uniforms and playing practical jokes on the freshman — sending them to the store for speckled paint and left-handed monkey wrenches. He played the part of Santa at the Christmas celebrations.

I remember these as happy years of my childhood — a time of swimming in irrigation ditches, riding the stray donkeys which wandered into town, making forbidden candy with friends, snitching watermelons, waiting for the ice to come in from Roswell so that we could make ice cream and the one big treat of going to town on Saturday night to visit with all of our friends.

We attended the First Baptist Church. Mother was very active in the women's work of the church. I can remember the big revival meetings which were well attended by almost everyone in town. Grandmother and Mother were members of a women's club — the L.C. Club. One of my treasures is a quilt top made of blocks embroidered by each member and given to my mother when she left Hagerman for California.

By 1928 my grandparents had moved to our place south of town. A heart condition demanded that Dad move to a lower elevation. We moved to Hermosa Beach, California. Dad became a school janitor there. Mother had been in ill health for several years and finally passed away in 1932. Dad's heart condition continued to plague him and he passed away in 1938. They both lie at rest in a peaceful cemetery in Redondo Beach, California.

My grandparents continued to live south of town. We came back to Hagerman to visit them and our friends. In 1936 Grandfather died. Grandmother died in Roswell in 1955. They both lie at rest in the Hagerman cemetery.

James Ogle now lives at 8138 Duesller Lane, Downey, California. He is an assembly line foreman for the General Motors plant in Southgate. He married Maxine Dixon and they have three children — Beth, Bill and Shelley.

Veva Ogle Knoblock now lives at 104 N. Manville, Boise, Idaho. She married Robert Knoblock, who is now retired from the Bureau of Land Management. They have three children — Ken, Nancy and Mike and four grandchildren.

SLAYTER — DRAGOO FAMILIES

Information from John Henry Slayter and Mary Slayter Thomas
Written by a friend, Helen Curry

Mr. and Mrs. L.C. Slayter and Mrs. Slayter's parents, Mr. and Mrs. J.W. Dragoo, came to New Mexico from Miami, Oklahoma, in 1906. Mr. Slayter was a Methodist minister in Miami. Mr. Dragoo was a partner in a general store there. He sold the store and both families came to New Mexico to homestead on a 160 acre dry land farm across the Pecos River east of Hagerman.

They sold the farm in 1910 and moved to Hagerman where Mrs. Slayter was in charge of the local telephone exchange which was located upstairs in the bank building over the post office. She kept that position for eighteen years until her death in 1928.

Mr. Slayter was a very able speaker and would often give illustrated lectures to schools.

Mrs. Slayter was very efficient as operator of the telephone exchange and was highly respected by all the citizens.

Mr. Slayter and Mr. Dragoo both passed away a few years after moving to town.

The Slayters were parents of two children, John Henry and Mary. Both attended the Hagerman school. John Henry was also an able speaker, having been taught by his mother. She too, on rare occasions, would give readings. There was hardly ever a program at school or church at which John Henry did not give a reading.

After graduation from high school John Henry attended Park College at Kansas City, Missouri, graduating in 1926. He married Marian Paddock in 1928. Their only child, Betty, was born in Clovis in 1936. She is married and the mother of three children and lives in El Paso, Texas.

John Henry taught in several different school systems and retired from the Alamogordo school in 1962. He was a tutor for several years. Marian taught for several years and has been active in many organizations.

Mary graduated from Park College in 1929. She was married to Chandler Thomas in 1935. She taught for several years and retired from the Albuquerque school system in 1972. Marilyn, their only child, resides with her husband and two children in San Jose, California.

Many New Mexicans will remember Chandler Thomas as Grand Lecturuer and Grand Secretary of the Masonic Grand Lodge of New Mexico until 1971.

I, the writer, would like to add some memories I have of the Dragoo and Slayter families. I first became acquainted with them through the Sunday School and church.

I visited in their home many times. They lived in rooms adjoining the telephone exchange. I always was made welcome and became good friends of the family.

Somehow it became a custom for me to eat dinner with them on the Fourth of July. Always we had a big layer cake with chocolate frosting made by Grandmother Dragoo.

Mary and I would shoot firecrackers (often bought with money given to us by Dad Losey). Then we would go to the park where some kind of celebration was being held.

As I grew older I became acquanited with Marian Paddock and her family. It was a privilege to have known all of them.

THE SMITH AND COX FAMILIES

There were five of the Smith brothers, all bachelors. They lived in Texas and at one time had five hundred head of horses. A drought came so they drove the horses to south Texas where the grass was green. An epidemic struck and all but three of the horses died.

At another time they were partners with a banker in a cattle venture which turned out better than the horse deal. At other times they prospected in Guatemala and Honduras and mined in Idaho. They stuck together most of the time.

One of the brothers, Edmund, worked for years in a bank in Texas. The others decided to see the Pecos Valley in New Mexico which was being so highly advertised at that time. So they came, liked what they saw and settled near Lake Arthur. George and Charlie ran a hog ranch. Later they went into the sheep business and did quite well for a time. About 1920 prices dropped about fifty percent and many ranchers and banks were wiped out.

Alfred and Arthur came to Hagerman where they opened a Tin and Plumbing Shop in 1905. The shop was located on South Cambridge. They operated the shop until about 1920. Later the building was used for a meat market operated by Mr. Plattor and Sons. Bud Lawing bought the building and moved it to Argyle Street near where the post office now stands. He had a meat market and grocery store. The building stood vacant for a while, then one Thanksgiving or Christmas Day, it caught fire and burned. All that remained was a shell which had to be torn down.

Alfred and Arthur were joined in Hagerman by their two sisters, Harriet Smith and Mrs. Annie Cox and her three children. Stafford Cox was graduated from Hagerman

High School in 1911. A year later he died of burns received when a fire pot exploded in the tin shop. He and Edmund Smith are buried in the Hagerman Cemetery.

Lester Cox was graduated with the class of 1912, other members being Julia Boyce, Vivan Hall, Tessie Swann, George Parks and Worthy Newsom.

Lester earned a B.S. degree in mechanical engineering from what is now known as New Mexico State University in 1917. He worked for the Bureau of Ordnance and Naval Gun Factory in Washington, D.C., for five years. He then moved to California where he worked for thirty-two and a half years in the Engineering Department of the City of Los Angeles. He retired to acting engineer of Mendocino County for another four and a half years, retiring again to consulting engineer for Mendocino County for another four and a half years.

Laleah Cox married a Roswell man, George Hinson. Shortly afterward they moved to California where she served as postmistress for a number of years at Hayes, California. Laleah and her husband were the parents of one daughter. Laleah passed away a few years ago.

— Information from Lester Cox

THE STINE FAMILY
By Mrs. Edith Stine

Earl Stine, his wife, Edith, and son, Kenneth Earl, came to Hagerman in 1921. They made the trip by train, riding on the Narrow Gauge Railroad from Alamoso, Colorado, as far as Santa Fe. They were seeking a better climate as Mr. Stine suffered from asthma.

When they first arrived they stayed a short time with Mrs. Camp, then moved to a farm one and one quarter miles northeast of town. They raised alfalfa, some grain and cotton. Cotton was just beginning to be raised here so Mr. Stine hauled their first crop of a few bales to Roswell to have it ginned. No cotton gin had been built here. He used a team and wagon, starting from home at 4 A.M. and returning around midnight. Little Kenneth, four years old, went along just for the trip with Daddy.

Later dairy cattle were added to the farming.

All of the Stines were active members of the Methodist Church. Mr. Stine served on the official board, also taught a Sunday School class of intermediate boys. Mrs. Stine belonged to the Missionary Society and taught in the Primary Department for many years.

Mr. and Mrs. Stine served on all kinds of election boards.

Mr. Stine owned and operated one of the first Hagerman school buses, starting in the fall of 1930.

He began land leveling when he used a one horse scraper to take off high places. Later he started using a new Fresno and used a four horse team. Before starting to terrace and level his farm just south of the Felix River, Mr. W.E. Bowen, assisted by Kenneth Stine, surveyed the fields for him, then work began.

Mr. Stine passed away in 1946.

Following the disastrous flood of 1954, the land had to be leveled again. Mrs. Stine had the work completed by 1955 and became the first woman to receive a Banker's Award for Soil Conservation.

Kenneth received his grade school and high school education in the Hagerman school. His first teacher was Mrs. Stella B. Palmer, who taught many years in the Hagerman school. E.A. White was school superintendent while Kenneth was in school.

Kenneth was the first member of the Future Farmers of America in the Hagerman school to receive the State Farmers Award.

Kenneth went on to attend the University of New Mexico at Albuquerque and received a degree in mechanical engineering.

Kenneth was married to Margaret Slade, daughter of the late Rev. and Mrs. J.W. Slade, one time pastor of the Methodist Church here. They were the parents of two daughters, Ann and Earlene. Kenneth passed away in 1944, leaving his wife and two little girls.

At the time of his death, Kenneth was in Washington D.C., serving in Civil Service as Mechanical Engineer in the Ordnance Division of the War Department. His office was in the Pentagon.

Mrs. Stine continues to live in West Hagerman in the same place which has been the Stine home since January 1, 1924.

One incident Mrs. Stine will never forget occurred in 1921, when they were on the farm northeast of town. Across the road from them was the Delavan place where Mrs. Stine witnessed the "shoot-out" when Mr. Parks was killed and Guy Robinson was wounded. She furnished bedding to make a stretcher on which Mr. Robinson was carried to safety.

One of Earl Stine's first school buses, 1930.

THE EDWARD VAN SWEATT SR. FAMILY
By Edward Sweatt

E. Van Sweatt and his wife, Ada, moved from Barstow, Texas, in 1924 to Hagerman. The family included Edward Van Jr., Carolyn and Mearl.

Mr. Sweatt, his father and two brothers, Jack and Gene, had farmed large tracts of land in Ward County, Texas, and owned a mercantile store and a gin. The Pecos River water began to become scarce and salt was coming into the river from Malaga Bend. The Sweatt's sold their Texas lands and moved to New Mexico.

The Van Sweatt family moved to the Felix Ranch to farm. Mr. Sweatt dug an Artesian well in 1927 that was a good well. A small four and three eights off-size German make casing flowed into a reservoir from the well. Many people traveled for miles to get a tank of the sweet soft water. Mr. Sweatt piped water to stock tanks, workers houses and the family home. This was before many people in the town of Hagerman had water piped into their houses.

There were apple orchards on the northeast and southeast forty acres of the section. Most were old trees and didn't produce enough for commercial use. Mr. Sweatt immediately started cutting the orchards out. This was a difficult job since the roots were so large. Dynamite was used to blow the trees out of the ground and a winch rigging and a good three horse team were used to rid the land of the trees.

The big Felix ranch house with the porch all around was a joy to live in and a precious memory to the family and cousins and friends who came to visit. Mr. Sweatt hired a teacher, Violet Woodmas, to teach the Spanish workers' children to speak English.

While he lived in the Hagerman area, Mr. Van Sweatt was president of the school board for several years, owned an interest in the Hagerman gin and was president of the Drainage District System Board of Directors. He assisted in many civic projects and helped the underprivileged sometimes when he could not afford it. He was a likeable person and good to his many friends, hired men and family. Mrs. Sweatt was interested in culture for the town. She was instrumental in bringing music teachers to the community.

Looking back at Hagerman I can remember many interesting people and occurrences: Grandpa Miller's store and the way he liked to tease Mr. Harshey; Dad Losey was a cornerstone and solid rock of the community; Col. Tom McKinstry was exceptionally interesting to me; Pat Summers went after a sixty pound catfish with his bare hands. Nobody calls Royce Lankford "britches" anymore; Ike Boyce could throw a bale of hay higher than anyone and place it correctly from a hay wagon; Bob and Harry Cumpsten could lay the best hardwood floors in the county. Bay Curry was a mainstay and could repair anything. My first love was Juacille Barnett; L.W. Garner grew a finger nail on his little finger that measured exactly one inch. The 40° below zero weather in 1933 that split the cottonwood trees; "Vetta" Brown, "Teeds"; the time Mr. Jim Williamson was wounded in the leg by a desperado thought to be connected with Bonnie and Clyde Barrow. My mother missing church to prepare dinner, hoping to make a match between Doris Deter and Raymon Welborne.

I felt roots in Hagerman that I've felt no other place. I now live in Roswell with my wife, Merrell. Our oldest daughter is named Elizabeth Ann, and our second daughter is Mary Merrell.

My sister, Carolyn, is Mrs. Jimmy LeConey of Dayton, Ohio. She has two sons, Douglas Edward and Jon Tiffany. My other sister, Mearl, lives in Artesia, New Mexico, with her husband, Jabo Rich. They have a daughter, Margaret Rose Bean, and a son, Sammy Rich. They also have one grandson.

My father, Van Sweatt, died at the age of sixty. He was managing the Harroon Farms, Malaga, New Mexico at the time of his death. My mother, Ada Sweatt, is living in Artesia, New Mexico with my sister, Mearl.

THE JACK SWEATT FAMILY

By Lois Jean Sweatt Wiggins

The beautiful green Pecos Valley with its abundance of water, a promise of summer rain and warm winter days brought Jack and Sallie Sweatt from West Texas to farm cotton in Hagerman. Water had become scarce in the Pecos, Texas, area where Mr. Sweatt was involved in banking, farming and ranching.

In 1924 the Sweatts, along with two young daughters, Bernice and Dorothy, and their son, Van, came to Hagerman to live in an apartment above the bank building. Mr. Sweatt and his teen-age son returned to Texas to drive their cattle on foot to New Mexico. They brought along many hired men, but the cattle drive took several days due to a distance of about 140 miles.

The Buffalo Valley farm, east of Hagerman, was leased by the family. Later a house in town and the farm were bought by the Sweatts from a Mr. Abrams of Dallas, Texas.

After the family lived in New Mexico a while another daughter, Lois Jean, was born. All of the Sweatt children graduated from Hagerman High School with the exception of Van who attended New Mexico Military Institute.

Mr. Sweatt was an active and honorable man of business in the Pecos Valley. Always approachable and known for his shrewd practical commonsense, he was a just and upright citizen. He served on the Town Board as a trustee from 1930 to 1932 and again from 1940 until 1956. An active democrat, he enjoyed politics. His willingness to accept a job for his church, country, state and town was a great asset to Hagerman.

Mrs. Sweatt was active in civic and social clubs. She was a gracious hostess and her fine southern manners were admired by everyone. "Miss Sallie" was a relative of N.J. Fritz, who was sometimes referred to as the father of Hagerman because of his many years as a commissioner and because he was the town's first mayor.

Mr. and Mrs. Sweatt lived to celebrate their golden wedding anniversary in 1954. During their years in Hagerman they were lovingly called "Uncle Jack" and "Aunt Sallie" by young and old. This was brought about by a nephew, Jim Wheat, who came to live with the Sweatts.

Jack Sweatt.

Sallie Sweatt.

THE TANNER FAMILY
By LaRue Tanner Gibbs

Sometime during 1891, my grandfather, Oscar R. Tanner, left Birlington, Kansas, for the Pecos Valley of New Mexico. He was looking for a place that showed promise for the future, good farm land with plenty of water and a place for his children to grow up. He found what he was looking for and 1892 found him and his wife, Dillie, son Charles, who was six, and Ethel, four, on the newly opened railway bound for the Pecos Valley of New Mexico. The emigrants receipt for household goods and stock is still in my possession. They settled first in Otis, but a short time later moved on to Hagerman, where he opened up a real estate and insurance office, which he continued with until his death in November, 1936. He was interested in civic affairs, working for statehood for New Mexico and was the first Sunday School Superintendent for the Methodist Church. At one time he ran on the Republican ticket for State Representative and was Town Clerk in Hagerman for many years. Just before his death, he told me he hoped he could live to vote one more time in the national election, however, he didn't make it for he died on the Sunday before the election on Tuesday. His choice would certainly have been Alf Landon, for he was a stauch Republican.

Dillie Reed Tanner was born in Illinois, her mother and father had traveled from Vermont. As a young girl she attended Rockford Seminary for Young Ladies, which is today known as Rockford College in Rockford, Illinois. The Dillie Tanner I knew was not a very social person, she read a lot and played the organ. I remember when my father wired the house for electricity, she would turn it off and light the kerosene lamps. She also continued to dress in the old way. She died at eighty-eight.

Charles Tanner was a man of many talents and had an inquiring mind. After finishing school at Hagerman, he attended New Mexico Military Institute for three years. He was in the second graduating class. The next few years he had the first mail route between Artesia and Hope. During that time he married Pearl Lawrence and later they moved to Hagerman. Four years after their marriage, Pearl and Charles were divorced. There was one child of that marriage, Pauline, who is now Pauline Knouse and lives in Oklahoma City.

The following years, Charles Tanner operated a light plant and furnished Hagerman with electricity for eleven years. He also gave Hagerman the first silent movies in an outdoor theater. I remember he always referred to Mary Pickford as his favorite. "America's Sweetheart," he said. He bought his first auto (the first in town), married again, and, when I was born, moved to Chicago, where he was employed at the University of Chicago as an electrician. Sometime previous to this he had attended Coyne Electrical School. These were the years of bootlegging, short skirts and bobbed hair in Chicago. Somewhere along the line my mother was caught up in Aimee McPhearson's religion, which brought Charles and Ethel to the parting of their ways in 1928. My father and I left Chicago and came back to Hagerman. That was the time of the Great Depression. Grandpa had his own problems, and my father was fortunate to get a position as beacon light inspector for the U.S. Airways. One summer I went with him, slept in isolated hangers in Wyoming, Utah and Nevada, seeing the Great Salt Lake and other natural wonders. After several years of being single, he decided to remarry and chose a lady in Battle Creek, Michigan, Grace Ramsey. I guess you could say he settled down to becoming an electrical contractor, a tool salesman, and later, after my grandfather died, "keeper of the bees." These things filled his life. Grace Tanner died in 1970. He followed her in death in 1972.

As for me, I married in 1940 and came back to Hagerman during the Second World War with my two daughters. I still think of Hagerman as my home. The old place is still there (since 1894) and holds a lot of history. I now reside in Colorado.

Charles' sister, Ethel, went to Fairmont School for Girls, in Kansas and later to a school of nursing. She became a graduate nurse and married Ray Hyde of New York. They had four children. She never returned to New Mexico, and it is not known if she is still living.

MISS LUCY THOMAS
By her neice, Merrill Bush Allen

Miss Thomas came to the Pecos Valley in the early nineteen hundreds. She first lived with Miss Grace Wetherald, who was proving up on a claim near Greenfield. They both taught in the Greenfield school. Miss Thomas was a primary teacher. Then she taught in Lake Arthur. Her parents, Rev. Eli N. Thomas and Margaret Minerva Thomas, came out from Girard, Kansas. They then moved to Hagerman and she bought a piece of Mr. Ames' apple orchard and built a small house on it. It is still there on Argyle Street about two blocks west of the railroad tracks. While there she had several children living with her and going to school. One was a nephew from Kansas, named Charles Johnson, then my brother, Leslie Bush, from Hanley, New Mexico.

In 1909 I came and attended school, and I'm in a picture of the pupils of Hagerman High School, class of 1910, which is in this book. I was one of the members of the choir of the First Baptist Church, of which Roy Walworth was the director.

Miss Thomas taught in Artesia later and then to Roswell where she retired. She lived past ninety-three and is buried with her parents and half-brother in the Hagerman Cemetery. Her pallbearers were former pupils or husbands of former pupils. On her grave marker are the words "she went about doing good."

Hagerman High School, Class of 1910. 1. Vivian Hall 2. Julice John Boyce, 3. Hallie Robertson, 4. Lucy Clemer 5. Mary Boyce 6. Loveta Swann 7. Mae Jack McCoy 8. Chloe Camp 9. Tessie Robertson 10. Blanche Michelet 11. Tessie Swann 12. Prof. Adair 13. Arthur Wimberly 14. Virgil Parks 15. Daphne Lewis 16. Lulabee Williamson 17. Mabel Swann 18. Merrill Bush 19.Opha Bowen 20. Rose Michelet 21. Johnnie Clark 22. Prof. Paddock 23. Harold Miller 24. Ethen Parson 25. Gus Clemer 26. John Jacobson 27. Aron Clark 28. Maynard Tessler 29. Worthy Newson 30. Floyd Taylor.

THE R.N. THOMAS FAMILY
By R.N. Thomas

I first came to New Mexico in 1921 when I filed on a homestead at Hope. In Texas, my native state, I had been teaching school and ranching after serving in World War I. Upon returning to Texas from Hope I married beautiful, vivacious Velma Whittenton, with whom I had been teaching for three years. We both taught again, there in Texas, the fall of 1921 through the spring of 1922 before I accepted the position as Principal of Elementary Schools at Dexter as well as the baseball and basketball coaching job.

Mrs. Thomas preceded me in coming to New Mexico that summer of 1922 — her excuse being to help hold the claim on the homestead, but, candidly, she did attend school at Las Vegas during the summer.

After we taught one year at Dexter the Hagerman Board of Education offered both Mrs. Thomas and me positions if I would take the coaching job. We moved to Hagerman for the 1923-24 school year; Mrs. Thomas was the fifth grade teacher and I taught the eighth grade.

That school year, 1923-24, was a great year for basketball in Hagerman. We won the State Championship. I gave up the coaching job after this triumphant year but continued teaching for eight more years in Hagerman.

Mrs. Thomas was loved by all and was sought after, and thus agreed to sponsor the senior classes for the five years that she taught. She was active in several clubs and faithfully served as Girl Scout leader. We were members of the Methodist church.

I managed to stay busy during those years. Besides teaching, I owned a service station for two years, farmed some four years while running some sheep. I was also Boy Scout master.

We made many lasting friends in Hagerman, whom we left to teach and ranch in Eddy County. In 1938 I was elected as Eddy County Superintendent of Schools. Mrs. Thomas and I alternated in this same office for sixteen years. Later I worked in Carlsbad's Administration Offices until retirement. We now live at 1031 North Mesa Street, Carlsbad, New Mexico.

Our first child, Roy Newton, was born while we lived in Hagerman. He married and had two sons. Roy Newton died in 1960. His sons live in El Paso. Our other son, Jimmy, lives with his wife, son and daughter in Las Cruces.

TRUITT* — LEMON FAMILIES

Laura Greer, 1867-1947, sister of J.W. Greer, was born in Keene, Texas. At the age of twenty-one, she married D.R. Lemon and to this happy couple were born a daughter, Tola, and a son, Clay. Early in 1893, Mr. Lemon passed away.

In 1899 Mrs. Lemon was married to George L. Truitt, a widower with three sons and two daughters. To this union were born three daughters, Mintie and Minnie (the twins), Edith, and one son, Earl.

The family moved to Hagerman from Texas in 1904 and settled on a farm three miles west of Hagerman. Close neighbors were the Newsom, Heitman, and Jenkins families. Lois Titus remembers the Truitt home as a "picture book" home, with a white, two-story house, red barns, vine-covered windmill tower and beautiful flowers. This lovely home was completely destroyed by fire in 1941, nothing was saved, but no one was hurt.

"Uncle George" and "Aunt Laura," as they were affectionately called by many of their friends, were faithful workers in the Seventh Day Adventist Church. This church had its own grade school and the Truitt children attended this school in Hagerman until they were sent to Keene, Texas, for high school and later to college.

Several members of this family remained in church work. Ernest Truitt served as a missionary in Puerto Rico, later became an optometrist in California, and Florine Truitt McHenry was a missionary in India. Minnie and Mintie Truitt worked in the General Conference of the Seventh Day Adventist Church in Washington D.C., from 1921 until their retirement a few years ago. Edith Truitt Burchfield's husband, Raleigh, served as treasurer for several church conferences and Oda Truitt married Arthur Lickey, a minister and author of the book, "God Speaks to Modern Man." Tola Lemon Blakley was a teacher.

Following Mrs. Truitt's death, Mr. Truitt went to California to stay with a daughter and remained there until his death about 1950. They are both buried in the Hagerman Cemetery.

Information from Mrs. Clay Lemon, Lois Jenkins Titus and a story on the Hagerman Seventh Day Adventist Church by Grace Cole Greer.

HENRY CLAY LEMON
By Dorothy Devenport West

Clay Lemon, 1891-1965, was born in Savoy, Texas, and moved to Hagerman with his mother and step-father, George Truitt. He was married to Iola Gertrude Devenport in 1917 and their daughter, Ida Bea, was born in 1919.

Clay started to work for the Hagerman Irrigation Company in 1915, as a ditch rider, and retired from the company after forty-eight years of service. During most of those years he served as superintendent, also secretary-treasurer, as well as being a ditch rider. His early day ditch riding was done with a horse and cart.

In an interview for the Roswell Daily Record, at the time of his retirement, he told of some of the changes. He said, "The water is way down from what it used to be. The Felix River flowed plenty of water. North and South Spring Rivers had enough water, so that boat loads of people could be taken for rides. In those days water was $2.00 an acre, now it sells for $12.00, but there wasn't as much land under cultivation then."

The Lemon's daughter, Ida Bea, was married to Sanford Knoll in 1937. They farmed west of Hagerman until they moved to Lovington, New Mexico, in 1952. They continue in farming. They are parents of two sons and a daughter.

Clay and Iola were faithful members of the Church of Christ, and it was Clay's voice that often led the singing. Generous with their time and money, kind with their words, they were loved by many people.

After Clay's death in 1965, Iola moved to Lovington to be near her daughter and her family. She remains faithful to her church, family and friends.

UTTERBACK FAMILY HISTORY IN NEW MEXICO
By W.E. Utterback

My father, J.A. Utterback, moved to Roswell from Hubbard, Iowa, in April of 1903. My mother had died in Iowa, and Dad batched and raised us three boys. I was the oldest, fourteen at the time; Burt was twelve and Winfred nine. Dad rented a small twenty acre farm near the Country Club in Roswell.

As we grew up we began to scatter out. Winfred started in as a printers devil at the old Register Tribune, working under Bill Robertson. The Hall brothers worked there at about the same time. Winfred (Dutch) was a printer all of his life and finally owned a job printing shop in Oklahoma City. He was married twice but had no children. His widow still runs the Utterback Type Setting Co. on South Walker, Oklahoma City.

Burt worked at several different jobs. At one time he worked for the Telephone Company under Frank Markl. He married and had one daughter, Mrs. Robert Metzner, Phoenix, Arizona. Burt died in Phoenix in 1966.

I worked on farms all my life and at one time worked for John Stone south of the Country Club. In 1910 Dad and I moved just south of Greenfield. Burt and Dutch stayed in Roswell. It was here I met a brown eyed filly of the Lathrop family who had just moved to Greenfield from Ohio. I darn near camped at the Lathrop place until she said yes. We were married April 10, 1912. We have four children, Tom, Ruth, Stanley and Robert.

Tom married Pauline Duncan, is retired from the U.S. Forest Service, lives in Oragon City, Oragon, has a son, a daughter and five grandchildren.

Ruth married Harlan Brown (deceased), is teaching in the Las Vegas, Nevada, school system, has a son, two daughters and five grandchildren.

Stanley married Vivian Hadley, they have a son, four daughters and four grandchildren.

Robert married Edna Johnson and they have two sons and two daughters.

Stanley and Robert bought all the Utterback farm land between Hagerman and the Pecos River and live here east of Hagerman.

In my family this all adds up to four children, fourteen grandchildren and fourteen great-grandchildren.

Mr. and Mrs. W. E. Utterback.

Mr. and Mrs. Utterback on their
Golden Anniversary, 1962.

THE UTTERBACKS AT HAGERMAN
By Stanley Utterback

Hope Lathrop Utterback and W.E. (Ernest) Utterback, my mother and father, moved to Hagerman in 1915. They farmed rented land for several years before settling in one place and buying a farm. The Stewart place was their first Hagerman home. From there they moved to Buffalo Valley, then back across the Pecos River to the Harter farm. Their next move was to the Elliott place and in 1924 they bought 200 acres from The Union Central Life Insurance Co. This was the site of the family home while we were growing up. Through the years, they bought forty acres from Noah West, forty acres from Ralph Walker, forty acres of the Hall tract and eighty acres of drainage land. In 1951 Mom and Dad bought the Mayre Losey Stewart home and are still living there.

The early years were busy years. Everyone worked hard and put in long hours. Mom sold cream and butter, raised turkeys and chickens, sold eggs and even took her turn on the horse drawn mowing machines. Many days she spent at the pump on the river to be sure the old Primn engine kept running and the irrigation would be uninterrupted.

Church work has always been an important part of Mom's life. She was a member of the Christian Church, taught a Sunday School class and was pianist. At one time she organized a church band within the youth group. When the Christian Church closed its doors, she joined the Presbyterian Church and is a faithful member and a diligent worker in the Ladies Aid.

Years ago she was a member of the Rebekahs, the Ladies Co-Operative Club, the Hagerman Woman's Club and is still a member of O.E.S., being Worthy Matron in 1939 and serving as treasurer for twenty-eight years.

After starting to expand the family farm Mom and Dad continued to rent some additional land, and Dad did a great deal of custom hay baling and seeding.

As farming became more mechanized and he no longer had to care for and work horses and mules, Dad was able to become more active in civic affairs. He was a member of the Oddfellows Lodge, the Young Farmer's Club, Lions Club, served as a charter Board Member of the Farmers Co-Op Gin Association, as well as a board member of the Soil Conservation District. He is a charter member and past president of the Chaves County Farm Bureau and served on the County Board for several years.

In 1951 he entered politics and served one term in Santa Fe as Representative from Chaves County.

Dad is known as "Waterback" and "Water Utterback" to many people through out the state due to his knowledge of, and limitless hours spent in the interest of, the Pecos Valley waters. He helped organize the Pecos Valley Pumpers Association.

In the early 1930's Dad played catcher for the Cowboy softball team at Hagerman. It was one of several teams and they had the first lighted field in New Mexico.

His love of baseball is still with him and when the Little League program was to become a reality for Hagerman, he worked long and hard with everyone to get the park laid out, fenced and grassed. He is honored by having the park named "Utterback Field." To this day he is still the No. 1 "bush shaker" when the annual fund raising time rolls around.

In retirement he has renewed his interest in collecting anything he feels is becoming obsolete. He has old harness, hand tools, pictures and numerous small items stored at home. On the farm he has parked his old machinery. There you can find a buck rake, dump rake, a horse drawn mower, three threshing machines, of which two were once used by Mark Boyce, and four old balers. The 1910 Eagle horse power baler has been restored and Dad gives demonstrations at the annual Hay Shows in the state, thus keeping alive a part of the past that is so rapidly being forgotten.

All four of us children graduated from Hagerman school and continued our education at New Mexico A&M, presently known as New Mexico State University.

THE GEORGE WADE FAMILY

George E. Wade was born in Ladonnia, Missouri, and moved with his family, at the age of three, to the Indian Territory which is now Oklahoma. He started to school in Miami, Oklahoma. The family moved to New Mexico in 1907 for his father's health. They homesteaded east of Dexter.

George continued his education at Spring Mound Valley school. He went through the eighth grade there then rode horseback to Dexter to attend high school.

During his growing-up years he learned to ride and rope well. When he was seventeen he broke horses for $1.50. For $1.00 he would ride anything with a saddle on it.

In 1916 he married Mable Lawing, daughter of Tom Lawing. When they married they had twenty dollars plus the cost of the marriage license. With this money they bought a table and oil cook stove from a second hand store. George's father gave them a mare and colt and Mr. Lawing gave them a cow, a calf and a pig.

The Wade family moved to Hagerman after having bought a forty acre farm. The whole family worked on the farm. When they were not busy on the farm they did all kinds of hauling, house moving and dirt moving. At times when the canal would become choked with sand or weeds they would dredge it.

The next year they bought an adjoining farm which had a two-story house on it. (This was known as the Tom McKinstry place, now owned by Mrs. Max Wiggins.) Through the years George would buy land until his farming operation totaled more than four hundred acres.

The Wade children, Grace, Ruth, George Jr. and Mable Jo, all attended the Hagerman school and all graduated from the high school. Grace and Ruth attended Texas State College for Women at Denton, Texas. Grace went two years, but Ruth obtained her degree. She taught for a time in Hagerman, then went to Roswell and has been a teacher in the Roswell schools for many years.

George Jr. attended the New Mexico Military Institute. He farmed at Hagerman for a while then moved to Carlsbad where he had an implement agency.

Grace married Irvin (Rip) Coleman. They are the parents of a son, George. They made their home in Dexter for a number of years but now reside in Roswell.

Ruth married Richard Burl O'Neal of Roswell. They have a daughter, Peggy. Mr. O'Neal is now deceased.

George Jr. married Evelyn Heinrich. Their daughters are Susanna, Brenda and Karen. They now live in El Paso, Texas.

Mable Jo married Ivo Paul Weber. They have five children, Ronnie Paul, Cecilia, Sharon, Linda and Carol. They make their home in Albuquerque, New Mexico.

While living in Hagerman the Wade children attended the Presbyterian Church.

Later Mr. Wade went into the ranching business and was owner and operator of several large ranches all the way from Quemado to the Caprock.

In 1966 their children honored them with a reception at the Roswell Inn on their fiftieth wedding anniversary. Both George and Mable are now deceased having passed away within a few months of each other. They were laid to rest in South Park Cemetery at Roswell.

THE F.G. WALTERS FAMILY
By Leo Walters

Frank G. Walters and wife, Josephine, came to Hagerman to make their home in 1906 from Winfield, Kansas. They had two sons, Joseph Anthony and Leo James. The information concerning this family came from Leo who now lives in Wichita, Kansas.

He wrote that his mother and the two boys stayed the first night in Hagerman at the hotel which was then under the management of a man named Bryant. Then they stayed with a Davidson family whose farm adjoined the one his father had bought. His father came on the freight train with the household goods, three horses and one cow.

Leo remembered that he and some friends were swimming in the Felix River near the site of the dam being built when a cave-in occurred burying two men.

Leo wrote, "It was tougher in those days but I believe we all looked after one another and were more happy than today. Today everything is upside down — too much greed. I always considered Hagerman my first love and regretted leaving there. After we moved to Roswell I used to go back to help Mr. Wranosky on the ranch."

The Walters family were Catholics and faithful to the church.

THE OSCAR WALTERS FAMILY
By Bernice Walters West

Sara Ann Stafford married Liberty Walters and lived in Missouri. Later they moved to the San Saba, Texas, area and then lived in Dexter, New Mexico, for many years. Their children were: Oscar, Osie, Estella, Omer (or Omar), Otto, Ora, and Olga.

Oscar Walters married Zantha Orlena (Lena) Gavness in Cherokee, Texas, in 1885. They moved to Roswell, New Mexico, in 1896, coming via covered wagon. Oscar was born in Missouri in 1874 and died in 1955. Lena was born in Texas in 1874 and died in 1950.

Oscar worked for the Turkey Track Ranch for years. In earlier days, about 1902-1905, he ran a chuckwagon for the ranch. A picture of Oscar with his chuckwagon and six cowboys eating lunch appeared in the *Western Horseman* magazine about 1970.

After several years Oscar Walters accumulated his own herd of cattle and ranched east of Hagerman and Dexter, New Mexico.

Children of Oscar and Lena were: Floyd, 1896-1918; Roxy Ann (Mrs. Clayton) Moore, 1897-1971; Lester who married Beryl West and had a daughter; Ealen (Mrs. Howell) Gage, 1900; Bernice (Mrs. Guy A.) West, 1903, who had a daughter; Bessie (Mrs. Ray) Carey, 1906-1971; Joe, 1912-1950 who married Mildred Jordan and had son; and Edgar, 1915, who married Joe's widow, Mildred.

All the children of Oscar and Lena Walters were able ranch hands, participating in roundups, brandings, etc. They spent much of their time on horses. On one occasion Roxy was sitting on her cow pony in front of the bank in

Hagerman, chatting with friends, when along came a run-a-way team of horses hitched to a hack running east on main street. Roxy unfurled her lasso and gave chase. She layed it on the run-a-ways and pulled them down and led them back to town.

On another occasion when Roxy was in school and had beaten all the girls at foot racing, Roy King was the men's champ and a challenge developed matching the two for the school championship. They ran in front of the schoolhouse and Roxy took the honors.

Oscar and Lena used to provide free music for the cowboy dances. Later son Floyd assisted. Oscar and Floyd played fiddle and Lena played piano and mandolin. Floyd may have seconded on the mandolin at times. The dances usually lasted all night, breaking up at dawn. Some of these events took place in Hagerman, others on various ranches from time to time.

On occasions when the cowboys were in town, various kinds of diversion were followed. There were what were known as "tenderfoots," meaning greenhorn cowpokes. The older hands had a lot of sport picking on the tenderfoots. One of the old time favorite stunts was to talk up a bite fight between a big bulldog and a badger. They would try to dare some neophyte to take on the job of pulling the badger, which consisted in pulling the "badger" by rope from under a wash tub. The dog was standing by in readiness. Some one lifted the edge of the tub a bit while the tenderfoot dragged the "badger" out in the open. At that point every one except the tyro died laughing. The "badger" was a common chamber pot half full of beer in which was floating a hot dog or sausage! Some fights usually ensued but not between the dog and the "badger!"

THE WALWORTHS

Roy and Edward Walworth came from a fertile agricultural area near Mazon, Illinois, early in 1906. Both were in search of land, and Roy was also searching for a climate which would improve his health.

The brothers settled on adjoining half-sections three-fourths of a mile south and five miles west of the Hagerman business district. Roy took possession of the east half of Section 23, Township 14, Range 25 East on March 1, 1906. Edward, on March 28, 1906, acquired the south half of Section 14, Township 14, Range 25 East.

The residence was a sheet metal barn about forty-five feed wide and ninety feet long located on Edward's property. Inside the barn, in the southeast corner, a large tent was set up, divided into four rooms and comfortably furnished. The remainder of the barn was used to house implements and ranch products.

It is not clear whether a sister, Lois, accompanied Ed and Roy to Hagerman or whether she came a short time later to keep house for them. Lois returned to Illinois in 1908 and another sister, Jessie, came to take her place. In the course of time, Jessie also became a property owner in the area. From time to time other members of the Walworth family visited in and around Hagerman.

The Walworths were active members of the Hagerman Baptist Church. For a period of time Roy directed a choir which was composed of persons from the Baptist and Presbyterian congregations. Since services were held on alternate Sundays in the two churches, the choir served the church in which the meeting was being held.

Roy married Tessie Parks, daughter of John W. Parks of Hagerman, in December of 1911. In the spring of 1912 they moved to Pine Lodge in the Capitan mountains, which Roy managed for ten years.

Edward married Frances Hines, also of Hagerman. They eventually returned to Illinois.

Jessie married Harlan Boyce of Hagerman in 1916. They moved to Iowa in 1918.

The above was written by Harlan W. Boyce, son of Jessie and Harlan Boyce, aided by legal documents and interviews with Tessie Parks Walworth and others who knew the Walworths personally.

Walworth family. Front row, l. to r: Mary Boyce, Jessie Walworth, Tessie Parks, Nellie Hines. Back row, l. to r: Ollin Waters, Harlan Boyce Edward Walworth, Roy Walworth.

THE WARE FAMILY
By Hal W. Ware

Robert M. Ware and Caroline Waughop were married in Chicago, September 27, 1881, and raised a family of four: Ellen, born 1882; Jo, 1884; Hal, 1886, and Alice, 1891.

R.M. Ware and E.A. Paddock came to the Pecos Valley on a Talmadge excursion train in 1904 to look over the country. They both were anxious to get away from city life. They were favorably impressed and decided to make the change. They secured a section of land about five and half miles northwest of Hagerman and two miles west of Greenfield.

The Paddocks came down in the spring of 1905. They built a home and got things started. The Wares waited until school was out and started in July. Ellen had married Sterling Goddard and did not come to New Mexico. Mr. and Mrs. Ware and Alice came by train in late July and brought a carload of furniture. Jo and Hal started the first of the month by freight train in an immigrant car and landed in Greenfield about a week later. It was a most memorable trip. We had nine horses in one end of the car and the other end was filled with miscellaneous equipment, such as a farm wagon (knocked down), a buggy, a windmill, plows, fence posts and wire for a corral and lumber for a shed plus a couple of hundred bundles of shingles for the house we were going to build. The space between the doors was our bedroom — mattress on the floor with pillows and blankets, suitcases, and, believe it or not, we also had two dogs.

We loaded the car in Riverside, a residential suburb of Chicago, and in the evening we were picked up by a through freight and landed in Kansas City the next day and switched to another train. At Wichita, Kansas, we received a severe bump and the horses were piled up against the partition and broke it down and messed things pretty badly. They switched the car to the stockyards and we unloaded the horses — one was hurt so badly we had to leave her. We patched up the damage and moved on the next day. From there on we unloaded the horses at the stockyards each night and it made things easier for all concerned. We landed in Greenfield on July 8, and moved everything out to what was to be "home." There was so much to do. We had to have water for domestic use so a well was drilled and a windmill with a water tank put up. A barn with corral was built for the horses and a shed for the folks who were coming soon. The land was all range land so it all had to be fenced to keep the cattle out.

Dad sent a carpenter down from Chicago and the foundation for the house had to be completed when the lumber arrived — two carloads shipped from Texas.

The folks arrived the last of July and took up residence in the shed. Jo and I lived in a boarded up tent.

An artesian well was drilled (nice fresh flowing water) and a reservoir was built. Ditches were made and plowing was going on most of the time — getting ready for spring planting.

The house was finally completed and we moved in soon after the first of the year (1906) and life in New Mexico began for the Wares.

At this time this country gave every evidence of being a fruit country. There were many apple orchards throughout the valley. Each year many carloads of apples were picked, packed and shipped out, making lots of work for people wanting it.

After all, other farm crops were needed and everyone grew lots of alfalfa hay and sorghum grain, oats and barley. All this farming was done with horsepower. Harvesting a hay crop was quite a chore; mowing, raking, baling and hauling to the railroad with horses was hard work. Methods of farming improved all the time; new and better machinery and tractors.

The climate and weather were not so favorable for growing fruit. There was frost in the spring and an increasing need for spraying. The older orchards were dying and a good many of the younger orchards were abandoned.

Fortunately cotton was soon introduced and a new cash crop developed and took hold.

The living was rather crude then — coal or wood stoves for cooking and heating; washtubs and washboards for laundry; candles, lamps and lanterns for light. Soon gas and electric power were brought to the farm and times improved.

Anytime anyone wanted to go to town a horse and buggy had to be hitched up, or a surrey or wagon, or possibly just a horse and saddle. But low and behold, Model T came along so the roads had to be graded and gravelled or surfaced and more and more cars appeared until before long the little "Puddle Jumper," (train) had to give it up. It had served the public of the Pecos Valley well for many years. When the schedule was right one could go to Roswell in the morning, tend to his business or shop and come home that evening. It was much easier than driving a horse and buggy, which made a long day on the road with little time in Roswell. It also connected with the main line for anyone going east or west by train.

As a family we had many good times — lots of friends in both Dexter and Hagerman, with many parties and picnics, etc. Mother Ware was interested in the Hagerman doings — Thursday Club and card clubs and other things. Our home life was always interesting, too, with all the children around during the summers. Alice grew up and married Roger Elliot in 1910 and they had three children. Ellen, who lived in Chicago, was married to Sterling Goddard in 1903 and they had five children. They were often here in the summers. The Paddocks had four girls. In 1912 Louise Thode and I were married and we contributed three. They were not all here at the same time but we had many jolly picnics and parties. We had our Thanksgiving dinners with the Paddocks and Christmas was a merry time with the Wares.

Mother and Dad grew old on the farm, and he died in 1942 just before his eighty-fifth birthday. Mother lived on for several years on the farm and in Chicago with Ellen. She died in Chicago in 1954. They are both buried in South Park Cemetery in Roswell.

Louise and I and the kids were in Idaho for about eight years and returned in 1934. Dad was getting too old to work so we took over, and when the folks died we bought out the other heirs. We developed more water and put in more land.

As the children grew up Margaret took a nurses training course in Denver General Hospital. After graduation she went to the Navy Hospital in San Diego and met Ted Ivers, a chief petty officer in the Navy. They married in 1940 and raised two fine sons.

Robert graduated from the Naval Academy at Annapolis in 1937, took flight training and went through the war with Japan. After returning he married and later retired from the Navy. He and his wife, Edie, now live in Guadalajara, Mexico.

Hal Jr. graduated from high school in Hagerman and went to New Mexico A. and M. After time out for war service in Italy in the Air Force he graduated in 1947. He married Blanche Egerton and they now live in Tucson, Arizona.

We sold the farm to T.H. Boswell III in 1964 and retired to Artesia where we bought a house next door to Ted and Margaret and are living there now.

REV. ANGUS E. WATFORD

The Reverend Angus E. Watford and his wife, Ruby H. Watford, came to Hagerman in 1928 from Davis, Oklahoma. They brought with them five children, Paul, Elwood (deceased), Marguerite, Wilbur and Joyce. All the children married. Two of them married local young people. Elwood married Joyce West and Marguerite married James Burck (deceased).

The Reverend Watford was minister in the local Methodist Church and was a thirty-third degree Mason. He retired from the Oklahoma Methodist Conference in 1929. He had come to New Mexico for his health and died in 1929. His wife, Ruby, died in 1969.

THE WEST BROTHERS

Arkansas was home to John Allen West, his wife, Elizabeth Clement West, and their ten children. The boys were James, Noah, Ben Jack, William, Greenberry, Joe, J. Tolliver, H. Earl and Charles. There was one daughter, Ella. All of the children, except Greenberry, lived in Hagerman at one time or another. The father had died before any of the family came to New Mexico. The mother lived here only a short time, but she died here in 1937 while staying with the B.J. West family. Three of the boys, Noah, Ben Jack and Tollie, remained in Hagerman to raise their own families. Will's family left for several years but returned to Hagerman.

THE NOAH WEST FAMILY
By Guy West

I was born in Arkansas in 1898, but the family moved to West Texas about 1902. In 1904 we moved on to New Mexico by train, I think. My father was attracted by the apple growing industry in the Hagerman area. We located on what later became known as the Pomona Farm, about two-thirds of a mile north of Hagerman.

My father was married to Martha (Mattie) Mullis, daughter of Duke and Betty Mullis. They had eight children, Harvey, Guy, Beryl, Joe, Roy, Jack, Jeff and Ruth. He served as Mayor for one or more terms and was a member of the school board for many years. We were Methodists.

I did not go to school the first year, as an older neighbor girl had told me the brush field through which I would have to walk was full of mad dogs. My mother taught me my ABC's from an old flour sack while she did her churning and other chores. Later I managed to catch up with my class and graduate on time.

My boyhood days were spent working on the farm when school was not in session. In 1917 I volunteered for service in World War I and served for nearly two years. Harry and Robert Cumpsten, George and Vergil Parks were some of the others serving at the same time.

In the old days the two artesian wells provided sulphurous water for the town. I recall seeing one well shoot water at least fifty feet high!

When we first moved to Hagerman herds of antelope came nearby, but they soon learned to stay away. On a recent visit to Hagerman I was shocked to find the Felix River dry. As a small boy I caught ninety perch in one afternoon near the "little dam," a half mile or so above the old bridge. Also, I've killed hundreds of rabbits east of the Pecos River. It is sad to think that this thrill is denied the boys of today.

In 1922 I married Bernice Walters, daughter of Oscar and Lena Walters, and began my teaching career at the Lake Arthur High School (then a two-year institution). After one year I moved to Silver City and worked in colleges and universities there and elsewhere for the next forty-two years. I retired in 1965 as President Emeritus (and founding president) of the California State University at Sacramento. We have one daughter and are now living in Dallas, Texas, near her and her family.

My parents moved from Hagerman to San Jose, California, in 1946 to be near their children and died there (my father at age ninety-four).

The following is a brief report on my brothers and sisters who are still living: Beryl West Walters is retired and lives in San Jose. She has one daughter. Joe West, retired Dean Emeritus of the California State University at San Jose. A twelve-story residence hall at the university bears his name. He lives at Sun City, California, and has one son. Roy lives in San Francisco and has one daughter. He owns and operates two apartment buildings there. Jeff retired as Assistant Superintendent of the Stockton, California, City Schools. He has one son. Ruth West Jung lives in San Jose. She and her husband own a jewelry store and have two daughters.

We have many fond memories of the early days in the pioneering atmosphere of Hagerman and the Pecos Valley.

BEN JACK WEST
By Ray West

It was cold and windy when the B.J. West family came to New Mexico about 1906. They traveled in a covered wagon from Plainview, Texas, and the roads were very bad. When we came to the Caprock, Dad had to lock the back wheels on the wagon with a chain to keep the wagon from running over the team.

After arriving in Hagerman we settled on what is now known as the E.E. Lane farm, north of the Felix. Some of Dad's brothers were already in Hagerman, so he helped them bale hay with a foot-feed hay baler. Later Dad bought an Auto-Fedan baler and then he baled some for the public.

He sold apples and hay off the farm. He hauled them to town by team and wagon and loaded them on box cars. Later, after the alfalfa mill was built, he could haul the hay loose in the wagon.

I rode to school on a burro, and later, when my sister started school, we both rode the burro. Later Dad let us take a horse and buggy. We had great fun to and from school with the other kids.

Dad sold the farm and moved near West Plains, Missouri. We stayed about six months, then moved back to Hagerman and bought a farm just north of the one we'd sold before going to Missouri.

My mother passed away in 1920. There were three children, Thelma (Mrs. Fred Parrish) of Silver City, New Mexico; Ruby (Mrs. Eckrey) of Salmon, Idaho; and myself, Ray West. I live in Dexter and retired after eighteen years with the Farmers Cooperative Gin Association. I have twin sons.

In 1922 my father married Eva Swann Powell. They lived at 400 E. Sterling for many years. He was a successful farmer and very active in many organizations and the community. They left the area in the early forties and he died in Las Cruces in 1947. Eva West returned to Hagerman to make her home.

W.P. WEST FAMILY
By Verna West Curry

William Pickens West, a bachelor, came to Hagerman from Pine Bluff, Arkansas, in 1905, to join his brothers. He was a ditch rider with Burt Bailey for the Hagerman Canal Co. until he became an ordained minister in the Methodist Church in 1911.

In 1906 Will wrote a letter, a brief proposal of marriage, to Flora Ethel Wilson, a school teacher in Rison, Arkansas, telling her, "This is the most wonderful country in the world. I am coming back to marry you and bring you out here." She accepted his proposal and they were married in September of 1906.

Their first home was a small house, owned by the Hagerman Canal Co., between Greenfield and Dexter. Their first child, Tennie Ethel, was born here in 1907. Their next two children, John Williams (1908) and Verna (1910), were born while living in a house just north of the Felix River bridge.

While they were living in this house a big flash flood came down the Felix and nearly washed the house away. It was a frightening experience, as the water was filled with snakes, so the house was moved to the top of a hill, a little farther north, and added to a house formerly owned by Arvid Johnson.

After being licensed as a minister, Will and the family moved to their first pastorate in Elida, New Mexico. While serving there another son was born, Wilson Pickens (1912). He was to have been called Wilson, after Flora's sixth cousin President Woodrow Wilson, but people were soon referring to him as "little Woodie" so his mother quickly decided to use his middle name of Pickens.

Will preferred to move from a church every two years as he felt a new minister added life to a church. Following the pastorate in Elida, he served in Melrose (1913-1915) where their fifth child, Emma Joyce, was born here in 1914; Dayton (1915-1917) serving the church at Weed too, during this time. His last church was at Dexter (1917-1919). Ill health forced him to resign in October of 1919.

During the years of the ministry, Will and Flora supplemented their meager salary. While in Dayton, Flora worked peeling tomatoes for a local cannery. She was a frugal, capable person and sewed beautifully. She made all the family clothes, including Will's shirts, as he was over six feet tall, and could not be fitted with ready-made shirts. While in Dexter, Will worked as night watchman for the Pecos Valley Milling Company and grew enough vegetables so that the surplus could be traded at the local grocery stores for the family staples.

Following the complete failure of Will's health, the family spent some time at Port Aransas, Texas, hoping this would be a benefit to him, but this did not help. Following a short stay near relatives in Rison, Arkansas, they returned to Hagerman.

He was growing weaker and knew he would not live long. They bought the fifty acre farm north of the Felix River bridge where they had lived once before. He wanted a place where Flora could live and raise five kids after he was gone. It was a familiar, but sad sight, to see Will driving a buggy around the farm teaching Flora how to plant, irrigate, cultivate and harvest the crops. He died in September of 1921.

His widow carried on and her success can best be told by excerpts from a story written by Rev. Harold Dye (Baptist minister) and published in The Hagerman Messenger in December, 1933.

"I saw her out in the field the other day as she drew the sleeves of her blue shirt across her brow which was moist with the sweat of hard toil. It was getting dark and for twelve hours she had been at labor on her farm, and now she turned homeward, body tired, but soul satisfied that she had played the game yet another day.

"She did not ask for the admiration of men — she had it. She did not deal in flirtation to win their love — they brought it unsought and laid it at her feet — the deepest, most abiding form of love — honor, reverence and respect."

Flora was active in the Methodist Church. She was a charter member of the Woman's Society of Christian Service and her Life Membership pin went with her to her grave. She lived a happy useful life to the end and died in 1968. She had achieved her life's ambition of seeing her children educated and married and had been surrounded by love from family and friends.

Ethel graduated from Hagerman, attended Texas Woman's College in Fort Worth, Texas. She married Alva Lloyd (Ted) Curry, son of pioneer couple, Mr. and Mrs. C.W. Curry, in 1926. He worked for the Santa Fe Railroad in Loving, New Mexico, and then in Roswell. Ethel worked as a ticket agent for the Santa Fe from 1943 to 1972. She lives in Roswell. They had one son.

John graduated from Hagerman and attended McMurray College in Abilene, Texas. He helped his mother on the farm and was employed at the Hagerman Gin when he died after a long bout with sugar diabetes in 1932 at age twenty-one.

Verna graduated from Hagerman and attended Texas Woman's College in Fort Worth, Texas, then worked as a bookkeeper for the First National Bank in Hagerman. She married Vinton Curry, brother of Ethel's husband, in 1930. He taught in Colorado until he retired as Professor Emeritus of Accounting from the University of Colorado in 1971. She worked in various banks and businesses as a bookkeeper for many years. They now live at Mercer Island, Washington.

Pickens graduated from Hagerman and McMurray College. He was employed, immediately following graduation, as a bookkeeper for Pecos Valley Milling Company and was later promoted to mill manager. He worked in mill management for twenty-seven years, mainly in Lamar, Colorado. He now runs his own Real Estate and Insurance Company there. He married Mary June Grace in Rupert, Idaho, in 1938. She died in June of 1975.

Joyce graduated from Hagerman and married Elwood Watford, son of Rev. and Mrs. A.E. Watford of Hagerman. They farmed for several years before going into the grocery business in Hagerman and operated this store until Elwood's death in 1969. Joyce is now employed as a bookkeeper for Keeth Gas Company in Hagerman. They had two sons and a daughter.

J.T. WEST FAMILY
By Dorothy Devenport West

John Tolliver "Tollie" West came to Hagerman in 1907. He settled on a farm northwest of town, across the Felix River. His mother, a brother, Charlie, and sister, Ella, lived with him for a time until they returned to Arkansas.

In 1909 he married Edith McKinstry. They moved to 303 N. Oxford in Hagerman, and Tollie worked for the Joyce-Pruitt store until it burned; then he sold insurance. Their second home was located east of the cotton gin. This home had been a Hagerman Ranch Line Camp and was set in a forty acre farm. They had four children, Loveta (1910), Donald (1914), Sara Beth (1919) and Robert (1923).

About 1925 he started the J.T. West Feed and Seed business, located just west of the railroad tracks on Argyle. This was a varied business. In the early years he shipped in flour by the boxcar load for the grocery stores, bought and shipped cream in ten gallon cans by rail. He cleaned and ground grain, including corn meal, bought and cleaned alfalfa seed, shipping it all over the country. In a few years a garage and filling station were added to the business, also a cotton seed delinter. In 1937, he obtained the contract for the Hagerman school buses and retained this until his death in 1952. He sold the feed and seed business to his son, Robert, in 1946.

Tollie was generous in his support of the Presbyterian Church. He was active in the Masonic Lodge and the Order of Eastern Star. He loved to hunt and fish. He will be remembered best for his service to the town of Hagerman. He served as Mayor for a total of fifteen years, and his famous temper was often used to fight battles for the town. Many projects (such as water and sewer) were started and concluded during his administration.

John Tolliver West.

Edith was a capable homemaker and a talented worker in many organizations. She became a member of Harmony Chapter #17 O.E.S. in 1909 and remained a member until her death in 1973. She was active in Missionary-Aid Circle of the Presbyterian Church, Woman's Club and Thursday Club. She loved gardening and her yard was a mass of beautiful flowers. She was the town's authority on horticulture and she always participated in the garden clubs. In 1962 she moved to Carlsbad to be near her daughter.

Loveta married J.C. Hearn in 1929. He had come to Hagerman as a bookkeeper for Pecos Valley Milling Company. Later he became President of the National Dehydrating Mill Company in Lamar, Colorado. He owned and operated his own insurance and accounting business in Chandler, Arizona, for several years preceding his death in 1974. Loveta remains in Chandler. They have two daughters.

Donald and Frances Welborne were married in 1937. They are parents of a son and daughter. He worked in various areas of Oklahoma and New Mexico, until he returned to Hagerman in 1955. In 1953 Donald and his brother, Robert, combined their businesses for several years. This partnership was dissolved in 1963, and Donald remained owner of the school buses. Following his divorce in 1968 he sold the buses. He served two terms as Mayor of Hagerman. He and his present wife, the former Bernice Tulk Hardin, live in Roswell and Chama, New Mexico. Frances West continues to live in Hagerman.

Sara Beth and Lewis Wakeman were married in 1940. He was an engineer with the construction company installing the first R.E.A. lines in the Hagerman area. Following Lewis' return from overseas after World War II, he joined Southwestern Public Service Company, Carlsbad office, and remained there until his retirement in 1972. They are parents of a son and daughter and still make their home in Carlsbad.

Robert returned to Hagerman following his service in the Air Corps during World War II and bought the feed and seed business from his father, and it continued in the same tradition until he decided to close the business in December of 1973. Robert has served on the Hagerman Town Council since 1952. In 1946 he and Dorothy Devenport were married and they have two daughters and a son.

E.A. WHITE, SUPERINTENDENT OF HAGERMAN SCHOOLS, 1920-1942

Information furnished by his daughter, Mrs. Clint Smith, of Las Cruces, New Mexico, and a brother, Ben White, of Lubbock, Texas

E.A. White, usually known as "E.A.," "Prof." and Dick to family and close friends, came to Hagerman as school superintendent in 1920 from Farwell, Texas, where he had been superintendent and county attorney. His tenure was lengthy, from 1920 until he retired in 1942.

"Prof." began his duties at Hagerman in what developed as a critical era. World War I had ended only two years previously. As in countless thousands of other communities of similar small population many people had left to take advantage of war related jobs, in addition to the men who had gone into military service. The local ad valorem property tax was, at that time, almost the sole support for schools. Whether farm prices were high or low, it was felt more by owners of farm and ranch property than any one else.

Through periods of prosperity and later through the tough years of the Depression of the 1930's, when cotton sold for six cents a pound, E.A. White was a guiding hand in developing school programs and building projects which were important to the Hagerman community. Certainly this could not have occurred without community support and strength lent by progressive members of a board of education. "Prof.'s" leadership was vital at all times but its effectiveness was made possible by the teamwork of the superintendent and school board.

E.A. (Ernest Alexander) White was born in 1882 at Gatesville, Texas. He died at Las Cruces, New Mexico, in 1959. His family was of the typical pioneer Texas type and lived on the same farm in Hamilton County for almost two generations. After completing high school he prepared for teaching, and early in his professional career he was superintendent at Gomez and Tahoka, Texas, before going to Farwell, Texas, then to Hagerman. Along the way he earned a bachelor's degree at the former New Mexico Normal School at Las Vegas (now Highlands University); qualified in Texas as a practicing attorney and received a master's degree at Colorado State Teacher's College at Greeley, Colorado. In addition to his high school duties at Hagerman he served the field of education in New Mexico by being a member of the State Board of Education in 1923 through 1935, an unusually long tenure in that capacity, as the position was then appointed by the Governor. He was president of the New Mexico Educational Association in 1927. Shortly after his death he was elected to the New Mexico Education Association Hall of Fame in 1960, the honor being accepted in his name by his daughter, Vene (Mrs. Clint Smith) of Las Cruces.

The above remarks by no means do justice to White's valuable services as Hagerman superintendent. Many who are now Hagerman residents recall that era of community and school affairs. There were many sidelights. The Hagerman schools emphasized basketball, in common with most other small and large systems. In those days Hagerman had no coach most of the time, and that chore was done by any of the faculty who had the aptitude. During the early 1920's "Prof." himself coached one of the two successive years that the Hagerman team won the state championship. The second year R.N. Thomas was coach. In those days there was an official national tournament.

During White's tenure Hagerman started one of the first school lunch programs — a "home grown" venture, not the school lunch program of the present day. Most foods and supplies were contributed. Preparation was done by the home economics department even though many times (quoting his daughter) the experience was good for all concerned.

It was well known that E.A. thought the first two years of a child's school experience were the most important. For that reason he put more emphasis on the selection of teachers for those grades than any others. And without getting in the teachers' way he visited those rooms frequently, formed personal friendships with all the pupils and paid careful attention to how the work in those rooms progressed. Years later he told his daughter that if one learned well how to read and write in early school years, and use arithmetic competently, how to study in high school, and found out when finishing college he didn't "know a hell of a lot," a person was well on the way to becoming educated.

Many anecdotes have been told about "Prof." Lots of them are true literally, others in essence and some have a ring of truth whether apocryphal or not. In keeping with his well known belief in the importance of the first year or two of school there was one anecdote about a second grade boy who was asked in class who was the President of the United States. He didn't ponder long before responding, "It's either Professor White or Jesus Christ."

Many stories have been told about "Prof.'s" original method of discipline. Robert West remembers one time when he and several friends decided to play hookey from school. They were having a relaxed time in the local poolhall when they looked up and there stood "Prof," carrying several books. "Prof." said, "Since you boys would rather be here than at school, we will just hold class right here," and he proceeded to teach the class. At noon he marched them to school for lunch, then returned them to the poolhall for afternoon classes. It seemed to the boys that every father in town decided to visit the poolhall that day. This cooled any desire, in that group of boys, to play hookey for quite some time.

John Garner and Glynn Knoll both laughingly recall the "Sylvia Gatignol" prank. John was the captain and had

Glynn and George Heick as lieutenants. It was the noon hour at school, and as usual the study hall was full of pupils visiting, having fun, and that day just waiting to enjoy the prank. They tied a rope to a bookcase and to the door knob of the door at the north end of the hall, so that when the door was opened, the pull would bring all the books and bookcase crashing down. It was time for Miss Gatignol to arrive. John held the south door tightly closed from the inside. As expected Miss Gatignol couldn't open it, so she walked on down the hallway to the north door with her unmistakeable steps. Everyone in the study hall was quietly waiting for the inevitable disaster, and they sure were not disappointed. It was a total Disaster! The fun was short lived for the three boys. Miss Gatignol, quickly deciding that John was the ring leader, marched him into "Prof.'s" office. "Prof.," looking at John with a mean look in his eyes, said, "Now, just tell me all about what happened." John, scared half to death, did explain (he thinks). Finally "Prof." just had to laugh and said, "John, you want to try to not make these old maids so mad." Then it was the other two nervous boys' turn to report to the office. Glyn recalls that he looked at them sternly but that they detected a twinkle of laughter in his eyes. Nevertheless, performing his disciplinarian duty, he did give them a very strong and firm lecture.

Mrs. White still survives her husband and lives in Colorado. This was a second marriage, after the death of his first wife. Their daughter lives at Las Cruces, as indicated above. A son, Gene Rex, lives in Colorado, and a son Bruce, lives in California. Two sons lost their lives in tragic incidents early in life.

THE WIGGINS STORY

Joseph William Wiggins traded his Missouri farm for the Bogart farm (also called the Fife farm) five miles southwest of Hagerman. He made a contract of trade without seeing the Pecos Valley first. The shock of the unusually hard and distasteful gyp water, strong and hardy mesquite bushes to be cleared and the blowing sand seemed an impossible situation after living in Missouri.

Will Wiggins and Grace Mitchell Wiggins, their three young children, Spurgeon, Max and Ruth, and the family's household possessions came by train to Hagerman in 1923. W.E. Bowen took the family by car to the W.A. Bogart farm some five miles from Hagerman.

The old adobe house (now over 100 years old) then consisted of two large rooms, a lean-to kitchen and a long sleeping porch. The original two rooms on the west still stand, though the house has been remodeled several times. One of the family's first clear memory of the house was seeing a large cast-iron pot on the table in the northwest room. A tin dipper in the pot was used to ladle out the red beans, which were apparently the mainstay of the two Bogart boys who had remained in the house until the new owners arrived.

The devastating freeze of 1933 meant the end of the orchards and the beginning of the production of cotton. Mr. Wiggins and his two sons cleared the land of mesquite bushes over a number of years to prepare for more cotton acreage.

Will and Grace Wiggins had strong constitutions and worked long and hard to build their farm into a profitable business. They were quiet people with a strong faith. Their home was a welcome place to friends and neighbors.

All of the children graduated from Hagerman High School and all attended college. Spurgeon attended New

Mexico State University and Texas Tech. He eventually returned to farm and ranch in the Hagerman vicinity. He passed away in 1965. Max received a mechanical engineering degree from New Mexico State University at the age of nineteen. Later he served as a pilot in World War II, was shot down over Germany and spent two years in a prisoner of war camp. After the war he returned to Hagerman to farm and ranch. At the time of his death in 1968, he was a board member of several different farming organizations. Ruth graduated from New Mexico Western University. She lived in many different states but returned to the Hagerman area to build a home. She was employed by the State Health and Social Services when she passed away on April 14, 1975.

— Ruth Wiggins Strixner, Lois Jean Wiggins, Retty Wiggins

Grace and Will Wiggins.

THE JIM WILLIAMSON FAMILY

James Williamson, his wife, Lula Cartwright Williamson, and their five children arrived in Greenfield, New Mexico, on January 7, 1904. They had come from Crandall, Texas, and by freight train from Pecos, Texas. There was a severe snowstorm that day and the children were delighted and excited about the snow. A man in a hay wagon from the Felix Ranch met them at the train.

Before moving to the Hagerman area, Mr. Williamson, as an unmarried man, had driven a herd of cattle to New Mexico and worked as a cowboy in the Organ Mountains. During the winter months he and others lived in a cave in the mountains. He was a typical Texan, generous to a fault, quick to resent an affront, but charitable toward all and forgiving to an enemy. Although he was brought up amid the association of cattlemen, he turned his attention to the growing of alfalfa and his rare good judgement soon made him one of the most successful farmers in the district. As the manager and part owner of the Felix ranch, he tackled a difficult proposition. He also served as deputy sheriff and game warden in the Guadalupe Mountains for many years.

Mrs. Williamson was a lovely hostess, and she entertained often. The fish fries, picnics, hay rides and slumber parties at the Felix Ranch will be remembered by many people. Even though she had nine children of her own, neighbor children and friends were overnight guests almost every week. One night during a hard rain, the visitors who had come for a party stayed the night and pallets were made all over the house. One of Mrs. Williamson's many loves was flowers and she once won a prize for having the most flowers blooming in her yard. The prize was 75¢. She was a gold star mother, charter member of the Womans Missionary Society and a life member of the American Legion Auxiliary. Both Mr. and Mrs. Williamson lived to celebrate their golden wedding anniversary in 1940. They had nine children, Alline, Sydney, Kittie, Lula Bell, Roberta, Olan, Mary, Jimmie Lee and Alyce.

The Williamson children rode to the Hagerman school in a buggy. When the river came down they had to stay the night in town. Each morning Mr. Williamson loaded hay in the buggy to be fed to the horses at noon, but the children were always busy playing after lunch and forgot to feed them. Rather than take the hay home and be caught, they gave the feed to Rev. Cumpsten's milk cow. The children claimed she was the best fed cow in the country. There was a low buggy bridge at what was known as the Harshey crossing and a cow that liked to lie down on the bridge. Before the children could cross they had to stop and run the cow off. One day Sydney Williamson told the other children that if the "ole heifer" was on the bridge that day, he was going to run over her. He did so, shattering the staves, scaring the cow and breaking the buggy in two. All the way

Mrs. Jim Williamson.

Mr. Jim Williamson.

home the children tried to think of what they would tell their father. There was no need, for the owner of the cow had already called Mr. Williamson.

Buggy races among the young were not uncommon in that day. One race, well remembered, was with the Blythe children. When the race was nearing the end both buggies got up to full speed and ran down into the Felix River, side by side. In another fast ride a friend fell from the side of the buggy and no one missed her for ten or fifteen minutes. Needless to say, the friend was very angry and wasn't anxious to ride with the Williamsons again.

Sydney was the first soldier from Chaves County to die in World War I. He and Floyd Walters went to Deming, New Mexico, in June of 1918 for training, and in September Sydney was sent to Camp Dix, New Jersey. He became ill from the flu and his father left to be with his son. The horrible flu epidemic killed 125 soldiers as well as Sydney one night.

One week later Lula B. died from the flu also. Everyone in the family came down with the flu except the mother. Friends were so afraid of contacting the germ that no one came to help except Grandmother Mason, leaving Mrs. Williamson with little rest for weeks.

Shortly after the epidemic, Mrs. Williamson, along with Mrs. Oscar Walters, who had lost her son, Floyd, from the flu also, went from door to door collecting donations to beautify the cemetery. Soon afterward the Cemetery Association was reorganized.

— Bob Williamson Michelet

WILLIAM JOSEPH WILSON FAMILY

By Florence Wilson Loudon

My father, W.J. Wilson, was a foreman for J.J. Hagerman and helped in the development of the Pecos Valley. He helped in the survey of the townsite of Hagerman and planted the cottonwood trees. He was also a deputy sheriff under Pat Garrett.

My mother, Jessie Marie Cowan, came directly to Hagerman with her family for her health. Both parents came originally from Iowa. My mother's family took up homesteads south of Hagerman and also built two homes in Hagerman. She taught school in Dexter and one year in the Oklahoma territory. She died when I was a baby on the South Spring Ranch where my father was employed. My brother, Raymond, died in childhood. I believe my grandmother's family was one of the first, if not the first, family to live in what is now Hagerman.

I was raised by my grandmother, Mary S. Cowan, until her death. I then lived with my Uncle Jim and Uncle Harry Cowan until I finished high school. My life in Hagerman was uneventful. I graduated from Hagerman High School in 1917 as valedictorian, then went to live with my father in Arizona. From there we went to California where I attended college and worked until I married. My father died in Los Angeles in 1923 as a result of an auto accident. I married C. Thomas Loudon May 30, 1923, in Los Angeles, California, where we lived until we moved to Ruidoso, New Mexico, our present home. We have one daughter, two grandchildren and one great grandchild.

THE J.E. WIMBERLYS
By Frank E. Wimberly

The J.E. Wimberly family moved to Hagerman from Hale Center, Texas, in the fall of 1904 by train, probably loading their goods and much of the equipment first used to publish the *Messenger*. Arthur and I were left with relatives and my father returned to the plains to get us. He rented a horse and buggy rig at Bovina, the only short range travel used in those days.

Being just more than five years old at the time I recall that trip quite well including a herd of antelope running across the road in front of us during the ride. Certainly a lad that age would remember seeing a train for the first time, particularly coming around the bend at Bovina. I don't remember anything else about that trip — the stop-over at Clovis, arriving at Hagerman — but that steam engine coming around the curve impressed me like few natural or man-made wonders since.

My parents came to Hagerman for the purpose of publishing the *Messenger*. It should almost certainly be assumed he had made one or more trips to Hagerman before deciding on the move. The Pecos Valley was being promoted as an irrigated farming area.

I do not know when my father started publication of the *Messenger* at Hale Center, Texas. He had been a ranch hand. His formal education was limited. He used to say he finished the seventh reader but he was an avid reader, a student of history and politics. Political discussions and arguments were even more common then than later and were frequently heated though almost always friendly. Later, while continuing publication of the weekly newspaper he began carrying the rural route mail from the Hagerman post office. The family also made a short-lived attempt at

Mrs. J.E. (Margaret Wilson) Wimberly, 1873–1965.

homesteading on a tract east of town but it didn't take long to decide that it would not be practicable to continue and "prove up."

Electricity, when first used in Hagerman, was a major innovation to nearly everybody as few people had previously used it. Charlie Tanner strung poles over quite a bit of the town and generated electricity a few hours each evening, direct current instead of the customary A.C., using a horizontal diesel engine for power. The "chugs" of the engine accompanied the "juice" through the distribution lines.

My father, Joe Edward Wimberly, was born in 1874 in Arkansas. My mother, Margaret (Maggie) Wimberly, was born in Tennessee in 1873. They were charter members of the Presbyterian Church in Hagerman. My father served on the church session and once attended the annual General Assembly of the Presbyterian Church in the United States as a delegate from the Hagerman congregation.

There were four children born to the family in this order:

Arthur was born in 1896 and died at Hagerman in 1921. He married Helen McBride, the daughter of a family who lived in the Pecos Valley for many years. He was appointed postmaster in Hagerman after returning from serving in the army in World War I.

Frank, born in 1899, was married to Ola White. After graduating from college in 1921, he returned to Hagerman to teach agriculture and science. He now is in the commercial radio broadcasting business in Altus, Oklahoma.

Will Harrington was born in 1899 and married Myrth McCurley. He followed in his father's footsteps in journalism and in recent years was inducted into the Oklahoma Journalism Hall of Fame. He is the owner and publisher of the *Duncan Banner* in Duncan, Oklahoma.

Margaret (Mrs. Floyd Childress) was born in Hagerman in 1906. She has lived in Roswell, New Mexico, for many years. She taught music in the Hagerman schools before her marriage.

J. E. Wimberly, 1874–1943.

B.H. WIXOM FAMILY
By Ethel Brown and Alice Roth

When there was a land boom in 1905 in the Pecos Valley, Mr. and Mrs. Wixom bought a farm near Hagerman. They brought their family from Illinois to live in New Mexico.

Mr. Wixom was a member of the Board of County Commissioners of Chaves County for a number of years. He was once appointed by the governor to fill a vacancy of the state tax commissioner and served one year. He was vice-president of the First National Bank of Hagerman for awhile. Mrs. Wixom was a busy, home loving mother with many friends. The family had lived in the tall corn state and there were many new experiences in moving to New Mexico.

Of the five Wixom children only two are living, Mrs. Ethel Brown and Mrs. Alice Roth, both of Phoenix, Arizona.

Ethel and Alice well remember the day they went out riding, saw a pretty cactus and decided to take one home. The girls took turns digging it up and succeeded in ruining one pair of shoes plus a pair of gloves. Their hands were scratched and full of stickers and they received a good lecture about cactus which they haven't forgotten.

Cotton picking, too, looked interesting. They tried that for half a day. The eighty cents they earned bought aspirin for headaches, linament for backaches and tape for sore hands.

W.P. WOODMAS FAMILY
By Violet Woodmas Sweatt

My mother, father, brother, Marlin, and I drove to Roswell in an Overland car in the summer of 1921 from Quenemo, Kansas, a town about the size of Hagerman, forty miles from Topeka. I was thirteen years old at the time and my brother three years younger.

I'll never forget that trip, especially the day it rained. We made twenty-seven miles and spent the night at Liberal, Kansas, sleeping on tables at a camp ground to get away from the water dogs. There were no paved roads and no motels.

In 1922 we moved to Hagerman from Roswell as my father, Percy Woodmas, had a chance to buy a dry goods store in a building that had once been a saloon. He had been in the mercantile business in Kansas. We bought our home from J.T. and Edith West.

Hagerman looked very different then. There were apple orchards, flowing artesian wells and dirt roads. When the winds blew, and it seems they blew more then than now, the sandstorms were unbelievable. We would have to shovel out sand before we could eat.

Even so, I preferred all that to the cylcones and terrific electric storms in Kansas. I remember the lightning coming down the telephone on the wall and shooting across the floor. My mother would put my brother and me on a feather bed until it was over. The houses had lightning rods. The farmers had storm cellars but we weren't farmers. Once the wind blew a large tree down in front of our house. I missed the sledding and ice skating but I could stand the sand stinging my legs as I walked to school in preference to cyclones.

There was a flowing mineral well in Hagerman across from the depot. People used to come for miles to get containers of the water for it was supposed to be good for a number of ailments. It contained a lot of sulphur. Later they built a swimming pool and filled it from the flowing well.

In 1929 when the Depression hit, my parents sold their store. Lawrence Garner bought their home and they moved to Santa Ana, California. This was about the time the highway to Roswell was built and it was taking too much trade from Hagerman. My good-hearted father had too much on the books after furnishing numerous students with books and clothes which he never got back.

Strange as it may seem, we came to New Mexico for my mother's health. She was having throat trouble and her doctor advised a dry climate. At the present time, February 24, 1975, she is ninety-two years old. My father passed away in 1938 and my brother about five years later.

My mother and father were active in the Presbyterian church. He was superintendent of the Sunday School and she was a Sunday School teacher.

THE WRANOSKYS
By Helen Curry

Republic County, Kansas, lost some of its fine citizens when the John S. Wranosky family moved to Hagerman in the spring of 1905. His wife was formerly Christie Grace Pelesky. They were the parents of seven children, Mabel, Winnie, Anna, Sylvia, Ernest, William and Marguerite.

The family lived in the second house on the highway, just south of the intersection of Argyle Street and State Road 2. Mr. Wranosky built a small house to the south for his parents who came in 1907. The Winters' house was on the corner. South and across the road from Wranoskys, lived the Warren Perry family, also from Republic County.

The fruit trees surrounding the houses were a thing of beauty. Many people who came west for health reasons, especially "consumptives" as they were called, lived in tents in the orchard and yard. Mr. Wranosky had great faith in the future of Hagerman as a health resort.

In 1913 after selling their farm to Mr. and Mrs. Randolph of Roswell, the family moved to the house on West Argyle which burned a few years ago, on the property owned by Paul Robinson. Later the family moved to a place south of town.

Frank Wranosky, a brother to John, moved his family to this town at the same time as John. He lived in the house across the street from the Robinsons, which is now owned by Louise Brown Sleeper.

John Wranosky was instrumental in building the first Catholic Church here, especially for his parents. Mabel wrote, "Although Papa was Catholic, we girls attended other churches, especially The Presbyterian. Mr. Alter was the minister."

William is the only one of the children not living. Mabel married Tom Reed and lives in Kansas; Winnie is married to Kenneth Keeble at Freer, Texas; Anna is Mrs. Glen Gardner, Uvalde, Texas; Sylvia's first husband died and she is now Mrs. George Luning, living in Panama; Ernest married Essie Moreland and is in Corpus Christi, Texas; Marguerite's first husband died, she remarried and is Mrs. Grady Copeland, Woodsboro, Texas.

A part of southwest Hagerman became known as the Wranosky Addition.

The family left the valley about 1920.

Information by Mabel Wranosky Reed

THE ADAM ZIMMERMAN FAMILY
By Mabel Zimmerman Alston

Adam Zimmerman, a German emigrant, and Stella Foster were married in Odessa, Texas, in 1900. They immediately began traveling westward in two covered wagons. Approximately thirty-five miles east of Hagerman, just under the Caprock, they filed on and homesteaded a claim.

While living in tents they built themselves a rock house. This house is still being used today as a bunk house.

They had five children, Clyde, Mabel, Bill, Ruth and Hazel. Clyde and Mabel were born in Midland, Texas, because there were no doctors available in this area. They made these two trips to Midland in a covered wagon. Bill was born on the ranch with a midwife in attendance. When they discovered that another child (Ruth) was on the way, they bought a house in Hagerman. Ruth was the only one born in the Hagerman house. Hazel was born on the ranch. A doctor came there to deliver her.

We owned the old house in Hagerman on South Manchester Street for about sixty years but had it razed four or five years ago.

Clyde attended school in Hagerman for a part of the winter when Ruth was born. But the Zimmermans, as did most of the ranching families, employed governesses to teach their children on their ranches. After the children reached the upper grade levels, Stella would move to Hagerman each winter while Adam stayed out at the ranch. The separation of our family for nine months every year was indeed one of the most dreaded and actually the saddest times of our lives. In addition to the fact that our parents were extremely lonely being seperated, we, the children, had to leave our beloved horses and our riding which was the only life that we had ever known. But, as we grew older and began dancing and having fun in general, we soon learned that there was nothing as enjoyable as having friends and to participate in activities.

Adam died on the ranch in 1940. Clyde died in 1957, Mother in 1962.

I, Mabel, live in Lovington; Bill in Texas, and Ruth and Hazel in California.

POST SCRIPT

There were many other families who lived in Hagerman and contributed to its growth and culture. Some of them are mentioned in one or more stories, but many are not. We had no way of contacting living relatives in some cases. We cannot name them all, but those who knew them will remember them. They are included among the pioneers to whom this book is dedicated.

www.ingramcontent.com/pod-product-compliance
Lightning Source LLC
Chambersburg PA
CBHW030124240426
43672CB00005B/18